RANDOLPH SCOTT
A FILM BIOGRAPHY

by
Jefferson Brim Crow III

Published by
Empire Publishing, Inc.
Box 717
Madison, NC 27025-0717
(910) 427-5850

Empire Publishing, Inc.
Box 717
Madison, NC 27025-0717
(910) 427-5850

Randolph Scott / A Film Biography copyright © 1987, 1994, by Jefferson
Brim Crow III

Originally published as *Randolph Scott / The Gentleman from Virginia* by
WindRiver Publishing Company, Carrollton, Texas

ISBN Number 0-944019-17-X
Library of Congress Catalog Number 94-61281

Published and printed in The United States of America

1 2 3 4 5 6 7 8 9 10

INTRODUCTION

Randolph Scott made 100 movies over a career spanning 34 years. From 1950 to 1953, he was rated among Hollywood's top ten film stars by the Motion Picture Herald Poll. He is one of the most fondly remembered actors of Hollywood's Golden era: the 1930s to the late 1950s. While he played in musicals, comedies, romances and war movies, he is best remembered as a western star after 1947.

The majority of his films were for Columbia Pictures and Warner Brothers, yet his versatility brought him many roles at other studio lots. During his career, he worked at virtually every studio in Hollywood and appeared with such legendary greats as Henry Fonda, Humphrey Bogart, Betty Grable, Fred Astaire, Marlene Dietrich, and John Wayne.

Scott was one of those rare actors who never signed with a major studio. While other film stars labored under contracts which gave them little freedom, Scott was generally free to cut his own deals. His business acumen was legendary, negotiating his own contracts and investing in real estate, oil and gas, and other commercial ventures. Following his retirement from films, he amassed one of the largest personal fortunes in California.

Randy Scott, as his friends affectionately called him, was a western hero in the truest sense of the word. His portrayals of tall, soft-spoken, hard-fisted Westerners who stood by their principle of right over wrong, provided a role model for millions of youngsters. These same middle-aged men today will tell you that Randolph Scott personified the kind of man they all wanted to be.

Contents

Acknowledgements

Dedication

Prologue: THE KID FROM DALLAS   xiii

Part I   I: ENTER RANDOLPH SCOTT   1

           II: ZANE GREY   7

          III: THE DRAWING ROOM   17

           IV: A RETURN TO THE SADDLE   25

            V: WHEN THE DALTONS RODE   33

           VI: THE WAR YEARS   43

Interviews   57

Part II   VII: THE WESTERN ERA   71

         VIII: THE WINDS OF CHANGE   87

           IX: THE MAN IN BLACK   91

            X: THE GOLDEN FIFTIES–THE TOP TEN   101

           XI: THE SHAPE OF THINGS TO COME   123

          XII: THE GOLDEN YEARS   129

         XIII: RIDE FOR THE SUNSET   161

          XIV: RIDE THE HIGH COUNTRY   183

     Epilogue: EXIT RANDOLPH SCOTT   195

The Song: "Whatever Happened to Randolph Scott"   201

Selected Articles and News Items   205

The Reviews   211

The Films   245

Bibliography   285

Index   293

Photographs in this book are reproduced courtesy of the following companies:

Allied Artists Inc.
Columbia Pictures Industries Inc. / Coca Cola
Metro-Goldwyn-Mayer Inc.
Paramount Pictures Corp. / Gulf & Western
RKO General Inc.
Twentieth Century-Fox Film Corporation
Universal City Studios / MCA
United Artist Inc.
Warner Bros. Pictures / Warner Communications

Abbreviations used include:

AA	Allied Artists
ABC	American Broadcasting Company
CBS	CBS Inc. (formerly Columbia Broadcasting System)
Col	Columbia Pictures Corporation
Fox	Twentieth Century-Fox Film Corporation
Lip	Lippert Pictures
MGM	Metro-Goldwyn-Mayer Studios
Mon	Monogram Pictures (now Allied Artists)
NBC	National Broadcasting Company
Par	Paramount Pictures Corporation
Pathe	RKO Pathe Pictures
Rep	Republic Pictures Corporation
RKO	RKO Radio Pictures Inc.
UA	United Artists Pictures
Univ	Universal Pictures / Universal-International Pictures
WB	Warner Bros. / Warner Bros.-First National Pictures

ACKNOWLEDGEMENTS

Acknowledgements proved the hardest part of this book by far. So many people helped. Some to a great extent, some only a little, but they each gave freely and willingly to contribute to the contents of these pages. The encouragement was constant. The people named here only skim the surface. To those of you I have failed to mention, know that I am, and always will be grateful.

Thanks to author David Rothel of Sarasota, Florida, who gave encouragement to a total stranger and gave him guidelines on where to begin. Without David's help, this book might still be just a dream. Thanks to B.D. "Bo" Duncan of Duncan Poster Service in Dallas who had so many fine stills. He has even found stills for Mrs. Randolph Scott. To Guy Steele of The Movie Collection who got out and hustled about 200 more when I needed them most. A special thanks to the Fine Arts Department of Dallas Public Library, George Henderson and Robert Eason for tirelessly digging up those obscure facts and loaning me some rare stills.

Thanks also to Travis Jordan, Director of Media Services, Fondren Library at Southern Methodist University in Dallas for his help in digging out some of those obscure credits.

Thanks to Don Reid of the Statler Brothers who gave me a big moral boost when I needed it. To Donald Curtis, Noah Beery, Claude Akins and Roy Huggins who either sent notes of encouragement or granted interviews. To Denver Pyle and Mariette Hartley who wanted to do interviews but could not clear their busy schedules.

Thanks to Ileta Bodie who took the original manuscript in it's most primitive form and translated it into something workable.

A very special thanks to my 'second generation' experts who helped me so immensely when it came time to make a book out of the various parts. Mel Duus and Gwen Lee of Haag Photo Services who took stills that were in various states of self-destruction and made 250 quality, even-tones photos from them. To Bill Thornton who took a true novice and showed him the ropes. To Neil Summers for his special contribution. And to Marilyn Ross of About Books, Inc. who showed me selling is an art and proved it by pre-selling to a major book club.

The Nevadan (Columbia-1950).

Fort Worth (WB-1951) with David Brian.

Thunder Over The Plains (WB-1953) with Lane Chandler.

Riding Shotgun (WB-1954).

DEDICATION

To my wife Pattie and my daughters Vicki and Sherrie. They encouraged me, helped me, gave constructive criticism, kept me on a forward course and, when the going was roughest, encircled me in an envelope of love.

PROLOGUE

THE KID FROM DALLAS

As a child growing up in Dallas in the late 1930s and early 1940s, I had three great loves. Radio, war movies and westerns. I would rush home from school every day and sit glued to the radio from 4:45 until 6:00 pm. as I listened to *Hop Harrigan, Terry & The Pirates, Captain Midnight, Superman* and *Tom Mix*. Those were my favorites and I thought missing an episode a singularly dreadful disaster.

Promptly at 6:00 p.m., I would go tearing out of the house to spend the next couple of hours being Superman or Hop Harrigan or whoever I was that particular afternoon. On Mondays, Wednesdays and Fridays, however, this time was shortened because at 6:30, you-know-who was back in front of the radio to listen to *The Lone Ranger*. And so it went.

The second thing I loved was westerns. We loved westerns. All kinds. Any kinds. Almost from the time I could walk, I knew beyond the shadow of a doubt, I wanted to be cowboy when I grew up. Every Saturday would find the whole gang scurrying to the Varsity Theatre and plunking down our precious dimes to see a double feature western. Sometimes it would be Bill Elliott. Other times it would be Bob Steele or John Wayne or Johnny Mack Brown. We didn't particularly care as long as it was a western. We would sit in the darkened theatre for several hours and completely lose ourselves as we became the hero on the screen. It was all a growing boy of eight or nine could ever hope for. We were sure this must be what Paradise was like.

As we grew older and the mid-forties were upon us, we each began picking our favorites. Maybe Jimmy decided he liked Wild Bill Elliott best.

Rolly might have liked Bob Steele. Larry wanted to pattern himself after young John Wayne or Don Barry or Lash LaRue or Sunset Carson or . . . .

For me, there was never a question. He had started riding a beautiful Chestnut horse and would later start dressing all in black. He spoke with a genuine southern drawl he never lost in 100 films spanning over thirty years. He was my favorite then, he is my favorite now. He was loved as a man of honor. A man of action. A man a boy of eight or ten could well pattern himself after for he never let us down. He was Randolph Scott. An original. I still like him best!

The Kid from Dallas aboard his trusty mount (about 1939).

Hangman's Knot (Columbia-1952).

Decision At Sundown (Columbia-1957).

Decision At Sundown (Columbia-1957) with James Westerfield (bartender) and Noah Beery Jr. (in striped shirt).

Buchanan Rides Alone (Columbia-1958).

Tall Man Riding (WB-1955) with William Ching.

A Lawless Street (Columbia-1955) with Angela Lansbury.

With Gail Russell in Warner's *Seven Men From Now* (1956).

Thunder Over The Plains (WB-1953).

Shoot-Out At Medicine Bend (WB-1957) with Gordon Jones (left) and James Garner.

Shoot-Out At Medicine Bend (WB-1957).

Shoot-Out At Medicine Bend (WB-1957) with Dani Crayne.

A Lawless Street (Columbia-1955).

Fine portrait from *Hangman's Knot* (Columbia-1952).

PART I

CHAPTER I

ENTER RANDOLPH SCOTT

Randolph Scott began his motion picture career in a film called *Sharp Shooters* in 1928 and retired from the screen 34 years later, in 1962, after making what has now been recognized as a milestone western, *MGM's Ride the High Country*. In the interim, Randolph Scott made 100 films.

While he made all kinds of films from romantic comedies to musicals, it is his western films that are indelibly etched into the memories of those millions of fans who sat through those thousands of movies in the decades of the thirties, forties and fifties. If you were a western fan, those were the golden days and Randolph Scott was the panacea.

It would seem Scott was a star from the beginning. That isn't really the case. While his success lasted many years, it was just as elusive and discouraging in the beginning as it has been for countless others.

George Randolph Scott was born January 23, 1898, in Orange County, Virginia, the only boy of six children. His prominent family were direct descendents of Virginia's early colonizers and his primary and secondary education were at private schools. Upon graduation he entered Georgia Instutute of Technology (Georgia Tech) where he played football. Sustaining a back injury that ended his football playing, he transferred to the University of North Carolina where he graduated with a degree in textile engineering and manufacturing.

Fully intending to pursue a career in textiles, Scott, decided to take a year off and tour Europe. A career in his chosen field was not to be, however. In the year since graduating from college, he had decided he wanted to be an actor. Having an understanding father helped. So, with a letter of introduction from his father to Howard Hughes, thirty-year-old Randolph Scott headed west to Hollywood.

Hughes did help Scott get a job as an extra in the George O'Brien film

1

The black outfit and a beautiful chestnut horse, Randy's trademark. Scene is from *The Bounty Hunter* (WB-1954).

Ten Wanted Men (Columbia-1954).

Sharp Shooters. The year was 1928. This was followed with bit parts in two more Fox films, *The Far Call* and *The Black Watch*, but instant stardom did not come to the young Virginian. He tested for the lead in Cecil B. DeMille's *Dynamite*, but the part went to another aspiring, young actor named Joel McCrea. Scott had to settle for another bit part.

During this period in 1929, Scott studied acting at the famous Pasadena Playhouse. While there he was hired by Paramount to give Gary Cooper voice lessons for his upcoming role as *The Virginian*, the second of three times Owen Wister's classic novel would be brought to the screen.

Feeling his career was going nowhere, Scott decided he'd had enough. But luck chose this time to smile upon him and he was cast in a play, *Under a Virginia Moon*, receiving good, if not great, reviews. Two more stage roles, *Oh Judge* and *The Broken Wing*, the latter with Leo Carrillo, earned him four motion picture offers. He accepted an offer from Paramount that was the start of a long and successful association that would last for seven years and twenty pictures. His contract was not exclusive, however, and during this period, from 1931 to 1938, he also made features for Monogram, RKO, United Artists, Columbia, Twentieth Century-Fox and Universal.

While negotiating his contract at Paramount, Scott appeared in a programmer *"The Women Men Marry"* (Headline Pictures-1931). After that Paramount was ready for him, and, in 1932, he joined Nancy Carroll and Cary Grant in a non-western called *Hot Saturday*. It was during this time that Scott and Grant became friends.

Hot Saturday, released in October 1932, was a big boost to Scott's ascending star. It was a romance and Scott got the girl and compliments from the NEW YORK TIMES reviewer who said " . . . Randolph Scott is solidly virtuous as the boyhood sweetheart."

In 1933, then 35 years old, he shared a beach house with his young friend, Cary Grant. Their bachelor quarters were the subject of numerous layouts by fan magazines of the day.

In February 1934, Grant married 26-year-old Virginia Cherrill in London and informed the press that he and his new wife would live a "quiet, simple life". Things appeared to be just that until September 1934 when it deteriorated into one of the stormiest marriages in a town known for such things. They were divorced on March 26, 1935.

Again at liberty, Grant moved in with his friend, Randolph Scott. This

With Forrest Tucker in *Rage At Dawn* (RKO-1955).

Tense scene from *Rage At Dawn* (RKO-1955).

With close friend Cary Grant in the late thirties.

The Nevadan (Columbia-1950) with Forrest Tucker.

time their home was a house on West Live Oak Drive which became known as "Bachelor Hall". Newspaper columnists, probably with some prompting by the Paramount publicity department, had a fun time trying to guess which of Grant's current girlfriends (Ginger Rogers, Mary Brian, Mary Carlisle, Phyllis Brooks) he would marry. Grant said, "There'll be no marriages for me. It will be five years before I'm ready for that." Scott said, "Cary will never know peace as long as his name spells news. I've seen him actually lose sleep and weight after reading certain items that touched upon his personal life." True to his word, Cary Grant didn't marry again until 1942.

Scott himself was next at the altar. In 1936 he married Marianna duPont Somerville. This marriage lasted until 1939, ending in divorce. Five years later, in 1944, he married Marie Patricia Stillman, a union that has lasted until this day. The Scotts have two children, Christopher and Sandra. While the press had a field day with most married actors and actresses, Mr. and Mrs. Randolph Scott gave them little to gossip about as they succeeded in living a truly normal life while Randolph set out to do what he did best—truly professional acting—and a career that would last another 18 years until he voluntarily put a stop to it in 1962.

The Nevadan (Columbia-1950) with Dorothy Malone.

CHAPTER II

ZANE GREY

Zane Grey (1875–1939) was or was not a great writer depending on your point of view. Critics of the day panned his books with alarming regularity. The public loved them and, from about 1909, they have continued to sell year after year. Countless millions have been sold worldwide.

In his lifetime he wrote 89 books and countless short stories. How many millions of copies of his books have been sold would be impossible to determine but the figure would be astronomical. His books have never been out of print. Zane Grey and American western literature have become synonymous. Randolph Scott, meet Zane Grey.

Zane Grey is, and probably will remain, the most filmed western storyteller. His western films date from 1918's *Riders Of The Purple Sage* through *The Maverick Queen* (Republic-1956). Feature films have been made from his books 96 times. There were also two movie serials, *King Of The Royal Mounted* (Republic-1940) and *King Of The Mounties* (Republic-1942) and a television series *Dick Powell's Zane Grey Theatre* (CBS—1956–1962, 145 episodes) that used little more than Mr. Grey's name. So it was not all that unusual, when in 1933 Paramount decided to cast their tall, lean Virginian in a series of Zane Grey westerns. A great western star was about to become a reality.

After his big-time debut with Cary Grant in 1932, Paramount had loaned Scott to Warner Bros. for a featured role in *A Successful Calamity* (1932) which starred George Arliss. His stock as an actor went up considerably with the film community as a result of his performance in that film. Also, on the theory that a little notoriety never hurt, the fan magazine had a great time playing up Randy's alleged romance with Mexican actress Lupe Valez. Because of the sudden increase in Randolph Scott stock, Paramount assigned him the leads in two pictures, *Lusitania Secret* and *Lone Cowboy*. For some

A Lawless Street (Columbia-1955).

With Ruth Donnelly in *A Lawless Street* (Columbia-1955).

reason these films were never made and Randy went directly into the Zane Grey series.

In 1932, he made the first of ten Zane Grey westerns he would make for Paramount over the next two and one-half years. These pictures, while truly "B" westerns in the strictest sense of the term, were really much more. They kept the cost down by using action footage from the Jack Holt-Zane Grey series of ten years earlier. This was first class action footage and, neatly edited into the film, deprived the audience of absolutely nothing. This left virtually all the budget for actors and directors. The end result was a series of programmers with class.

The first in the series, *Heritage Of The Desert*, was released in September 1932. It was directed by a 34-year-old former juvenile actor named Henry Hathaway who would go on to indelibly leave his mark on the pages of motion picture history as one of the greatest directors of all time. It is undoubtedly this directorial quality combined with the fine acting ability of Randolph Scott that gave this series its better than average quality. Support in the first picture gave a clue to the caliber of support Scott got throughout the series. Included in *Heritage Of The Desert* were veterans J. Ferrell McDonald (who made over 300 pictures in his long career) and Gordon Westcott. Also in the cast was a young Guinn Williams who would come into his own in the next few years as Big Boy Williams in a series for RKO and some independents.

The second Randolph Scott-Zane Grey picture was released in November 1932—*Wild Horse Mesa*. It was again directed by Henry Hathaway who would direct the first seven of the series. In the cast were Sally Blaine (who had been in *Heritage*), Fred Kohler (a bad guy's bad guy), George Hayes, Jim Thorpe, Charley Grapewin, Buddy Roosevelt and James Bush.

The Zane Grey series continued in 1933 with four more films. The first, released in March of 1933, was *The Thundering Herd*. Again, a who's who cast that included Barton MacLane, Judith Allen, Harry Carey, Buster Crabbe, Raymond Hatton, Noah Beery, Sr., Monte Blue and Al Bridge. In May, Paramount released the second Grey of '33, the fourth in the series, *Sunset Pass*. Harry Carey again offered his support along with Fuzzy Knight, Tom London, Tom Keene, Noah Beery, Sr. and Kent Taylor of Boston Blackie fame. The last 1933 entries in this series were *Man Of The Forest* and *To The Last Man*. The supporting casts in the pictures had by

The Stranger Wore A Gun (Columbia-1953) with Claire Trevor.

Thunder Over The Plains (WB-1953).

now become a more or less standard repertory company of the best Paramount had. There might be a change of ingenue and a character or villain, but the nucleus remained—Harry Carey, Barton MacLane, Larry "Buster" Crabbe, Noah Beery, Sr., Jack LaRue, Fuzzy Knight, Tom Kennedy and Guinn "Big Boy" Williams to name a few. Also, from time to time an unknown would appear on their way to success. Two such appeared in *To The Last Man.* One was a lovely 22-year-old actress named Gail Patrick who was to go on to become quite a popular leading lady of the 30's and 40's and later Executive Producer of the "Perry Mason" television series. The other, also an actress, was a five-year-old named Shirley Temple. Her part in *To The Last Man* was just one scene, but she impressed director Henry Hathaway. He told Paramount to sign her to a contract. Paramount decided not to sign her and released her after the picture was finished. Twentieth Century-Fox then signed her to a long-term contract and the rest is history.

Frank Gruber, writing in his 1969 biography, *Zane Grey*, relates an incident that occurred during the filming of *Man Of The Forest* that almost brought Randolph Scott's career to an abrupt close before it ever really got started.

In *Man Of The Forest*, there is a scene where the hero (Scott) is riding home and gets "attacked" by a cougar. Only later does the audience discover that the big cat is actually tame and the 'attack' only a playful scuffle. However, the cougar hadn't read the part in the script that said this was all an act, and, right on cue, pounced on Scott and went to work for real. He sank his teeth and claws into Scott's back and shoulders. Scott, frightened as never before, lay perfectly still. The trainer, aware of what was happening, did not attempt to pull the cat off Scott until the scene was finished.

The doctors attended to Scott afterwards and the cat, although restrained by a short chain, continued to try to get to him. A rather incensed Randolph Scott asked the trainer why he hadn't helped him and the trainer is said to have replied that he didn't want to spoil what was obviously a good scene. Further investigation revealed that the cougar was fed a diet of horsemeat and that Randy Scott smelled of horse after many hours in the saddle.

Only two entries into the Zane Grey series were made by Paramount in 1934. They were also the only pictures Scott made of any kind in 1934 after making a career-high, nine pictures in 1933, an unheard of output for a star.

A Lawless Street (Columbia-1955) with Don Megowan.

Seven Men From Now (WB-1956) with Walter Reed and Gail Russell.

His film output would increase in 1935 and he would continue to make three or four pictures a year for nearly 30 more years, his second highest output coming in 1955 with a series of six westerns.

The first 1934 Grey film was *The Last Roundup* adapted by Jack Cunningham from Grey's *The Border Legion*. It was the last of this series directed by Henry Hathaway. With the release of *The Last Roundup* in May, Randolph Scott-Zane Grey fans had to wait until September for the next entry into the series. That was *Wagon Wheels*, an adaptation (by Cunningham) of Grey's *Fighting Caravans*. Charles Barton signed on as director for the first two pictures he would do in this series. Gail Patrick returned for the second time as female lead, Barbara Fritchie having done so in *The Last Roundup*.

Home On The Range (released February 1, 1935) and *Rocky Mountain Mystery* (released one month later on March 1, 1935) ended the Randolph Scott-Zane Grey series for Paramount.

Home On The Range, directed by Arthur Jacobson, was an adaptation of Grey's *Code Of The West*. Feminine lead went to an up and coming young actress named Ann Sheridan, who would become a major star in just a few years and remain so for the next twenty-five. Included were Dean Jagger and former child star Jackie Coogan. *Rocky Mountain Mystery* held over Miss Sheridan from *Home On The Range*, but otherwise it had a completely new supporting cast, the first time Paramount had deviated from its policy of using the same basic repertory company, with only minor changes, throughout the series. The cast for *Rocky Mountain Mystery* included Charles (Chic) Sale, Leslie Carter, Kathleen Burke, George Marion, James Eagles and Florence Roberts. Charles Barton directed this final effort.

It has been said that Randolph Scott was an avid reader of Zane Grey's books and that he looked upon Grey as the best adventure writer of his or any time. It has also been said that Scott credits the Paramount series of Zane Grey stories with giving his career its biggest boost. This is probably so. Hardly a boy ever grew up in this country who didn't read at least some of Zane Grey's books. Few western films were made that weren't influenced in some way by Zane Grey's stories. Many a career was indeed launched by an actor appearing in a Zane Grey western. They were filmed and re-filmed and retitled and re-filmed for over fifty years.

With the departure of Scott, Paramount reduced the series to

Randy assists a lady in distress, in this case Phyllis Kirk, in *Thunder Over The Plains* (WB-1953).

It wasn't all chasing bad guys. This is lovely Joan Weldon in Warner's *Riding Shotgun* (1954).

programmer status and continued with Larry "Buster" Crabbe and Tom Keene, while Randy Scott moved on to other endeavors as an "A" star. He did, however, play in Zane Grey stories two more times before he finally hung up his .45's. In 1941 he starred with Robert Young in Twentieth Century-Fox's big budget production of *Western Union*. While not particularly faithful to Grey's book, it was nevertheless an exciting film with lots of action and a decent story. Six years later he made his last film based on a Zane Grey story. It was *Gunfighters* (Columbia-1947) based on the book *Twin Sombreros*.

In all, Randolph Scott made twelve films based on Zane Grey. It all seemed so natural. He looked the part. He sounded like you would expect a Grey hero to sound. He had a natural grace and athletic ability. Above all, he had talent, the indispensible ingredient for a successful acting career. By 1935 Randolph Scott had arrived.

Sugarfoot (WB-1951) with John Hamilton, S. Z. Sakall and Robert Warwick (from left).

CHAPTER III

THE DRAWING ROOM

While appearing in the Zane Grey series at Paramount, Scott also appeared in four non-western films for them, one for Monogram and one for Columbia.

One Paramount film was *Hello Everybody!* (1933) with radio personality and singer Kate Smith. Smith made a number of pictures in the 1930's and 40's while also appearing regularly on radio. Her motion picture popularity never reached that of her radio show, however. *Hello Everybody!* was a typical vehicle for a radio singer in the 30's. Wicked guys from the power company want to build a dam. The dam will flood the valley and so the farmers must be bought out. Kate refuses to sell so the power company sends Randolph Scott to romance Kate and get her to sell. Randy really does fall in love with Kate's sister, Lilly (Sally Blaine) and switches to the farmers side. This is really Kate Smith's picture and it is she who saves the day when she enters a talent show and is heard by a famous impresario (Ted Collins) and signed to a lucrative contract. With the money she forces the power company to back down and save the valley and farms.

Continuing at Paramount, Scott went into *Supernatural*, an eerie film about spirits taking over innocent people. Also in the cast were H.B. Warner, William Farnum, Vivienne Osborne and Beryl Mercer. Female lead (and top billed player) was Carole Lombard in her pre-light comedy days, an actress on the verge of real success.

"A gruesome, but thoroughly engrossing murder mystery. Lionel Atwill is an insanely jealous husband", wrote the New York Times, "Is almost too convincing for comfort".

"By whose hand did death strike?" read the posters for *Murders In The Zoo*. Back-to-back thrillers.

1934 brought even greater boosts to Scott's ascending star. A popu-

Portrait still from *Hello Everybody!* (Paramount-1933).

Supernatural (Paramount-1933) with H. B. Warner (left), Carole Lombard and Allan Dinehart.

larity poll was taken that year in which fifty popular actresses were asked to list their ten favorite male stars. Randolph Scott was one of the ten along with such well established actors as Ronald Coleman, Clark Gable, James Cagney and Joel McCrea. Such stalwarts as Gary Cooper were not even on the list.

1934 also brought about a marked decrease in the number of Randolph Scott films from nine to two, both westerns in the Zane Grey series. 1935, however, saw the number increase again to six films, including four non-western.

Randy's non-western output for 1935 was a truly mixed bag of films. Included were the musical, *Roberta* with Fred Astaire and Ginger Rogers and dramas, *She*, based on one of a series of H.R. Haggard romantic fantasy novels from the late 1800's and *A Village Tale*, all from RKO Radio Pictures. Reviews were mixed. His non-western Paramount entry was *So Red The*

Follow the Fleet (RKO-1936). Visible over Randy's head is Frank Jenks.

Rose with Margaret Sullivan and Robert Cummings, a generally well received civil war love story.

Roberta was one of those great and unforgettable Astaire-Rogers films RKO Radio made in the 1930's. It had the music of Jerome Kern ("Smoke gets in Your Eyes", "I Won't Dance", "Lovely to Look At") and great dancing. It also had Randolph Scott. Fred got Ginger and Randy got Irene Dunne and the audience was rewarded with a shallow story that didn't hinder in any way the great music and dancing. *Roberta* was well received in 1935 by both the movie-going public and reviewers.

Scott's first release of 1936 was another Astaire-Rogers musical from RKO, *Follow The Fleet.*

Follow The Fleet was well received in 1936 and is still a terrific musical today. The cast, in addition to Fred Astaire, Ginger Rogers and Randolph Scott, included Harriet Hilliard (a young band vocalist who became Mrs. Ozzie Nelson), Astrid Allwyn, Harry Beresford and an up and coming young lady who would really come into her own in a few years—Betty Grable. Music was by Irving Berlin and direction by Mark Sandrich. Randy and Fred were a couple of sailors romancing Ginger and Harriet. The music flowed freely and such Berlin songs as "Let's Face the Music and Dance" and "Let Yourself Go". Fred and Ginger, Randolph Scott and Irving Berlin. RKO knew how to bring together a winning team. The movie going public was the ultimate winner.

Next came *And Sudden Death* from Paramount, the title referring to automobile safety rather than murder. Frances Drake was Randy's co-star in this little programmer. Scott turned in one of his best performances to date in James Fenimore Cooper's *The Last Of The Mohicans* (United Artists). It was directed by veteran director George B. Seitz and featured Binnie Barnes, Henry Wilcoxon, Heather Angel, Hugh Buckler and Bruce Cabot. This, the third screen version of Cooper's classic novel, remains a classic example of this type of film and compares quite favorably with *Northwest Passage* (MGM-1940) in this respect. As 1936 ended, Scott co-starred with Mae West in Paramount's *Go West, Young Man.* It featured such west dialog as "A thrill a day keeps the chill away".

High, Wide And Handsome (Paramount) with Irene Dunne, Dorothy Lamour and Charles Bickford, was the lone Randolph Scott film of 1937. The musical by Jerome Kern and Oscar Hammerstein was well received. Some-

Santa Fe (Columbia-1951) with Allene Roberts, Jerome Courtland and John Archer.

Carson City (WB-1952).

what dated today, with a corny plot, the Kern-Hammerstein score still holds up quite well.

By the end of 1937 Scott was a big star at a studio loaded with big stars.

CHAPTER IV

A RETURN TO THE SADDLE

Randy's first film of 1938 was a Shirley Temple picture for Twentieth Century-Fox, *Rebecca Of Sunnybrook Farm*. It didn't follow the book, but with Shirley Temple in it nobody cared. For Randy Scott, as with anyone who played with this captivating moppet, he could just hang in there, romance Gloria Stuart, look good and hope for the best. Randy would play in one other Temple picture the next year, *Susannah Of The Mounties* (Twentieth Century-Fox-1939).

Moving over to Universal for one film, he made *Road To Reno*. The story by Charles Kenyon and F. Hugh Herbert was about a girl (Hope Hampton) going to Reno to get her divorce while still being wooed by her husband (Scott), a westerner, and her husband-to-be (Alan Marshall), an easterner. This comedy was produced by Edmund Grainger and directed by Syvan Simon. The large cast included Glenda Farrell and Helen Broderick. Scott then swung his lanky frame back in the saddle for *The Texans*. Directed by James Hogan, *The Texans* was an adaptation of Emerson Hough's *North Of '36* and featured an impressive cast, Joan Bennett, Robert Cummings, May Robson and Walter Brennan (who, in 1936, would win the second of three academy awards he would win in his lifetime for *Kentucky*), good production values and enough action for any western fan. Set in post civil war Texas, the film was greatly helped by the presence of Randy Scott, who, it seemed, was a natural in western films. It was his last film of 1938 and his last at Paramount until 1948.

Twentieth Century-Fox had almost completely discontinued production of western films when they decided to make *Jesse James* in 1939. They had never really been involved with westerns to any great extent and had been somewhat less than overwhelmingly successful when they were. They never had a "B" unit, preferring to leave that to the other companies. Even

Action scene from *Frontier Marshal* (Fox-1939).

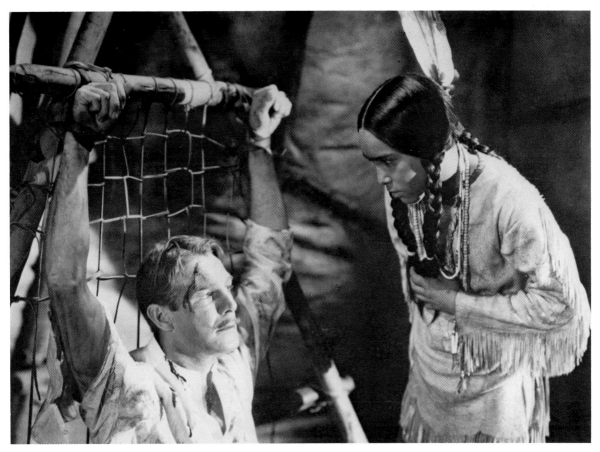

Randy in need of a little help in *Susannah Of The Mounties* (Fox-1939).

MGM had a fine "B" unit doing westerns in the 20's and early 30's, including very good series starring Tim McCoy. It was discontinued in the early 30's and they never returned to this type of film again.

Regardless of past problems in this area, Fox proceeded with *Jesse James*. It would be done in Technicolor. Daryl F. Zanuck himself, would produce. Nunnally Johnson would write the screenplay and Henry King would direct. Tyrone Power as Jesse and Henry Fonda as Frank headed a large cast that included Nancy Kelly, Henry Hull, Brian Donlevy, Jane Darwell, John Carradine and, of course, Randolph Scott. What evolved from all this was a rousing good western with enough action to please any fan and a film with enough story and plot to please anyone else. It proved to be a right move for Fox.

Wanting to follow on the successful *Jesse James*, Twentieth Century-Fox produced *Frontier Marshall* from the book *Wyatt Earp: Frontier*

Man In The Saddle (Columbia-1951) with Ellen Drew.

Carson City (WB-1952) with Lucille Norman and Richard Webb.

A lighter moment from *Riding Shotgun* (WB-1954) with Paul Picerni (center).

Hangman's Knot (Columbia-1952) with Frank Faylen and Monte Blue (on stagecoach) and Lee Marvin and Claude Jarman Jr. (right).

Rare still from *When The Daltons Rode* (Universal-1940) with Kay Francis.

Marshall by Stuart N. Lake. Lake's book had been filmed previously in 1934 with George O'Brien and would be filmed again in 1946 by John Ford directing. This version in 1939 comes off the well because of the presence of Randolph Scott as Wyatt Earp.

Scott's style of acting made him what everyone wanted their cowboy hero to be. "From Randolph Scott to Eddie Foy the actors fit their parts with perfection . . . ", said Bosley Crowther. Cesar Romero (as Doc Holliday) and Nancy Kelly rounded out the leads with support from Binnie Barnes, John Carradine, Ward Bond, Lon Chaney, Jr., Tom Tyler, Joe Sawyer, Edward Norris and Eddie Foy, Jr. This was, perhaps, Scott's best picture to date. It could only make the public hungry for more.

Randolph Scott was a full fledged star in star-laden Hollywood in 1939. *Gone With The Wind* (MGM, Selznick-1939) was being cast. Everyone seemed to sense that this picture was going to be something extra special, so casting was done very meticulously. Randy was seriously considered for the part of Ashley Wilkes, but lost out to Leslie Howard. It was said that, at the time, author Margaret Mitchell actually preferred Scott.

At the end of the 1930's, Randolph Scott had appeared in forty films starting with bits in films like *Sharp Shooter* (1928) and *The Far Call* (1929) and ending with starring roles in *Frontier Marshall* (Twentieth Century-Fox) and *20,000 Men A Year* (Twentieth Century-Fox-1939). Still to come were the 40's and the 50's and sixty good reasons to go out to a movie.

CHAPTER V

WHEN THE DALTONS RODE

In 1940 war was raging in Europe and movie attendance was on the decline in the United States. It would decline to its lowest point in 1941 (55,000,000 per week). By 1944, three years hence, attendance would increase to a whopping 100,000,000 persons per week. America wanted movies in the 1940's and it turned out to be a vintage decade.

If the 30's were good, the 40's would be better, moviewise. Moviegoers discovered in 1940 that if this year was any indication of what was to come, it would be a truly banner ten years.

Some of 1940's releases were *Of Mice And Men* (United Artists) which featured Charles Bickford, Lon Chaney, Jr., Burgess Meredith and Bob Steele; Alfred Hitchcock's *Rebecca;* MGM's *The Philadelphia Story;* Twentieth Century-Fox's *The Mark Of Zorro* and *The Grapes Of Wrath;* RKO's *Kitty Foyle;* Warner's *Meet John Doe* and *The Sea Wolf;* and John Wayne showing he really had talent in UA's *The Long Voyage Home.*

Randy Scott's film output continued to be varied. While he was now making westerns regularly (1945 would be the only year with nothing of this genre), he continued to show his versatility as RKO again cast him with his friend, Cary Grant and Irene Dunne in the excellent comedy, *My Favorite Wife.* Directed by Garson Kanin, this film is excellent and very funny today, and Scott's dry humor seems just right.

Also in 1940, Scott was teamed with Errol Flynn and Humphrey Bogart in Warner Bros.' *Virginia City.* Filmed in black and white and directed by Michael Curtiz, *Virginia City* was quite a good film. Flynn played a Union officer, Scott a Confederate officer and Bogart a Mexican bandit. It seems that Flynn wanted Scott's gold that was bound for the Confederacy to help in the war effort. Scott enlisted the aid of Bogart to help him get it there by attacking a Union garrison to create a diversion while the

Virginia City (WB-1940) with Russell Hicks (left), Humphrey Bogart and George Regas.

Virginia City (WB-1940) with (left to right) George Regas, Paul Fix, Humphrey Bogart and Moroni Olsen.

A Lawless Street (Columbia-1955).

gold was transported. It turned out that Bogart couldn't be trusted and he double-crossed Scott and killed him. Flynn then killed Bogart and decided to leave the gold hidden to help the South after the war. All very confusing? Not really. *Virginia City* turned out to be a good actioner, done justice by a good cast. It was the only time Scott ever worked with Errol Flynn or Humphrey Bogart. It is also interesting to note that this was the last of only two westerns Bogey ever made.

When The Daltons Rode (Universal), was based on a story by Emmett Dalton and Jack Jungmeyer, Sr. Emmett Dalton was the younger of the Dalton Brothers. The picture was directed by veteran action director George Marshall. Featured were Kay Francis, Brian Donlevy, Andy Devine, Broderick Crawford, Stuart Erwin, George Bancroft and, of course, Randolph Scott. All the ingredients necessary to make a good western.

The Daltons were a family of Kansas farmers who were forced by circumstance to become outlaws after one of them accidentally shot and killed a land grabber. It's a rousing, fast-paced western. The people come off as real people and you find yourself rooting for the Daltons (Donlevy, Crawford, Erwin and Frank Albertson) and their friend Tod Jackson (Scott) as they battle for survival against overwhelming odds, having both the bad guys and the law against them. The film comes to an exciting and inevitable climax in a livery stable in Coffeyville, Kansas, and it remains one of the highlights of the film. Randy Scott had really hit his stride now and regardless of what type of picture he would play in the future, he had established himself as a western performer of the highest caliber.

Scott's outlaw characterizations (as in *When The Daltons Rode*) always ended in justice being done, no matter how much we hated to see it. As Scott played him, a man could be outside the letter of the law, but still be a basically decent guy. That may have been pure pulp fiction, but it allowed Scott to give his fans a greater variety of roles while still giving them basically the same thing—RANDOLPH SCOTT. There were exceptions, such as *The Spoilers* (Universal-1942) when you were glad (if reluctantly) to see John Wayne give him his just desserts. Even in these pictures you knew this was no ordinary bad guy. This guy was cooler, smarter, more sure of himself. You knew that when the time came for Big Duke to do him in, it would be one hell of a contest. It always was.

With this characterization firmly established, Randolph Scott moved

Randy and everybody, including Claire Trevor in *The Stranger Wore A Gun* (Columbia-1953).

A serious discussion in *Riding Shotgun* (WB-1954).

Belle Starr (Fox-1941) with Joe Sawyer (left foreground), Chill Wills, Elizabeth Patterson and Owlin Howlin. Scott's arm is around Gene Tierney.

Gene Tierney, Randy Scott and Owlin Howlin in a tight spot in *Belle Starr* (Fox-1941).

into 1941 with two westerns from Twentieth Century-Fox. The first was an adaptation of Zane Grey's *Western Union*. It was Randy's first film based on the famous writer's books since his Paramount series in the 30's. Again, Fox went all the way with Fritz Lang directing, a good cast and Technicolor. Robert Young and Scott received top billing along with Dean Jagger and Virginia Gilmore. A good supporting cast included John Carradine, Slim Summerville, Chill Wills and Barton MacLane.

Western Union was a highly fictionalized version of true events, but still an exciting film. There were outlaws trying to prevent them from completing their tasks. There was even a big prairie fire. Add the rivalry between Randy and Robert Young for the affections of lovely Virginia Gilmore, and you had a good western that any red-blooded boy would be more than glad to pay his ten cents to see. A lot of them did. *Western Union* was very successful.

The war continued to rage in Europe and the Far East. It was even money that the United States would become involved soon. Those FOR entering the war ("war mongers") and those AGAINST ("isolationists") continued to debate the merits of each cause. Regardless of one's political beliefs, one needed entertainment. Among those qualified to provide this entertainment was Randolph Scott.

In 1941, Randy's second film was another "historical" western from Twentieth Century-Fox, *Belle Starr*. Again photographed in Technicolor, it was directed by Irving Cummings. The cast was impressive, but this time the results did not come off as well as in the previous films. Gene Tierney was a lovely Belle Starr and the rest of the cast included Dana Andrews, Chill Wills and Elizabeth Patterson. Scott was his usual, stalwart self, and the film, while not one of his best, was nevertheless an enjoyable big budget western.

December 7, 1941 and all the bickering between opposing factions on whether we should fight or not was settled once and for all. No longer were we divided. We were one. United we stand. So it was. Even now, in these dark times, as 1941 drew to a close, America's films were beginning to reflect just that. We were at war and Hollywood answered the call.

With Lee Marvin in *Seven Men From Now* (WB-1956).

7th Cavalry (Columbia-1956) with Jay C. Flippen.

Shoot-Out At Medicine Bend (WB-1957) with Dickie Bellis and Ann Doran.

CHAPTER VI

THE WAR YEARS

December 7, 1941 changed the world forever. Whole countries that existed before the war would never exist again. At least, not as they had been before. The far flung British Empire was entering its last years. The same was happening to the French, Dutch and Portugese. Most dramatic was the fact that the world had suddenly shrunk. Places whose names you may have only faintly remembered from your school geography classes suddenly became household words. Places you couldn't have cared less about were now of headline importance. The world had shrunk.

If movie attendance dipped just prior to World War II, it would now boom, reaching its peak in the postwar year of 1946. Then Hollywood, as the world had known it, would start to change forever.

It was all still a war away that fateful December. Right now Hollywood would be a busy, booming, furiously active place and would, in the next few years, turn out some of its finest motion pictures.

There were many fine war films, of course. MGM, with such veterans as Spencer Tracy, Lionel Barrymore and Franchot Tone, and talented newcomers like Van Johnson, Robert Walker and Robert Mitchum, would present such films as *A Guy Named Joe* (1943) and *Thirty Seconds Over Tokyo* (1944). Warners featured Humphrey Bogart and Raymond Massey in *Action In The North Atlantic* (1943), Errol Flynn and William Prince in *Objective Burma* (1945), and Cary Grant and John Garfield in *Destination Tokyo* (1943), a film about the submarine *Copperfin* that, early in 1942, sailed into Tokyo Bay to get weather information for the Doolittle Tokyo Raid. The film was so authentic the navy used it as a training film. Dramatically it is superb. The Doolittle Raid itself was authentically depicted in MGM's *Thirty Seconds Over Tokyo* based on the book by Ted Lawson and Bob Considine.

Twentieth Century-Fox made one of the best motion pictures of the

With Ralph Bellamy in *Coast Guard* (Columbia-1939).

To The Shores Of Tripoli (Fox-1942) with John Payne.

war years in 1944. Released in February as *The Sullivans*, it is the story of five brothers, how they grew up, married and went to war and were all killed in action—at the same time. It was the true story of Al, Frank, George, Matt and Joe Sullivan who grew up in Waterloo, Iowa.

Fox filmed the 111 minute picture with simplicity and honesty. Directed by Lloyd Bacon, the film featured Thomas Mitchell, Selena Royale, Bobby Driscoll, Ward Bond, Roy Roberts, Anne Baxter and Trudy Marshall.

On the heels of *The Sullivans*, Fox released another splendid war film, *The Purple Heart* (1944). With a fine cast headed by Dana Andrews and Richard Conte, it was a timely and moving story of the Japanese treatment of American prisoners of war.

There were so many more. *Guadalcanal Diary* (Fox-1943), *The North Star* (RKO-1944), *A Walk in the Sun* (Fox-1945) and on and on. There were also the non-war films. Warner Bros.' *Kings Row* (1942), the second Bob Hope-Bing Crosby-Dorothy Lamour "Road" picture *The Road To Morocco* (Paramount-1942), the classic western *The Ox-Bow Incident* (Fox-1943), *Lassie Come Home* (1943), *Meet Me In St. Louis* (1944), *National Velvet* (1944), *Anchors Aweigh* (1945), all from MGM. *The Lost Weekend, Going My Way, Laura, The Woman In The Window, Gaslight, The Adventures Of Mark Twain, State Fair*. This list goes on and, as with the war films, it is virtually endless. The 1940's produced the finest motion pictures in history. No decade can claim as many fine films back to back as the forties. Perhaps Hollywood knew what lay ahead for it in the not so distant future. Perhaps they knew and decided to give it their best shot. Maybe it was just the excitement of the war years, a time when the whole country was pulling together, that created a supercharged atmosphere that bred creativity. Perhaps it was because it was a decade when the movie industry wasn't bothered by mechanical innovations. Sound was now behind them and the multiple screen processes of the 1950's were yet to come, so they could concentrate on content. Whatever the reason, it was a banner decade and the war years (1942–45) were at the top of the list.

Randolph Scott made his first military film in 1939. He made two. *Coast Guard* (Columbia) and *20,000 Men A Year* (Fox), a story of the Army Air Corps. In 1941, with the war raging in Europe, he made his only non-western since 1939. *Paris Calling* (Universal) was an exciting story of

45

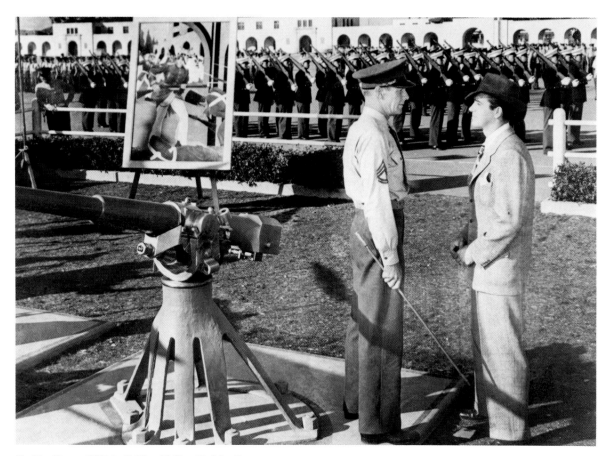

To The Shores Of Tripoli (Fox-1942) with John Payne.

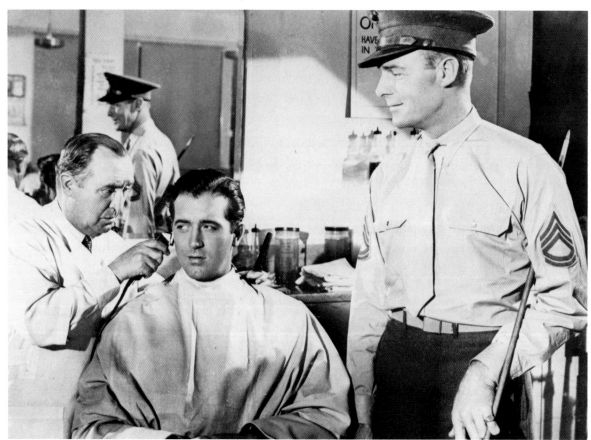

To The Shores Of Tripoli (Fox-1942) with John Payne (in chair).

the French underground resisting the Nazis. It featured Basil Rathbone, Gale Sondergaard, Lee J. Cobb and Eduardo Ciannelli. The female lead was Elisabeth Bergner. The cast was topnotch and the suspense nonstop.

Scott made three films in 1942 as he continued to be a very popular and well-liked actor. *To The Shores of Tripoli* (Fox) was a domestic war movie with all the action taking place at a marine training camp. One of the few films shot during the war years in color, the story concerned a spoiled, rich kid (John Payne) and Marine D.I. Randy Scott's attempts to make a man out of him, which he does at the end. Maureen O'Hara and Nancy Kelly provided the romantic interest in this bit of fluff.

The remainder of 1942, as far as Randolph Scott was concerned, was impressive. John Wayne, after years of serving his apprenticeship in countless programmers, had finally achieved a well deserved stardom in John Ford's 1939 classic, *Stagecoach*. Now he was getting first quality films. In 1942, two of them were with Randolph Scott.

Rex Beach's towering novel of gold mines and greed, *The Spoilers*, has been filmed (to date) five times. The Selig Company first filmed it in 1914 with William Farnum and Tom Santschi. It was again filmed in 1922 with the leads taken by Milton Sills and Noah Beery. Paramount filmed it for the third time in 1930 with William Boyd and Gary Cooper. Twelve years later Universal made the venerable story with John Wayne and Randolph Scott. Universal would also make it for the last time in 1955 with the leads taken by Rory Calhoun and Jeff Chandler, but the 1942 version is probably the best of them all, with one of the longest, best staged fights in cinematic history. Scott was the villainous gold commissioner, Alexander McNamara. Marlene Dietrich was the saloon girl in love with Wayne. Margaret Lindsay was the bad girl. Directed by Ray Enright, the cast included Harry Carey, Richard Barthelmess, George Cleveland, William Farnum (who had appeared in the 1914 version) and Russell Simpson.

On the surface, *The Spoilers* seems like just another western melodrama, but the classic fight scene (lasting the better part of a reel) between Wayne and Scott makes this film well worth watching. It set the pattern for years to come.

In August of 1942, Wayne and Scott were again teamed with Marlene Dietrich for the film, *Pittsburgh*.

Starting as miners and buddies, Wayne and Scott start to move up the

To The Shores Of Tripoli (Fox-1942) with John Payne.

Belle Of The Yukon (RKO-1944) with (l-r) Guinn Williams, Charles Winninger, Bob Burns and Robert Armstrong.

ladder of financial success. Wayne, however, becomes power-crazed and somewhat crooked. In the end he comes to his senses and the friends are reunited as World War II breaks out. Louise Albritton, Shemp Howard (of 3 Stooges fame), Thomas Gomez and Paul Fix were among the supporting cast.

The Spoilers and *Pittsburgh* were the only times Randolph Scott and John Wayne ever appeared in a film together, but it was not the only time they were associated in motion picture making. Down the road a few years, Scott would make one of his finest films and best westerns ever—for John Wayne.

1943 and the world continued to be engulfed by war. Hollywood continued to turn out some of the finest movies ever. At Universal, an already famous Alfred Hitchcock made a taut little thriller called *Shadow Of A Doubt*. It starred Joseph Cotten, Teresa Wright and Macdonald Carey. Twentieth Century-Fox released *The Ox-Bow Incident* with Henry Fonda and Dana Andrews. A somber, shocking western, it was received poorly at the box office when first released. Only later was it accepted for the fine motion picture it is. 1943 also saw *Heaven Can Wait* (Fox), *For Whom The Bell Tolls* (Paramount), *See Here Private Hargrove*, *The Human Comedy* and *Girl Crazy* (all from MGM). A vintage year. At Columbia, Scott made his first true, back-in-the-saddle western since 1941's *Western Union*. Photographed in Technicolor, *The Desperadoes* was his 50th film. Directed by Charles Vidor from a Max Brand story, *The Desperadoes* featured Glenn Ford, Guinn Williams, Claire Trevor, Edgar Buchannan, Irving Bacon, Evelyn Keyes and Glenn Strange. It told the story of an outlaw (Ford) who goes straight to help a marshall (Scott) clean up a lawless town. It was a good western with believable plot and action. Columbia's faith in the film was rewarded at the box office. The producer was Harry Joe Brown. *The Desperadoes* was his second film with Scott— first as producer. It marked the start of a long and successful partnership between the two (Scott-Brown Productions/Ranown Productions) that would produce some of the finest westerns ever during the next fifteen years.

After his lone western of 1943, Scott made three war films. *Bombardier* (RKO Radio) was a fine action film. Scott's co-stars were Pat O'Brien, Robert Ryan, Anne Shirley, Eddie Albert and Barton MacLane. The story of

Belle Of The Yukon (RKO-1944) talking to Robert Armstrong.

With Gypsy Rose Lee in *Belle Of The Yukon* (RKO-1944).

the training of B-17 pilots for daylight bombing raids on Japan, it was believable and good entertainment though not particularly well received at the time.

The second of the three films, and probably the best was *Corvette K-225*. Produced by Howard Hawks and directed by Richard Rossen, the film co-starred Ella Raines and James Brown, and had an extensive cast including Noah Beery, Jr., Barry Fitzgerald, Fuzzy Knight, Andy Devine, Thomas Gomez, Walter Sande and an up-and-coming Robert Mitchum.

Corvette K-225 was the story of one of the Canadian Navy's convoy escorts during an Atlantic crossing. The film had a documentary feel and the cast, headed by Scott, generally showed remarkable restraint.

Scott's fourth film of 1943 was *Gung Ho!* also from Universal. Released in December, *Gung Ho!* was the true story of Captain W.S. LeFrancois, USMC, and was produced by Walter Wanger and directed by Ray Enright. Appearing were Grace McDonald who, until now, had been relegated to musicals at Universal, Alan Curtis, Noah Beery, Jr., J. Carrol Naish, Robert Mitchum, Milburn Stone, Louis Jean Heydt and Rod Cameron.

Gung Ho! followed a group of Marine raiders from the beginning of their training through action in the South Pacific Theatre. The result was a typically interesting war film.

Scott made one film in 1944. It was a non-western film for RKO Radio *Belle Of The Yukon*. It featured Scott as a saloon owner (slightly crooked) who goes straight at the insistence of his girl, played by Gypsy Rose Lee. Not a musical in the truest sense, it nonetheless had music. Also in the cast were Dinah Shore, Charles Winninger, Florence Bates and William Marshall. Randy Scott in a cut-waist coat, the worst looking pair of striped pants the world has seen and spats, was almost too much. Despite all of it though, it wasn't a really bad picture. Just forgettable.

Also in 1944, Scott made a guest appearance in a film at Universal entitled, *Follow The Boys*. It was a musical about the forming of the USO shows in World War II. Dozens of Hollywood performers appeared in brief cameos. Scott appeared in the Hollywood victory sequence. The film is a treat to see because it contains most of the people who were performing in motion pictures in 1944. Some great moments and at 122 minutes there were many. It was his last film at Universal Pictures.

Belle Of The Yukon (RKO-1944) with Gypsy Rose Lee and friend.

China Sky (RKO-1945) with Ellen Drew.

Portrait still from *China Sky* (RKO-1945).

In 1945 Scott appeared in two films. Neither was a western. *China Sky* (RKO) again teamed him with director Ray Enright who directed many Scott films. *China Sky* was from a story by Pearl S. Buck and concerned a doctor (Scott) helping the Chinese fight the Japanese. Ellen Drew portrayed his worthless wife who is killed in the end. Featured were Richard Loo, Anthony Quinn, Carol Thurston and Ruth Warrick.

Scott's second film of 1945 teamed him with the famous Charles Laughton. Randolph Scott western fans would have to wait until another time. It was ho-hum time on the high seas. The film was *Captain Kid* (United Artists). Also in the cast were Barbara Britton, Reginald Owen, John Carradine and Gilbert Roland. Terrific cast, but it was all for naught.

So ended 1945. The best was yet to come.

Captain Kidd (UA-1945) with a rather formidable Charles Laughton.

Captain Kidd (UA-1945) with Charles Laughton.

INTERVIEWS

A handsome portrait of Randy and Lucille Norman from Warner's *Carson City* (1952).

"Randolph was truly a Southern gentleman of great charm and manner and everybody liked him very much."

Dr. Donald Curtis
Former actor, now minister
of Unity Church of Dallas
Dallas, Texas

"I worked with Randy many times and he
was and is a lovely man . . . "

Noah Beery Jr.
Co-star of "Rockford Files"
Universal/NBC

INTERVIEW WITH ROY HUGGINS

Roy Huggins is a name synonymous with fine entertainment. He has been a screenwriter—"I Love Trouble" (1948) with Franchot Tone and Janet Blair, "The Lady Gambles" (1949) with Barbara Stanwyck and Robert Preston, "Sealed Cargo" (1951) with Dana Andrews and Carla Balenda and "Hangman's Knot" (1952) with Randolph Scott and director— "Hangman's Knot" (1952). "Hangman's Knot" was Randy Scott's biggest moneymaker.

Mr. Huggins then took his talent into television where he created and produced such hits as "Maverick" (with James Garner and Jack Kelly), "The Fugitive" (with David Janssen), "Run For Your Life" (with Ben Gazzara), "Alias Smith & Jones" (with Ben Murphy and Peter Duel) and "The Rockford Files" (with James Garner).

Brim Crow: How many years have you known Randolph Scott?

Roy Huggins: I met him when I directed "Hangman's Knot." I have seen him only once since.

Brim Crow: How many times have you worked with him?

Roy Huggins: Only the one time.

Brim Crow: Was "Hangman's Knot" the only film you directed in?

Roy Huggins: Yes.

Brim Crow: Did you produce or write any other films for him or with him?

Roy Huggins:	No.

Brim Crow:	How do you regard Randolph Scott as an actor?
Roy Huggins:	He created the "Randolph Scott" character and played it to perfection. I'm not sure that's "acting." It may even be something superior to acting.

Brim Crow:	How was he regarded industry wide?
Roy Huggins:	Tolerantly.

Brim Crow:	How do you regard him personally?
Roy Huggins:	I liked him.

Brim Crow:	He always seemed so serious on the screen. Was he that serious off camera?
Roy Huggins:	He was the same off screen as on: reserved, humorless, polite, modest, unassuming.

Brim Crow:	Was he an easy actor to work with as a director?
Roy Huggins:	He was a pleasure to work with. I gave him only a half-dozen directions, all of which he followed without question and with ease.

Brim Crow:	How was he with other performers?
Roy Huggins:	He was friendly but reserved. He kept to himself.

Brim Crow:	Did he really seem to like acting?
Roy Huggins:	No, I think he looked on it as a way of earning a very good living. I don't think he thought of himself as an actor, certainly not as an "artist."

Brim Crow:	I cannot picture him being difficult. Was he ever?
Roy Huggins:	He was never difficult.

Brim Crow:	Was he really as good a horseman in real life as he appears on the screen?

Roy Huggins: Yes.

Brim Crow: Randolph Scott was in westerns exclusively from the late 1940s on. Was this something he chose or did it just turn out that way?

Roy Huggins: I believe he chose it, but there was probably no demand for him in other roles.

Brim Crow: Do you know if he preferred westerns to other types of films?

Roy Huggins: He obviously did, for himself.

Brim Crow: Do you know if he had a favorite co-star? Leading Lady? Character Actor?

Roy Huggins: I don't believe he did.

Brim Crow: Do you know his birthplace? Again I have two (Virginia and North Carolina).

Roy Huggins: I don't know.

Brim Crow: Was Harry Joe Brown his only partner? How long? How many films?

Roy Huggins: I think so. They made a great many films together over a long period of time.

Brim Crow: Do you still have contact with him today (business or social)?
Roy Huggins: No.

Brim Crow: Do you know anything about his activities today? His hobbies?

Roy Huggins: No.

Brim Crow: Do you have a favorite Scott film? Do you know if he does?
Roy Huggins: My favorite, naturally, is "Hangman's Knot." I would like to think it is also his. It made more money than his other

"Scott-Brown" films and was more favorably received. Even the *New York Times* praised it.

Brim Crow: Do you know if Randolph Scott ever acted on television? Appeared on TV?

Roy Huggins: I don't think he did.

Brim Crow: Do you know what kind of business he is in today?

Roy Huggins: Oil, *I believe.*

Claude Akins.

INTERVIEW WITH CLAUDE AKINS

Claude Akins is an actor who cannot be categorized. On one hand he is the best and blackest of villains that our Saturday hero ever had to face. Yet, he is equally at home on that white horse himself. He is a gifted comedy actor. Take your pick. Claude Akins has done it all.

Since his debut in motion pictures in 1953, Claude has made countless movies and television shows, including Randy Scott's fine 1960 film, *Comanche Station* (Columbia). His television credits include anthologies, comedy, drama, westerns and series including "Nashville 99" which co-starred Jerry Reed and the tremendously successful and popular "Movin On" which co-starred Frank Converse and "The Misadventures of Sheriff Lobo," based on the character he created in the hit movie and subsequent series "B. J. and the Bear."

Brim Crow: How many years have you known Randolph Scott?
Claude Akins: Since 1957.

Brim Crow: How many times have you worked with him?
Claude Akins: Once—*Comanche Station*.

Brim Crow: How do you regard Randolph Scott as an actor?
Claude Akins: More personality than actor.

Brim Crow: How was he regarded industry wide?
Claude Akins: With much respect.

Brim Crow:	How do you regard him personally?
Claude Akins:	Fondly—A real southern gentleman.
Brim Crow:	He always seemed so serious on the screen. Was he that serious off?
Claude Akins:	He was very pleasant and a little on the serious side.
Brim Crow:	Was he an easy actor to work with?
Claude Akins:	Yes, very easy.
Brim Crow:	How was he with other performers?
Claude Akins:	Gracious and helpful.
Brim Crow:	Did he really seem to like acting?
Claude Akins:	He read the *Wall Street Journal*, not Shakespeare.
Brim Crow:	I cannot picture him being difficult. Was he ever?
Claude Akins:	Not to, or with, me.
Brim Crow:	Was he really as good a horseman as he appeared on the screen?
Claude Akins:	I think so.
Brim Crow:	Do you know if Randolph Scott ever considered returning to films after he retired in 1962? How many offers he had? Did he plan to retire after *Ride The High Country* or did it just happen that way?
Claude Akins:	He joined the Los Angeles Country Club, which does not take actors. My understanding is that he promised not to perform again, in order to be accepted for membership.
Brim Crow:	Do you have a favorite Scott film?
Claude Akins:	*Comanche Station*, of course!!!

Brim Crow: Do you know what kind of business he is in today?

Claude Akins: Investments, I understand.

Superb action scene from *Seven Men From Now* (WB-1956), with Randolph Scott on the left and Lee Marvin.

Seven Men From Now (WB-1956).

PART II

CHAPTER VII

THE WESTERN ERA

The war was over. Sons and husbands and fathers and brothers were coming home. It had been a long, long four years. The world was picking up the pieces and trying to return to some semblance of normalcy. In this country, with wartime price freezes lifted, prices shot out of sight. Automobiles that sold for $800 new in 1941 now sold for $2,000 used. Housing was at a premium as GIs who had left as boys, returned as men and were starting their own families. But the war was over. We could live with the rest.

In 1946 television was still two years away. Radio was still king of the airwaves and going "out to a movie" was still the thing to do. And we did. 1946 was the best year for movie attendance in history. We did indeed go out to the movies. Some of the terrific movies we saw that year were Samuel Goldwyn's moving *The Best Years Of Our Lives* (RKO). Directed with excellence by William Wyler, it starred Myrna Loy, Fredric March and Dana Andrews. It was not to be missed. 1946 also saw Ray Milland's award-winning performance in Paramount's *The Lost Weekend*. MGM gave us *The Green Years* and RKO-Radio had *The Bells of St. Mary's* with Bing Crosby and Ingrid Bergman and Alfred Hitchcock's *Notorious* with Cary Grant. Twentieth Century-Fox had *Anna & The King Of Siam* with Rex Harrison and Irene Dunne. Warner Bros. presented Gary Cooper and Ingrid Bergman in the classic *Saratoga Trunk*. MGM also presented the musical *The Harvey Girls* with Judy Garland and John Hodiak, one of the best musicals of this or any year, and the deeply moving *The Yearling* with Jane Wyman, Gregory Peck and Claude Jarman, Jr. There were many, many more as the movie-going public was richly rewarded for its record attendance.

Randolph Scott swung his lanky 6'3" frame back into the saddle for the first time since 1941's *Western Union* and *Belle Starr*, for his first film of 1946. Released by United Artists, the film was *Abilene Town*. Directed by

Tall Man Riding Riding (Columbia-1955).

Besting Jock Mahoney in *Santa Fe* (Columbia-1951).

With John Archer (left) and Noah Beery Jr. in *Decision at Sundown* (Columbia-1957).

A vigilant Randolph Scott in *Decision at Sundown* (Columbia-1957).

Edwin L. Marin who had directed *Paris Calling* in 1944 and would direct several more, *Abilene Town* had all the right ingredients. Screenplay was by Harold Shumate from a story by Ernest Haycox and the producer was Jules Levy. Both Shumate and Levy had worked with Scott in the Paramount-Zane Grey series in the 1930s. *Abilene Town* also had a cast of veterans including Ann Dvorak, Edgar Buchanan, Rhonda Fleming, Lloyd Bridges, Hank Patterson, Eddie Waller and the villainous Dick Curtis. The story concerned the conflict between homesteaders and cattlemen in the years following the Civil War. It all worked. It was a good way for Randy Scott to start his "western years".

Scott's second release of 1946, *Badman's Territory*, came in April and must be considered a landmark film for two reasons. It marked the first association of Scott and producer Nat Holt, a pairing that would prove to be a productive one as Holt would go on to produce seven of Scott's best films, and it was a smash at the box office. The public was declaring that THIS was the Randolph Scott they loved and wanted to see. It was probably this single film more than any one thing that convinced Scott to concentrate on westerns during the second half of his career. With only three exceptions, all of his films from 1946 through 1962 were westerns. The choice was his. It is obvious that his choice was the right one for him and for the movie-going public.

Badman's Territory (RKO) was a truly good western but not an exceptional picture. What it did have as its most important ingredient was what must be called the Randolph Scott formula. It all clicked. Scott never deviated from it afterwards. The end result was a string of 38 top quality westerns. Directed by Tim Whelan, *Badman's Territory* told the story of the problems encountered by a U.S. Marshal in pursuit of outlaws who were getting away by entering land not under governmental control. A superb supporting cast featuring George "Gabby" Hayes, Ann Richards, Tom Tyler, Lawrence Tierney, Kermit Maynard, James Warren and Steve Brodie helped make *Badman's Territory* such a good film.

Moving back to Twentieth Century-Fox for the first time since 1942, Scott made the first of three non-western films that would mark an end to that phase of his career. It would also be his last film of 1946.

Home, Sweet Homicide was a mystery-comedy about the children (Peggy Ann Garner and Dean Stockwell) of mystery writer Lynn Bari who

7th Cavalry (Columbia-1956) with Russell Hicks.

7th Cavalry (Columbia-1956) with Frank Faylen (left) and Jay C. Flippen.

Randy seems quite unconcerned that Richard Boone has a gun on him in *The Tall T* (Columbia-1957).

A Lawless Street (Columbia-1955) with Angela Lansbury.

A business-like pose from *Buchannan Rides Alone* (Columbia-1958).

solve a local murder and find a new hubby (Randolph Scott) for Mom in the bargain. It was directed by Lloyd Bacon.

Trail Street (RKO) again joined Scott with producer Nat Holt and director Ray Enright. Scott Played Bat Masterson, in a fictional account of Masterson saving the town of Liberal, Kansas from corruption. Robert Ryan, Anne Jeffreys and George Hayes co-starred. It was Scott's first film of 1947.

In the spring of 1947, he returned to Columbia for *Gunfighters*. It was his first film at the studio since 1943's *The Desperadoes*. Adapted from Zane Grey's *Twin Sombreros* by Alan LeMay, who had done screenplays for the Paramount-Zane Grey series of a decade before, it was quite faithful to the original. Typical Zane Grey, it told the story of a gunfighter (Scott) who had sworn to hang up his guns only to find himself drawn into a range war. Directed by George Waggner, *Gunfighters* again teamed not only Scott and producer Harry Joe Brown, it also teamed him again with lovely Barbara Britton. Dorothy Hart, Bruce Cabot, Forrest Tucker, Charley Grapewin and Steven Geray rounded out a typically fine cast. *Gunfighters* ended Randolph Scott's Zane Grey series that had begun 15 years earlier in 1932.

After *Gunfighters*, Columbia scheduled a film called *Lona Hanson* with Scott, William Holden and Rita Hayworth. It was to be a large budget film in color and so forth, but Hayworth's personal problems caused an indefinite postponement, so Scott moved on to United Artists for *Christmas Eve*. *Lona Hanson* was never made.

With the sole exception of a brief cameo in Warner Bros.' *Starlift* (1951), *Christmas Eve* marked Randolph Scott's final appearance in a non-western film. All but forgotten, *Christmas Eve* concerns the story of a dowager (Ann Harding) who calls her family together for Christmas and the discovery by her stepsons that certain members of her family mean her no good. An attempt at comedy-drama, it was all rather slow moving. Others in the rather illustrious cast included George Raft, Joan Blondell, Reginald Denny and Virginia Field. It has been reissued as *Sinner's Holiday*. *Christmas Eve* was Scott's last film of 1947 and his last film ever for United Artists.

Badman's Territory (RKO-1946) and the beginning of "The Western Era."

Gunfighters (Columbia-1947) with Dorothy Hart (left), Barbara Britton and Bruce Cabot. Randy is on Steel, a favorite of many western actors.

Gunfighters (Columbia-1947) with villain Grant Withers.

Gunfighters (Columbia-1947).

Gunfighters (Columbia-1947).

Facing Bruce Cabot in *Gunfighters* (Columbia-1947).

Gunfighters (Columbia-1947) with Dorothy Hart, Charlie Grapewin and John Miles (left to right).

Christmas Eve (UA-1947) with Dennis Hoey (dark suit).

Christmas Eve (UA-1947) with Ann Harding (left) and Virginia Field.

CHAPTER VIII

THE WINDS OF CHANGE

By late 1947 you didn't have to be a genius to know that the Hollywood motion picture community was in big trouble.

The beginnings of Hollywood's problems came from a seemingly unlikely source—the Congress of the United States.

With World War II over and the country trying its best to return to some semblance of normality, Congress decided to go after the communists. Well and good except for one little thing. Instead of a true anti-communist program, Congress turned it into a witch hunt. Led by Congressman J. P. Thomas and his House Un-American Activities Committee, they turned it into a wholesale massacre of the motion picture industry. Many careers were ruined with nothing more than innuendo. A blacklist was distributed and, if your name was on it, you were unable to work. Guilt or innocence never entered into it.

By 1947 and 1948 the studio system that had so long dominated the industry was itself in jeopardy. Stars that had for so many years been associated with a certain studio were leaving when their contracts expired. Instead of going to another studio, however, they were remaining independent and forming their own production companies, and then contracting with major studio for distribution of the finished product. This was particularly true of stars returning from the Armed Forces after the war. Gene Autry, for example, chose not to return to Republic where Roy Rogers had become the king of the hill in his absence, choosing instead to move over to Columbia. In some instances the returning players were unable to pick up where they left off because of less than ideal films. Clark Gable had hit his ultimate peak in 1939 in *Gone With The Wind* (Selznick-MGM). Returning from the service in 1946, MGM put him in a string of mediocre films and his popularity dipped accordingly. As soon as he could, Gable left Metro for greener pastures.

With an anxious, but calm, Joan Weldon in *Riding Shotgun* (WB-1954).

Randy is "The Man in Black" in *Carson City* (WB-1952).

Similar circumstances affected Robert Taylor. Taylor did stay at MGM, although he never regained his prewar popularity.

Change was prevalent and, although it took fully another ten years for it to become complete, the erosion of the major studios had started.

In 1948 another change was taking place. All across America, a strange appendage was appearing on the rooftops of homes. As if Hollywood didn't have enough problems, with unhappy stars exiting and Congress giving them fits; an impertinent upstart named television arrived on the scene.

It was almost too much to bear. Radio with pictures. Perhaps if we just ignore it, it will go away.

But television didn't go away. It stayed. And grew stronger. And bigger. And the viewers were people who used to go out to the movies. The bottom fell out of attendance. It was the end of the movie industry.

Almost.

You don't get to be the best at anything without knowing what you are about. Hollywood did. They knew how to fight. In fifty short years the motion picture industry had come from primitive infancy to the state of the art that made it the world leader in entertainment. They weren't about to throw in the towel. Not yet.

And so Hollywood geared up to weather the storm. Ignoring television, of course, didn't work. Television had come to stay. And Hollywood's problems cost the industry some of their weaker companies. But when the smoke had cleared, what was left was the best Hollywood had to offer. And the movie-going public was the winner.

Randy is "The Man in Black" in *Carson City* (WB-1954).

CHAPTER IX

THE MAN IN BLACK

Despite the turmoil of the film industry during the late forties, some performers kept right on going without so much as a letdown. One such was Randolph Scott. His star continued to rise at a rapid rate. He had never been more popular. The movie-going public knew what it wanted. It wanted Randolph Scott.

It was now 1948 as he returned to his "home" studio, Paramount, for the last time. The film, released in February of that year, was Luke Short's *Albuquerque*. In Cinecolor, it was directed by Ray Enright (his fifth turn at directing a Randolph Scott picture) and featured a whole host of Scott regulars including: Barbara Britton (her third), George Hayes (fourth), Irving Bacon (fourth), Russell Hayden, Russell Simpson, George Cleveland (third) and Lon Chaney Jr. Scott was a Texas Ranger turned freight-line operator who is accused of the robbery of a gold shipment. A good western.

A return to Columbia Pictures again teamed him with director Ray Enright for the sixth time. (Enright would direct eight in all, including all 1948 releases). The film was *Coroner Creek* by Luke Short. Photographed in Cinecolor, it was released July 1, 1948. *Coroner Creek* served to introduce George Macready as a villain in Scott films. A worthy nemesis he would prove to be through several films. In *Coroner Creek*, Macready has killed Scott's fiancee and Scott is out to avenge her death. It is a good action western. Included were Marguerite Chapman, Forrest Tucker and Edgar Buchannan. The rest of the cast included many veterans from previous Scott films.

Coroner Creek marked the third time a Randolph Scott film had been produced by Harry Joe Brown (the first were *Western Union* in 1941 and *The Desperadoes* in 1943). In 1949, Scott and Brown would again team for the fourth and fifth times, and form a partnership that would produce 18 fine westerns over the next decade.

Coroner Creek (Columbia-1948) with Sally Eilers.

Coroner Creek (Columbia-1948) with Marguerite Chapman and a villainous Forrest Tucker.

Just 16 days after Columbia's release of *Coroner Creek*, RKO-Radio Pictures released one of the all-time classic westerns, Nat Holt's *Return Of The Bad Men*. Co-starring Robert Ryan, the film was a box office smash. "B" fan (and who wasn't) and "A" fan, this picture pleased nearly everyone. Scott was a marshal who encountered such villains as Billy the Kid, the Daltons, the Youngers, the Doolins (Scott would BE Bill Doolin in 1949), and a character familiar to movie-goers of the 1970's—The Sundance Kid. Anne Jeffreys, George "Gabby" Hayes and Robert Armstrong headed a large supporting cast. RKO really knew how to make a western in the period of 1945–1955. *Return Of The Bad Men* was one of their best examples. It also continued to prove that this was the Randolph Scott the public had really wanted all along. In two more years, he would be one of the top ten stars in Hollywood. 1948 was indeed a vintage year.

In 1949, Scott and Harry Joe Brown officially formed Scott-Brown Productions. An independent actor, making pictures for several studios rather than signing a long-term contract with just one, this gave Randolph Scott the actor, a much more solid base from which to work. Now he had a production company. Both Scott and Brown continued with outside ventures, but the bulk of film output for the period of 1949 through 1960 for either one of them, was Scott-Brown westerns for Columbia Pictures.

The formation of Scott-Brown did not preclude Scott's making films with (or for) Nat Holt. He would make two films for Holt in 1949 *(Canadian Pacific* and *Fighting Man Of The Plains)*, one in 1950 *(The Cariboo Trail)*, all for Twentieth Century-Fox release, and a final film in 1955 *(Rage At Dawn)* for RKO Radio. The Scott-Holt ventures produced some of the best films Scott ever appeared in. Holt, a prolific producer in his own right, with such films as *The Great Missouri Raid* (Paramount-1951) with Wendell Corey and Macdonald Carey and *The Denver And Rio Grande* (Paramount-1952) with Edmund O'Brien, Sterling Hayden and Dean Jagger, still produced his best westerns with Scott.

Canadian Pacific returned directorial duties to Edwin L. Marin for the fourth time. Marin would direct six of the next ten Scott features. Photographed in Technicolor, the film featured Jane Wyatt (who had been in *Western Union*), J. Carrol Naish, veteran heavy Victor Jory and a rather new, young actress, Nancy Olson. Scott was a railroad surveyor who had to fight Indians (and Jory) to complete the railroad. Misses Wyatt and Olson

The Doolins of Oklahoma (Columbia-1949) with Noah Beery Jr. (right).

The Doolins Of Oklahoma (Columbia-1949) with Lee Patrick (left) and Charles Kemper.

provided the romantic interest. *Canadian Pacific* was a good picture and a big moneymaker.

The first Scott-Brown production for 1949 was *The Walking Hills* for Columbia. Directed by John Sturges, who later directed such films as *Bad Day At Black Rock* (MGM-1955) and *The Magnificent Seven* (Mirisch-1960), *The Walking Hills* was a contemporary western rather than a period piece. The story concerned an ill-assorted band of people searching for a lost gold mine. It was a rather exciting, tense study of individuals, each after the same goal, each for his or her own reasons. There is a sandstorm sequence so realistic you can almost feel the grit in your own teeth. The impressive cast included Ella Raines, William Bishop, Arthur Kennedy, Edgar Buchanan, John Ireland, Jerome Courtland and folk singer Josh White.

Scott's third release of 1949 and second Scott-Brown production was the classic western film *The Doolins of Oklahoma*. Directed by Gordon Douglas, *The Doolins of Oklahoma* had all the classic elements to make it a truly memorable western film. It ranks as one of the all time favorite Scott westerns. The story of the infamous Bill Doolin and his brothers who became outlaws in the late 1800s and of the pursuit of a lawman who relentlessly hounded them and thwarted all efforts on Bill Doolin's part to leave his life of crime and settle down with his wife to a life of peace. In the end, all of the Doolins, including Bill, are killed by lawmen. There is an undercurrent of tension that runs throughout the picture. Through the use of black and white photography and shadows, the film creates an atmosphere that, until that time, had seldom been used in westerns. Using these techniques and keeping his actors underplaying their parts, director Douglas builds the film to a shattering, but inevitable climax.

The Doolins Of Oklahoma was box-office magic. Featuring Scott, clad all in black for the first time, as the ill-starred Bill Doolin and George Macready as the relentless lawman, it featured Noah Beery, Jr., John Ireland and Jock Mahoney as the Doolin gang and Louise Allbritton as Doolin's wife.

Topping a banner year was Nat Holt's *Fighting Man Of The Plains* (Twentieth Century-Fox). Written by Frank Gruber, who also did the screenplay, *Fighting Man Of The Plains* told the story of Frank James (Scott) out to avenge the death of his brother, Jessie. Featured were Bill Williams, Victor Jory, Jane Nigh, Douglas Kennedy and a young Dale Robertson in his most important role to date.

The Doolins of Oklahoma (Columbia-1949) with John Ireland (left) and Jock Mahoney.

Fighting Man Of The Plains (Fox-1949).

Fighting Man Of The Plains (Fox-1949) with Douglas Kennedy (standing at left) and Rhys Williams (at desk).

Jane Nigh prevents Joan Taylor from doing something foolish in *Fighting Man Of The Plains* (Fox-1949).

Sheriff Bill Williams holds a gun on Rhys Williams while Paul Fix, Barry Kelly, Randy Scott and others look on in *Fighting Man Of The Plains* (Fox-1949).

Randy Scott with Jane Nigh, Victor Jory and an unhappy Paul Fix in *Fighting Man Of The Plains* (Fox-1949).

Hollywood, September 28, 1949—Governor Frank Carlson of Kansas (right) pins a badge on actor Randolph Scott and commissions him a member of the Kansas State Peace Officers at a ceremony here yesterday. Scott and other principal players and executives were honored for their contributions to the movie "Fighting Man of the Plains", a story of Kansas frontier history of the 1870s. (Associated Press).

CHAPTER X

THE GOLDEN FIFTIES—THE TOP TEN

At the end of 1949, after a long string of critical and box-office successes, Randolph Scott entered the magic circle. He became one of the top ten motion picture stars in America. He would stay there through 1953, after which the poll was discontinued. The poll was the Motion Picture Herald Poll. In 1950 Scott was tenth. In 1951 he was eighth. He had found a formula the public liked. If Randolph Scott's name appeared on the marquee, it would be a good picture. His string of successful films would continue through 1962.

Elsewhere in Hollywood, the motion picture industry continued to do battle with television and a shrinking box-office. The low had been reached in the late 1940s and a new resurgence could be seen. MGM, which had been such a leader for years, continued to be so, but with less gloss more drama in their black and white films. Releasing such films as *The Asphalt Jungle* in 1950, they proved that Paramount, Warners and RKO had no exclusivity on stark, realistic dramas. The color musicals were still there, as only MGM could make them and a fine "B" unit was still turning out excellent programmers, but westerns still didn't seem to fit into MGM's plans and, although they made several good ones during this period, it seemed a lost cause.

At other studios, however, it was a different story. RKO continued to turn out some of the best of all kinds of films. Seeming to lean more toward black and white than some of the other studios, RKO Radio Pictures turned out a series of fine dramas with a good mix of westerns. Robert Mitchum and Jane Russell did yeoman service in both types of films. Mitchum, himself a graduate of westerns (some with Randolph Scott), was quite at home in the saddle. RKO also continued a good "B" series with Tim Holt, but it would not be for much longer. Columbia was very big in the western market. For starters, they had Randolph Scott and Gene Autry. They also had Charles

A tender moment with Phyllis Kirk in *Thunder Over The Plains* (WB-1953).

Starrett continuing in the Durango Kid series. Columbia also had a particularly good "B" unit. In addition to all of this, they released much of the product of independent producers. Columbia had long been regarded as something of a "stepchild" by some of the other majors. Columbia, along with Universal, Republic and some of the others were referred to as "Poverty Row" despite the fact that both Columbia and Universal were older than most of the others. Perhaps it was because Columbia produced more "B" product than the other majors. But time would prove Columbia was doing something right, because, in the 1970's when many of the giants were floundering, Columbia and Universal would continue to prosper.

Twentieth Century-Fox had eased off on the "A" westerns and were concentrating more on dramas and musicals, but had taken up the slack with a good series of "B's" using young performers such as Dale Robertson, Robert Wagner and Mitzi Gaynor. These were all in color and quite well made. Monogram was still two years away from becoming Allied Artists, and their main product continued to be series westerns (Johnny Mack Brown and others) and series comedies (Bowery Boys). Monogram, as Allied Artists, had the distinction of producing the last "series" westerns in 1954 with Wayne Morris.

At Republic the western was still king. Roy Rogers, Rod Cameron and Rex Allen were still in series. John Wayne, though he would soon leave and go to Warner Brothers, was still making films—and some good ones—for Republic. Herbert Yates, president of Republic, had elevated William Elliott to some color westerns (and some non-westerns) in an attempt to make him another Randolph Scott or Joel McCrea or John Wayne. But, regretfully, it never happened. In 1953, Republic would end their activity with series westerns as Roy Rogers moved on to television, John Wayne went to Warners, Rex Allen (and others) left for other ventures. They were continually trying to upgrade their product with more musicals and adventure pictures and less westerns. It didn't work and, regretfully by the 1950's Republic (along with RKO) was gone.

Universal (since the mid-1940's Universal-International) had stopped producing series westerns in 1946, but had stayed in the western market. Universal now had a young actor named Audie Murphy who would be quite popular over the next decade and a half, most of it in westerns. They also had such stalwarts as James Stewart and Dan Duryea. Not western actors before

Portrait (1953).

The Nevadan (Columbia-1950) with Forrest Tucker and Dorothy Malone.

With Forrest Tucker in *The Nevadan* (Columbia-1950).

1950, both Stewart and Duryea took to westerns like they were born in the saddle. Warner Brothers and Paramount continued to produce both "A" and "B" westerns (mostly "A") unabated. Warners would soon have John Wayne and they already had Randolph Scott. Later, in the fifties, both of them would make many fine westerns for the studio. Paramount had Gary Cooper who had appeared mostly in non-westerns in recent years but would return to that form of art shortly. Taking up the slack was Alan Ladd who made some good westerns in 1949 and 1950 and would make the classic *Shane* in 1953.

The others consisted mostly of products from Ron Ormond, Robert L. Lippert and a few others. They produced strictly programmers with varying degrees of success. United Artists, one of the pioneer companies, had fallen on hard times but would reverse the trend in the mid-fifties and by the late sixties become one of the top companies in the business.

The Nevadan kicked off 1950 on a high note. Directed by Gordon Douglas for Scott-Brown/Columbia, it was not up to Douglas' *The Doolins of Oklahoma*, but it was nevertheless a good picture. Filmed in Cinecolor, (all of Scott's films from this point on would be in color with the sole exception of *Shoot-Out At Medicine Bend*, released by Warner Brothers in 1957), the story told of an undercover U. S. Marshal after some stolen gold bullion. Along the way he meets an outlaw (Forrest Tucker) who is after the same thing. Scott also meets Dorothy Malone and falls for her, but she turns out to be the daughter of real villain, George Macready. All very complicated, but it works out before the 81 minutes has run its course. The film also featured a knockdown-dragout fight between Scott and Tucker in an old mine that ranks as one of the better screen fights.

In early 1950, Scott returned to Warner Brothers for the first time since 1940's *Virginia City*. The film was *Colt .45*. Produced in Technicolor, *Colt .45* was a big budget western such as Warners was making at the time with Gary Cooper. Randolph Scott was a big star at the box office and that was where it counted. Support was provided by the Warner Bros. stable of fine supporting and character actors. Zachary Scott, a really nice guy who played really bad guys, was the lead. Romance was provided by Ruth Roman. Also present were Lloyd Bridges, Alan Hale, Ian McDonald (who later played the infamous "Frank Miller" in *High Noon*), Chief Thundercloud (a real Cherokee named Victor Daniels) and Walter Coy. *Colt .45* was the

How to beat the high cost of living! *The Nevadan* (Columbia-1950).

Realistic fight scene from *The Nevadan* (Columbia-1950) with Forrest Tucker.

The Nevadan (Columbia-1950) with Forrest Tucker.

Cat and Mouse with villain George Macready in *The Nevadan* (Columbia-1950).

The Cariboo Trail (Fox-1950) with Karin Booth.

The Cariboo Trail (Fox-1950) with Dorothy Adams, Kansas Moehring and Bill Williams (in bed).

story of a gun salesman (Scott) whose merchandise (Colt guns) is stolen and used to arm a band of outlaws. An excellent picture.

Returning to Twentieth Century-Fox for the last time, Scott made *The Cariboo Trail* for producer Nat Holt. The film, directed by Edward Marin, featured many old-time Scott repertoire players plus many Fox players. Among those featured were Bill Williams, Victor Jory, Karin Booth (Mrs. David Brian), Douglas Kennedy and Dale Robertson. Co-star billing went to George Hayes, old "Gabby" himself. While Gabby Hayes is so well remembered as side-kick in many "B" westerns (he made more than 200, probably closer to 300 films) with such stalwarts as Roy Rogers and William Elliott, he also made a number of films with Randolph Scott. *The Cariboo Trail* must rank as his best. Director Marin wisely developed the relationship between the two men—Hayes an old prospector, and Scott a land buyer having to contend with corruption. The moments between Hayes and Scott are truly the highlight of this fine film.

1951 brought a change of pace for Scott as he took the character of *Sugarfoot* in the Warner Bros. film of the same name. Adele Jergens was the romance in Scott's life and Raymond Massey came aboard for the first time as the baddie. Along, in a fine character role, was S. Z. Sakall. *Sugarfoot* told the story of an ex-confederate army officer (Scott) who is now a U. S. Marshal working undercover to get the goods on Raymond Massey. The film derives its difference in Scott's performance. The normally stoic Mr. Scott plays a whining, less than heroic character so that he may gather information on the bad guys. This he does and, in due course, the real Randolph Scott emerges, dressed in black, astride that beautiful chestnut horse, and you know, beyond a shadow of a doubt, that the badmen are in deep trouble.

Colt .45 (1950) and *Sugarfoot* (1951) were both in issue when Warner Brothers went into the television market in 1955–56. When Warners developed television series using the titles of the Scott films, the features were retitled for theatrical release. *Colt .45* became *Chief Thundercloud* and *Sugarfoot* became *Swirl Of Glory*. Both films have now reverted to their original titles in all but the rarest of circumstances.

Starlift was an all-star extravaganza of the type studios used to issue to periodically film to show off all the stars they had working for them. Scott appeared in two such films. The first was Universal's *Follow the Boys* (1944). *Starlift* (Warner Brothers) was the other. The film starred Janice Rule and

Randy gets lots of care from Adele Jergens in *Sugarfoot* (WB-1951).

Sugarfoot (WB-1951) with Adele Jergens.

Santa Fe (Columbia-1951) with Warner Anderson.

Santa Fe (Columbia-1951) with Guy Wilkerson and Frank Hagney.

Santa Fe (Columbia-1951).

Santa Fe (Columbia-1951).

Dick Wesson. Scott, along with all of the other Warner's stars of 1951 appeared in brief cameo.

1951 would be Randy Scott's highest film output year since 1939 with five films. It would also be the highest output year for the rest of his career. The most he would make in any one year after 1951 would be 1955's four films. He would make three each in 1958, 1960 and 1962, and none in 1961. It is probable he wanted to retire from the screen at this time, but that opportunity to make one more picture with Joel McCrea (the only time they ever appeared together) proved too much of a pull.

Scott-Brown's *Santa Fe* started an interesting cycle. Whether by design or by accident, the next eight Scott films, covering the rest of 1951 and all of 1952 and 1953, would be alternately Scott-Brown and Warner Bros. films. A total of eight films. After two more films for Warners in 1954 and one for RKO at the beginning of 1955, the Scott-Brown/Warner cycle would resume for eleven more films through the end of 1957.

Santa Fe was written by Louis Stevens from a novel by James Marshall. Columbia had made the switch from Cinecolor to the better Technicolor and the films looked quite a bit better. The story concerned two brothers who found themselves on opposite sides of the law in the post-Civil War period. Janis Carter and Jerome Courtland (now a producer-director at Disney) co-starred.

Gary Cooper tamed *Dallas* (Warner Bros.-1950) so it was only fitting that Warners and Randy Scott cross the Trinity to do the same for *Fort Worth*. Released in July 1951, *Fort Worth* marked the last appearance of Edwin Marin as director of a Randolph Scott film. *Fort Worth* told the story of a gunfighter who becomes editor of a newspaper and tries to battle corruption with the pen. In the end, however, the citizens make Scott sheriff and it is the sword, used as a tool of the law, that frees the town from evil. In this film the bad guys are led by David Brian. The femme leads were lovely Phyllis Thaxter and equally lovely Helena Carter. While both *Dallas* and *Fort Worth* were pure fiction, they nevertheless presented western entertainment at its best.

A singing voice over the credits is quite common. Today it is done in many, if not most, pictures. The practice is not new. However, it seemed to gain a tremendous amount of respectability when Stanley Kramer used Tex Ritter singing over the titles of *High Noon* (United Artists-1952). Since then

114

Randy restrains Peter Thompson, Jerome Courtland and John Archer in *Santa Fe* (Columbia-1951).

Assisting an injured Peter Thompson in *Santa Fe* (Columbia-1951).

Protecting Janis Carter in *Santa Fe* (Columbia-1951).

Santa Fe (Columbia-1951) with Janis Carter.

Fort Worth (WB-1951).

Fort Worth (WB-1951) with Mary Anderson (left) and Helena Carter.

the practice has become common. But Kramer was not a pioneer. It was used as far back as the thirties. Many westerns of Roy Rogers and Gene Autry used the process although they were, admittedly, musicals anyway. RKO Radio used Tex Ritter to sing the title song for *Blood On The Moon* (1948) starring Robert Mitchum and Barbara Bel Geddes. Ritter did not appear in the film. Earlier, in 1946, Universal used Hoagy Carmichael to sing over the titles for *Canyon Passage* starring Dana Andrews and Susan Hayward. Jimmy Wakely did the voice over for *The Silver Star* (Lippert-1955) and Nat King Cole sang *The Blue Gardenia* (WB-1953). Tennessee Ernie Ford sang the title song for 1954's *River Of No Return* (Fox) starring Robert Mitchum and Marilyn Monroe. But prior to that, Ernie Ford sang the title song for *Man In The Saddle*.

Man In The Saddle was Randolph Scott's last entry into the 1951 movie sweepstakes. Released in time for Christmas (December 2, 1951), *Man In The Saddle* proved once again that Columbia could produce a film with the best of them. The Columbia/Scott films in the period of 1949–53 were probably, on the whole, better than the Warner Bros./Scott films. *Man In The Saddle*, from a story by Ernest Haycox who had written several earlier stories for Scott films, was basically, a standard western. The twist to the story, and something unusual for a Randolph Scott film, was a love triangle between Scott, Joan Leslie and Ellen Drew. Add to that the fact that this triangle causes a death and you have a very interesting story. The people who bought tickets thought so. At the end of 1951, Randolph Scott was eighth in the Motion Picture Herald Top Ten Poll.

Lawman Scott about to take care of business in *Fort Worth* (WB-1951).

Randy and David Brian fight the badguys in *Fort Worth* (WB-1951).

With Joan Leslie, Alexander Knox and Ellen Drew (l-r) in *Man In The Saddle* (Columbia-1951).

Man In The Saddle (Columbia-1951) with (l-r) Frank Hagney, Guinn (Big Boy) Williams and Frank Sully.

With Alphonso Bedoya in *Man In The Saddle* (Columbia-1951).

Ready for action in *Man In The Saddle* (Columbia-1951).

CHAPTER XI

THE SHAPE OF THINGS TO COME

"I like Ike" said everyone in 1952. We were a happy nation in 1952. Dwight Eisenhower became president. We had never been more prosperous. You could get a new 1952 Ford for as little as $1600 and a 1952 Lincoln won the grueling 2,000 mile Pan-American Road Race. On the racetracks around the country, Hudson Hornets were proving unbeatable as they took all comers. And in Hollywood, we were getting widescreen and lots of color. MGM made the classic musical *Singing In The Rain*. They made the dramatic *The Devil Makes Three* with Gene Kelly and lovely newcomer Pier Angeli. In westerns, MGM made the violent and believable *The Naked Spur* with James Stewart and Robert Ryan and, in an unusual approach, cast Robert Taylor with a virtually all-woman cast for *Westward The Women*. Universal was making high-grade programmers as fast as they could turn them out. They had one of the finest stables of young actors and actresses of any studio and felt that constant exposure would either make them stars or else. A young Brooklyn actor named Bernard Schwartz would prove himself equal to the task as Tony Curtis. Richard Long, Rock Hudson, Piper Laurie. The list was extensive. A young man named Audie Murphy was proving himself in a string of Technicolor westerns. His acting, if not award-winning caliber, was adequate and he had a winning personality. They made *Bend Of The River* with James Stewart and Arthur Kennedy. It must rank as one of the best westerns ever made. And they had Ma & Pa Kettle and all those kids. Columbia moved to the top of the class with *Death Of A Salesman* and *My Six Convicts*. RKO, still making black and white films as only they could, continued the Robert Mitchum-Jane Russell series with *Macao*. Mitchum also made a modern-day western, and perhaps the best picture ever made about rodeos, *The Lusty Men*. It co-starred Arthur Kennedy and Susan Hayward. RKO also filmed A. B. Guthrie's moving story of a keel-boat trip

Donna Reed in *Hangman's Knot* (Columbia-1952).

up the Columbia river in the 1840's, *The Big Sky*. Produced and directed by Howard Hawks, it was a splendid movie starring Kirk Douglas, Dewey Martin and Arthur Hunnicutt. RKO was still making series westerns with Tim Holt and Chico Martin, but it was fading fast. William Elliott had returned to Monogram for a series and Wayne Morris had also signed on for a series. Despite trying to phase into other areas, the western was still the staple at Republic. Rex Allen was still in a series and they produced others with various stars. John Wayne made *The Quiet Man* (a non-western) and by spring he was gone. Republic was never able to replace him. In the western area, Columbia still had a Charles Starrett series *(The Durango Kid)* but it was in its final year, after which the handsome and athletic Mr. Starrett would retire from the screen. And Columbia had Randolph Scott.

In 1952, the Cinerama Corporation dropped a bombshell on the entertainment world and changed movies forever. In the fall of 1952, a show opened in New York entitled *This Is Cinerama*. *This Is Cinerama* had no conventional story. It was, instead, a compilation of such things as an airplane ride through the Grand Canyon and a roller coaster ride. *This Is Cinerama* played for months wherever it was shown. The reason was not the story. The reason was the revolutionary process called Cinerama. Where a normal movie camera of that time captured a field of vision of about 30 to 40 degrees, Cinerama captured a field of 160 degrees—about 80% of the range of human vision. It was thrilling and combined with 360 degrees stereophonic sound, an exciting treat. Cinerama, however, had its drawbacks. It was totally impractical. It required extensive remodeling of the theatre to install the huge three-part screens and installation of the three 70mm projectors required to fill the three screens with the picture. With Cinerama, only a few theatres around the country could afford to make the change, for once changed, a theatre could not show conventional 35mm films. Only about four films were ever shot in the Cinerama process, but all were very successful.

Despite the shortcomings of the Cinerama process, it had been a true pioneer and had opened the door for other screen processes. They started coming fast and furiously. In early 1953, United Artists released a movie called *Bwana Devil* starring Robert Stack. It was a perfectly awful movie, but it was a box-office bonanza. The reason was a process called Natural-Vision. Natural-Vision was quite simply a three-dimensional process using polarized lenses from Polaroid Corporation. Unlike Cinerama, three-

Donna Reed in *Hangman's Knot* (Columbia 1952).

Lucille Norman seeks comfort from Randy Scott in *Carson City* (WB-1952).

dimensional films did not require remodeling of the theatre. All that was required was for the viewer to wear their Polaroid® glasses that brought together the two images being projected on the screen by the two projectors. The Natural-Vision/3-Dimension process, while not the greatest thing ever to happen to movies, wasn't really all that bad. However, any chance it had for survival was killed by Hollywood itself. After the popularity of *Bwana Devil*, the major motion picture companies jumped on the bandwagon with a vengeance. The byword was quantity, not quality. Don't worry about the story as long as there are plenty of objects flying off the screen into the audience. At first this philosophy worked. People stood in long lines to see a real 3-D movie. But in a few months, the novelty had worn off. You could only have so many tomahawks thrown at you before you got bored. So, by the time the motion picture industry got around to making some really quality films in 3-D, the marketability of the process was dead. At that time,

127

the studios decided to release the pictures shot in Natural-Vision in regular flat screen versions. Alfred Hitchcock's classic thriller *Dial M For Murder* (Warner Bros.-1954) was one of these films, as was *Stranger Wore A Gun*, starring Randolph Scott. Flirtation with three-dimensional pictures lasted but one short year.

Hollywood had proven that the public was ready for, and wanted, a really good screen process that gave huge viewing areas and depth. In 1952, Twentieth Century-Fox Film Corporation announced that they had developed, in conjunction with Bausch & Lomb Corporation, a process they were calling CinemaScope. The process was simple enough in concept. Film the picture in 70mm. Reduce it to 35mm. In the theatre, a standard 35mm projector would reverse the process using a special anamorphic lens developed by Fox and Bausch & Lomb. The end result was a huge image shown on a giant slightly curved screen. Hollywood had it's answer. While there would be a proliferation of processes over the next few years, CinemaScope would prevail and, eventually, all companies would use the process. The CinemaScope process lasted a good fifteen years until it was replaced by Panavision in the late 1960s.

The motion picture industry had come of age once more.

CHAPTER XII

THE GOLDEN YEARS

Randolph Scott's first release of 1952 was Warner Bros. *Carson City*. The story was about the building of the railroad and the problems encountered because some didn't want the railroad built. Raymond Massey was again the bad-guy-in-residence. Singer Lucille Norman co-starred in a non-singing role.

Hangman's Knot was, according to director Roy Huggins, the biggest money-maker of all Scott-Brown films. It was extremely popular and quite well received by reviewers, including the New York Times. *Hangman's Knot* was exciting. And tense. Scott was at his best. His stern, lean features were now showing maturity and that made him all the more plausible as a western hero. Donna Reed was at the peak of her career, as her star continued to ascend. Next year (1953) would see her make an Academy Award winning appearance in Columbia's *From Here To Eternity*. Supporting were Claude Jarman Jr., Frank Faylen, Clem Bevins, Richard Denning and Glen Langan. The "heavy", one of the most menacing ever, was Lee Marvin.

The story of *Hangman's Knot* concerned a band of Confederate soldiers who rob a stagecoach carrying a Union Army gold shipment. The Southerners, led by Scott, hole up in a stagecoach waystation. There, surrounded by a blood-thirsty posse that has every intention of hanging them; Scott realizes the futility of their mission and wants to return the gold in exchange for amnesty. Marvin wants no part of such a move. Therein lies the story.

Hangman's Knot was a simple story, simply told, but with honesty and directness and realism seldom seen at that time. *Hangman's Knot* had an excellent cast and much credit must go to director Huggins for getting the

Randy dressed for action in *Carson City* (WB-1952). Also pictured is Richard Webb.

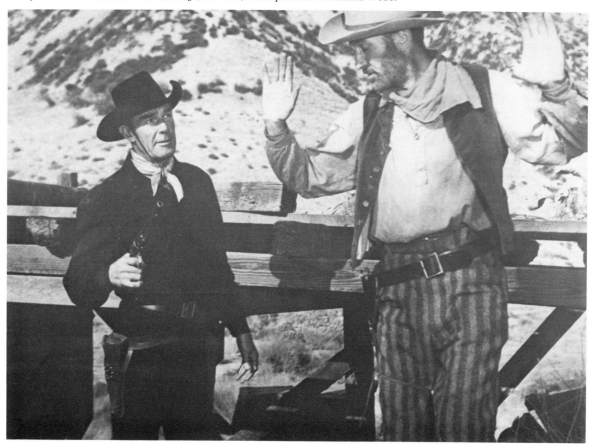

Our "Man in Black" giving a bad guy second thoughts in *Carson City* (WB-1952).

Portrait still from *Hangman's Knot* (Columbia-1952) probably Randy's most successful film.

Hangman's Knot (Columbia-1952), with (left to right), Frank Faylen, Claude Jarman Jr., Monte Blue, John Call (on ground) and Lee Marvin.

Hangman's Knot (Columbia-1952) with Glenn Langan (left) and Lee Marvin.

Dramatic scene from *Hangman's Knot* (Columbia-1952), a fine western directed and written by Roy Huggins.

Confrontation between Randolph Scott and Donna Reed in *Hangman's Knot* (Columbia-1952).

most from a good cast. This one film, perhaps more than any other, set the temper of all of Randolph Scott's remaining films.

The Man Behind The Gun (Warner Bros.) was officially released January 31, 1953. It marked the start of Scott's twenty-sixth year of movie making. It was his 82nd film. He had been a star since the mid-1930s. It was rather fitting that the story-line concerned the founding of the city of Los Angeles.

Some critics "panned" *The Man Behind The Gun* for the historical inaccuracies. However, when viewed as just a western adventure story, the film holds up very well indeed. It marked the first and only appearance of Felix Feist as director in a Scott film. Supporting were Patrice Wymore (Mrs. Errol Flynn), Dick Wesson, Philip Carey and silent western star Rex Lease.

Moving back to Columbia, Scott-Brown made *The Stranger Wore A Gun*. From the book *Yankee Gold* by John Cunningham, it marked the first of four appearances as director by Andre deToth. Filmed in Technicolor, it told the story of a man (Scott), befriended by an outlaw, who becomes involved in a life of crime before he can extricate himself. Co-star was Claire Trevor (who had ridden that famous *Stagecoach* with John Wayne fourteen years earlier). Featured were bad man George Macready, Joan Weldon (a Warner Bros. western veteran although still only 20), Lee Marvin and Ernest Borgnine.

The Stranger Wore A Gun was originally released in Three-Dimension on August 15, 1953, but 3-D films were becoming box-office albatrosses. After a short release in the three-dimensional process, *The Stranger Wore A Gun* was re-issued in regular flat screen. It was better than most films photographed in the process and not as good as some. It was the only film Scott ever did in 3-D but is best remembered for being a good western.

As the pendulum in the Columbia-Warner cycle swung back to Warner Bros., they released *Thunder Over The Plains*. Released in time for Christmas (December 12), *Thunder Over The Plains* told the story of a U. S. Cavalry officer (Randy Scott) who is sent to Texas to keep the peace because of the influx of carpetbaggers and assorted no-goods. Filmed in WarnerColor, it marked the first Scott film photographed in this process. WarnerColor was really Ansco Color and was quite similar to the old Cinecolor used in previous years by such studios as Columbia and Fox. MGM

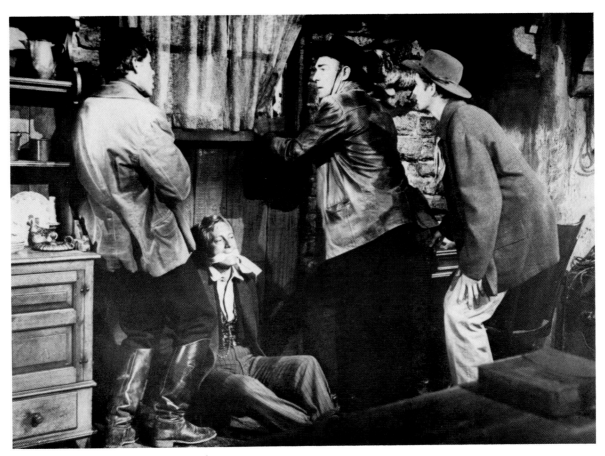

Hangman's Knot (Columbia-1952) with Lee Marvin, Richard Denning and Claude Jarman Jr.

Hangman's Knot (Columbia-1952) with Richard Denning (on floor), Lee Marvin and Donna Reed.

Hangman's Knot (Columbia-1952) with Jeanette Nolan, Richard Denning, Claude Jarman Jr., and Clem Bevins (from left).

Hangman's Knot (Columbia-1952) with Donna Reed, Lee Marvin (with gun), Richard Denning and Clem Bevins.

Particularly good action scene from Columbia's *Hangman's Knot* (1952) with (from left) Claude Jarman Jr., Jeanette Nolan, Donna Reed, Lee Marvin (directly behind Scott), Richard Denning and Frank Faylen.

With Frank Faylen and Claude Jarman Jr. in *Hangman's Knot* (Columbia-1952).

Randy politely asking Lee Marvin to unhand Donna Reed in *Hangman's Knot* (Columbia-1952).

Randy emphasizes a point to Lee Marvin in *Hangman's Knot* (Columbia-1952).

used Ansco and called it MetroColor. Twentieth Century-Fox called it Deluxe. Ansco was never as good as Technicolor, which most other companies (except Republic) continued to use and eventually most of the defecting companies came back to Technicolor or switched to Eastmancolor. *Thunder Over The Plains* co-starred former Tarzan, Lex Barker, with Phyllis Kirk, Charles McGraw, Henry Hull and Elisha Cook.

Breaking the alternating Columbia/Warners cycle, Scott stayed at Warner Bros. for both of his 1954 films. Both were directed by Andre deToth (his third and fourth), but had different producers. Both were photographed in WarnerColor.

Riding Shotgun was the first to be released on April 10, 1954. It featured Joan Weldon, Wayne Morris, Joe Sawyer and James Millican. Also in the cast was a young actor named Charles Buchinsky, who later became Charles Bronson. *Riding Shotgun* continued the string of westerns unbroken.

Scott's second release of 1954 was *The Bounty Hunter*. He played a bounty hunter with a special purpose. To track down three killers who had gone into territory beyond the reach of the law. With Scott on this western journey were Marie Windsor, Howard Petrie, Ernest Borgnine and British actress Dolores Dorn.

In 1955, Scott again increased his film output. He would make four films this year. The first, released in February, was *Ten Wanted Men*, a Scott-Brown production for Columbia.

Ten Wanted Men was set in the southwest cattle country and featured Randy Scott as a cattleman, who only wants peace, forced to take up arms against a gang of outlaws. The cast included Jocelyn Brando, Richard Boone, Denver Pyle and Minor Watson.

The second release of 1955 was Nat Holt's *Rage At Dawn* (RKO). It was Scott's last picture with Holt and his last at RKO-Radio. Directed by Tim Whelan, *Rage At Dawn* was from the book by Frank Gruber. Co-stars were Forrest Tucker, Mala Powers, J. Carroll Naish, Edgar Buchanan, Howard Petrie and Denver Pyle. All, with the exception of Powers, were veterans of previous Randolph Scott features.

Rage At Dawn was a straight-forward western, as all of Scott's westerns were. It told the story of the tracking down of outlaws by Scott. Straight-forward but never pedestrian.

Hangman's Knot (Columbia-1952) with Claude Jarman Jr. (left), Frank Faylen, Donna Reed and Lee Marvin.

With Richard Denning and Donna Reed in *Hangman's Knot* (Columbia-1952).

Frank Faylen restrains Lee Marvin as Randy embraces a very lovely Donna Reed in Columbia's *Hangman's Knot* (1952).

Peace at last for Donna Reed and Randolph Scott in *Hangman's Knot* (Columbia-1952).

A crowd at the old poker table including Paul Maxey (over Scott's right shoulder), Claire Trevor (over Scott's left shoulder) and Francis McDonald (sitting to Scott's left). The scene is from *The Stranger Wore A Gun* (Columbia-1953).

Randolph Scott's only 3-D film was Columbia's *The Stranger Wore A Gun* (1953) with Britt Wood, George Macready, Lee Marvin and Ernest Borgnine (all shown on Randy's left).

With Lex Barker in *Thunder Over The Plains* (WB-1953).

Thunder Over The Plains (WB-1953) with Henry Hull.

In June of 1955, Warner Bros. released Randolph Scott's third film of the year, *Tall Man Riding*. It was directed by a veteran western director usually associated with programmers, Leslie Selander. *Tall Man Riding* was NOT a "B", however, and director Selander distinguished himself very well indeed. The story concerned the opening of the Montana Territory for homesteading and of Scott's attempts to thwart greedy ranchers who desired to have it all for themselves. The film ran a tight 83 minutes, long enough to tell a good story, but not overly long. Appearing with Scott were veteran western players Dorothy Malone, Peggy Castle, William Ching, John Baragrey, John Dehner and Dub Taylor.

The Scott-Brown Christmas present for the year was *A Lawless Street* from Brad Ward's book, *The Marshal of Medicine Bend*. It introduced Joseph Lewis as director for the first of two assignments he would have with Scott and Columbia. Co-star for the film was Angela Lansbury.

In *A Lawless Street*, Randolph Scott played a marshal in the town of Medicine Bend charged with cleaning up the town. Miss Lansbury played a dance-hall girl whom Scott loves. Also in the cast were Warner Anderson, Jean Parker, Wallace Ford, Jeanette Nolan (Mrs. John McIntire in private life) and heavy Michael Pate who has since given up acting to devote his time exclusively to writing and producing.

1956 will probably be remembered more for rock'n roll music than any one thing. There was more, however. Dwight David Eisenhower was elected to a second term in the White House. A young man from Mississippi was making quite a splash. The young people thought he was great. The older ones said he wouldn't last. His name was Elvis Presley. Another young singer who was making his mark in 1956 and would still be going strong in the eighties was Johnny Cash. Some of the movies in 1956 were George Steven's *Giant* (WB), William Wyler's *Friendly Persuasion* (UA) with Gary Cooper, John Ford's *The Searchers* (Whitney/WB) starring John Wayne, Jeffrey Hunter and Vera Miles and *The Lone Ranger* (WB) with Clayton Moore and Jay Silverheels. Westerns were big in that year of over three decades ago.

John Wayne, like Randolph Scott, had been producing his own movies for several years. In partnership with Robert Fellows, he made some very good movies in the early 1950s. Later he made films without Bob Fellows under the name Batjac Productions. The name was derived from a John Wayne film of the late 1940s, *Wake Of The Red Witch* (Republic-1948) in

Thunder Over The Plains (WB-1953) with Lex Barker (left).

Thunder Over The Plains (WB-1953) with Lex Barker and Phyllis Kirk.

The Bounty Hunter (WB-1954).

With Dolores Dorn in *The Bounty Hunter* (WB-1954).

Randy deciding discretion is the better part of valor in *The Bounty Hunter* (WB-1954).

The Bounty Hunter (WB-1954) with Ernest Borgnine (far right).

The Bounty Hunter (WB-1954) with Marie Windsor.

Riding Shotgun (WB-1954) with Fritz Feld (center).

which the name of the shipping company was Batjak Limited. The film also starred Gail Russell. Which brings us to August 4, 1956 and the release of *Seven Men From Now*.

Seven Men From Now was produced by Batjac Productions for Warners. It starred Randolph Scott. It was to prove another turning point in his career. Produced by Andrew V. McLaglen and Robert Morrison, both known more as directors than producers, it was written by another director, Burt Kennedy. The actual director was Bud Boetticher. Budd Boetticher would direct another six films after this one for Randolph Scott. All of them would be considered among his finest films. Bud Boetticher and *Seven Men From Now* would indeed be a turning point as the career of Randolph Scott took another turn upward.

Seven Men From Now marked the first time Randolph Scott and John Wayne had worked together since 1942's *Pittsburgh* and *The Spoilers*. Wayne did not appear in *Seven Men From Now*, however. Co-starring with Scott was Gail Russell, who had appeared with Wayne in Republic's *Wake Of The Red Witch* (1949) and, earlier, *Angel And The Badman* (Republic-1947). A very beautiful young woman, Gail Russell was beset by personal problems that kept her off the screen for several years. *Seven Men From Now* was an attempt on the part of both John Wayne and Randolph Scott to help her make a comeback. She couldn't, however, and by 1961 she was dead at the age of 36.

Seven Men From Now told of a man (Scott) seeking the men who killed his wife. He meets a couple (Russell and Walter Reed) crossing the territory in a wagon, who are lost. Reluctantly he helps them because it is obvious the husband is not up to the task. He is weak and his wife despises him but is faithful to him. In the end, though, it is this very same man who helps Scott against the men who killed his (Scott's) wife. *Seven Men From Now* has it all. When westerns are remembered, it must indeed be this type of film that comes to the fore.

Moving back to Columbia for his next film, Scott made *7th Cavalry* for Scott-Brown Productions. It was directed by Joseph Lewis. The cast lacked nothing. Included were Barbara Hale, Jay C. Flippen, Jeanette Nolan and Denver Pyle. It was the third Scott picture in two years for Denver Pyle. A fine character actor who later made his mark in television series including *The Doris Day Show* (CBS), *Grizzly Adams* (NBC) and *The*

Riding Shotgun (WB-1954).

Riding Shotgun (WB-1954).

A young man named Charles Buchinsky about to do bodily harm to Randolph Scott in *Riding Shotgun* (WB-1954). Young Mr. Buchinsky was later to become Charles Bronson.

A slightly battered Randy with Joan Weldon in *Riding Shotgun* (WB-1954).

Scott tries to prevent Joan Weldon from breaking the law for revenge in *Riding Shotgun* (WB-1954).

Aftermath of a struggle in *Riding Shotgun* (WB-1954). Girl is Joan Weldon.

With Joan Weldon in *Riding Shotgun* (WB-1954).

Ten Wanted Men (Columbia-1955) with Tom Powers, Jocelyn Brando, Minor Watson and Louis Jean Heydt (from left).

Confrontation with Richard Boone in a tense scene from *Ten Wanted Men* (Columbia-1955).

Dukes of Hazzard. 7th Cavalry found Scott in a U. S. Cavalry officer's uniform in a story of a cavalry unit which thinks they have an officer in their midst who deserted the Little Big Horn battle, in which General George Custer and many of the Seventh Cavalry died. It was one of the best westerns of 1956. Suspenseful, taut and thoroughly believable.

So ended 1956. Randolph Scott had appeared in 92 films.

With Louis Jean Heydt in *Ten Wanted Men* (Columbia-1955). Minor Watson can be seen just over Scott's head.

Ten Wanted Men (Columbia-1955) with Jocelyn Brando, sister of actor Marlon Brando.

Ten Wanted Men (Columbia-1955) with Skip Homeier and Donna Martell.

William Forrest bandages Mike Ragan in *Rage At Dawn* (RKO-1955).

RANDOLPH SCOTT (1955).

Rage At Dawn (RKO-1955).

Rage At Dawn (RKO-1955).

Rage At Dawn (RKO-1955) with Denver Pyle & Mala Powers.

With Howard Petrie (left) and Edgar Buchannan in *Rage At Dawn* (RKO-1955).

CHAPTER XIII

RIDE FOR THE SUNSET

In 1957, the Russians put a satellite into orbit: Sputnik. The U.S. military went bananas. The Russians had beaten them into space. Little did it matter that, in twelve short years, it would be Americans walking on the moon. That was still Buck Rogers stuff in 1957. What the Americans wanted was to get their little grapefruit-size satellite into orbit.

In 1957 there was no NASA. It was, more or less, every man for himself. The Navy was first given the job of putting a satellite into space. As valiantly as they tried, however, they could not get the darn thing up. So the job was given to the Army. They did. Inter-service rivalry being what it is, it is highly probable that being in the Navy was rough in 1957.

In the world of entertainment, television was, or was not, depending on your point of view, better. If you were an exponent of live drama such as *Studio One* (CBS) or *Kraft Television Theatre* (NBC), you were not, in all likelihood, happy. Live television was at its lowest point ever. If you liked color, you were happy. And if you liked westerns, you were especially happy. The western era had finally hit television. With an, um bang.

Warner Bros. became the second major film company to really show any seriousness about television. Columbia had had a television subsidiary for some time, but as Screen Gems, not Columbia. In 1955, Warners, Fox and MGM all entered television with new shows that were nothing more than commercials for their big screen features. The shows were dismal flops. In 1956, however, Warner Bros. came back, cleaned up their act and gave us a western entitled *Cheyenne* (ABC) about a drifting cowboy who was raised by the Indians. It was strictly programmer stuff but had one very honest value; a new young actor named Clint Walker. *Cheyenne* is still running in syndication today. The next year Warners added another series and it too was a western but it was totally different from *Cheyenne*. The "hero" of this

Tall Man Riding (WB-1955) with Peggie Castle.

Tall Man Riding (WB-1955).

Tall Man Riding (WB-1955) with Peggie Castle.

Tall Man Riding (WB-1955) with Dorothy Malone.

With Wallace Ford in *A Lawless Street* (Columbia-1955).

A Lawless Street (Columbia-1955) with Ruth Donnelly.

one wore a black hat, a gambler's coat and a frilly shirt. If Cheyenne was a willing, if shy hero, this one was a reluctant hero, or so he wanted everybody to think. In reality, he was every bit as good and honest and willing to help as Cheyenne. He was, of course, Bret Maverick. *Maverick* (ABC) premiered in October 1957. The young star, James Garner, rode in the opening day parade of The State Fair of Texas that October and was present for ribbon cutting ceremonies to open the Fair in Dallas. He was a virtual unknown. A Warner Bros. contract player who had appeared in only a few films (including *Shoot-out At Medicine Bend* with Randolph Scott). His anonymity didn't last. *Maverick* was slotted on Sunday nights opposite the extremely popular *Steve Allen Show*. Maverick didn't ride in on his white charger and dispatch Steverino with one fell swoop of his trusty sword, but, not surprisingly, it did hold it's own. Westerns on television were here to stay. At least for a few years.

By 1957 Randolph Scott was King of the Westerns. No one could equal him. He was a fine actor, a tall, handsome hero and thoroughly believable. Nowhere did the old saying, "you're not getting older, you're getting better," hold more truth. Age only enhanced his weathered good looks. Those who worked with him say he was just as good and gracious off camera, as on. Directors say he was one of the easiest actors to direct. He was Randolph Scott. You could believe what you saw on the screen, because that was the real man. He played Randolph Scott. Director Roy Huggins *(Hangman's Knot)* suggests that "it may even be superior to acting."

On April 1, 1957, Columbia released *The Tall T*. It was no April Fool's Day joke. It was a treat. *The Tall T* brought director Budd Boetticher back for his second time. With but two exceptions, Boetticher would direct all of Scott's remaining films. Burt Kennedy again did the screenplay as he had done in *Seven Men From Now*. Richard Boone (still in his pre-Palladin days) again did the honors as villain. Boone was an excellent bad guy. The heroine was veteran actress Maureen O'Sullivan. Picking up the roles left vacant by Gabby Hayes was Arthur Hunnicutt. A better actor than Hayes, Hunnicutt had truly proven himself by getting an Acacemy Award Nomination in 1952 for Howard Hawk's classic *The Big Sky* (RKO).

The Tall T concerned an Arizona rancher (Scott) whose ranch is taken over by outlaws led by Boone.

Shoot-out At Medicine Bend was Randolph Scott's first black & white

Fight scene from *A Lawless Street* (Columbia-1955) between Randolph Scott and Don Megowan with Wallace Ford (with watch fob) looking on.

Randy and Don Megowan knocking each other all over town in Columbia's *A Lawless Street* (1955).

A Lawless Street (Columbia-1955) with Wallace Ford (left) and John Emery. Kermit Maynard is on the horse directly behind Ford.

Randolph Scott proves the better in a gunfight with villain Michael Pate in *A Lawless Street* (Columbia-1955).

With Angela Lansbury in *A Lawless Street* (Columbia-1955).

Wallace Ford prepares to avenge a prone Randolph Scott in Columbia's *A Lawless Street* (1955).

film since 1949. It was also his last. All remaining films would be in color. It was his 94th picture. Richard Bare made his only appearance as a director of a Scott film. Supporting players included James Craig, Angie Dickinson, Gordon Jones and a young, pre-Maverick James Garner in one of his earliest films.

Moving back to Columbia for a series of three pictures, Scott-Brown made *Decision At Sundown*. It was again in Technicolor as had been all of his Columbia films since 1951 when Columbia made the switch from the less desirable Cinecolor. *Decision At Sundown* was the story of a man (Scott) tracking down the men who assaulted his wife. He finds them in the town of Sundown only to discover that it was his wife who provoked the attack. Scott got excellent support from his cast. They were John Carroll, Karen Steele, Valerie French, Noah Beery Jr., Andrew Duggan and John Archer. Beery, Duggan and Archer, along with James Westerfield and Ray Teal were veterans of previous Scott films.

As 1957 ended, Randolph Scott had been in motion pictures for 29 years and had made 95 films.

Western entertainment reached its zenith in 1958. At least as far as growth. Eight years earlier, in 1950, one-fourth of all motion pictures produced were westerns. By 1958 that figure had risen to one-third. By 1958, there were no less than 37 western series on television and that figure does not include anthologies that had western stories or movies. In 1958, 110 million of the more than 300 million paperback books sold were westerns.

On television, we were enjoying such shows as Warner's *Maverick* (ABC) with James Garner. When it turned out that an hour a week was going to be too much for one actor, Jack Kelly was added to the cast. There were in fact, a total of FOUR Mavericks in the series during its run: James Garner, Jack Kelly, Roger Moore and Robert Colbert. Other Warners westerns, all on ABC, were *Colt.45* with Wade Preston and Donald May, *Cheyenne* with Clint Walker, *Sugarfoot* with Will Hutchins and *Bronco* with Ty Hardin. Most of them are still in syndication today.

ABC also had such shows as *Tombstone Territory* with Pat Conway and Richard Eastham, *The Life and Legend of Wyatt Earp* with Hugh O'Brien and *Lawman* with John Russell and Peter Brown, another from the Warner stable. NBC had *Wagon Train* starring character actor Ward Bond and young Robert Horton, but the famous *Bonanza* was still two years away.

A rare photo of the producer (John Wayne), the star (Randolph Scott) and the director (Budd Boetticher) on location for the filming of Warner Bros.' *Seven Men From Now* (1956).

With co-star Gail Russell in *Seven Men From Now* (WB-1956).

Seven Men From Now (WB-1956) with Gail Russell.

Seven Men From Now (WB-1956).

Seven Men From Now (WB-1956).

With Gail Russell and Walter Reed in *Seven Men From Now* (WB-1956).

CBS had cranked up *Gunsmoke* three years earlier, in 1955. It was the television version of a very popular CBS radio show that starred William Conrad as Matt Dillon, Parley Baer as Chester, Georgia Ellis as Kitty and Howard McNear as Doc. At first, CBS toyed with the idea of bringing the radio cast to television intact, but decided against it. They then offered the part of Matt Dillon to John Wayne. Duke declined, but suggested a young actor named James Arness. The rest is history. It is doubtful anyone knew back in 1955 what a tremendous show they had and that it would last 20 years in an industry where 13 weeks is considered a lifetime.

ABC also had *The Lone Ranger*. It was telecast from 1949 through 1961 and again in the summer of 1965. The television series starred Clayton Moore, except for a few entries starring John Hart who appeared as a replacement for Moore while he was having contractual problems. Probably the most popular western hero of all time, *The Lone Ranger* was also on the radio from 1933 through 1954.

There were many more. Thirty-seven is a lot of series. But, for the western lover, it was paradise. Like all good things, however, it was all too soon over. By the early sixties, most were gone. Since that time a number of series have come and gone, but the westerns have never again dominated the small screen the way they did in that period from 1957 through 1963.

If Randolph Scott had to make just one film in 1958, it is most fortunate for all of us that it was *Buchanan Rides Alone*. The story was adapted from Jonal Wood's book *The Name's Buchanan*. Wood's Buchanan books are must reading for any western buff. He is sort of a western Sam Spade. Alert, ready, stalwart, strong, but always with a twinkle in his eye. As Buchanan, Scott departed somewhat from the type of character he had played previously, because Buchanan was not all that serious a character. The story concerns Buchanan's defending a Mexican whom the townspeople want to lynch. He doesn't win any friends among the mob, but you'll cheer for him all the way. And you'll cheer for this picture. It's that good. It's a shame he didn't make any more films using the Buchanan character because it was great. Scott was tops. Co-starring was Craig Stevens (in one of the last films he made before becoming everybody's's favorite private-eye, Peter Gunn), Barry Kelly, L. Q. Jones and Peter Whitney. *Buchanan Rides Alone* on the trail but not at the box office. The film was a big hit.

1959 would see the release of two Scott films. The first, released by

7th Cavalry (Columbia-1956) with Barbara Hale.

7th Cavalry (Columbia-1956).

7th Cavalry (Columbia-1956) with Donald Curtis.

7th Cavalry (Columbia-1956) with Barbara Hale and Russell Hicks.

7th Cavalry (Columbia-1956) with Leo Gordon, Frank Faylen and Jay C. Flippen (from left.)

With Jay C. Flippen (left) and Frank Faylen in *7th Cavalry* (Columbia-1956).

Columbia on February 15, 1959, was *Ride Lonesome*, directed by Budd Boetticher. Produced by Burt Kennedy, it was in Technicolor and CinemaScope. It was a Scott-Brown production, but Scott-Brown was now known as Ranown. The cast again included many "regulars" as had most of Scott's western films throughout the years. It made the viewer feel comfortable with what he saw. This was the same technique used in series westerns. The names of the characters may be different, but the faces were familiar. This was towards the end of the era when studios had many young contract players on their payrolls and just wanted to use them. It is more likely that Scott and Brown, who had served their apprenticeship in the thirties, knew the value of familiar faces. The familiar faces in this film included Karen Steele, Pernell Roberts, James Best, Lee Van Cleef, James Coburn, Duke Johnson, Boyd Stockman, Roy Jenson, Boyd Morgan and Bennie Dobbins. The story concerned the efforts of a sheriff (Scott) in bringing in a young outlaw (Best). But more than that, it was a story of the loneliness a lawman knew in the wild days of the mid-to-late 1800s. Scott, with his handsome weathered face, seemed to epitomize this type of man. Virtuous, brave, dedicated, in a land where no one really cared. But, of course, people did care. At least the ones who purchased movie tickets.

Scott's second film of 1959 was Warner Bros.' *Westbound*. Again directed by Budd Boetticher, it was produced by Henry Blanke. It was in WarnerColor. Released April 25, it was the last in a long series of fine films Scott made for Warner Bros. dating back to 1933. In all, there were fifteen Scott-Warner Bros. films, all of them westerns except for *A Successful Calamity* in (1933) and *Starlift* (1951).

Westbound co-starred Virginia Mayo. Again featured was a real Scott regular, Karen Steele. Included were Andrew Duggan, who was one of the hardest working and most popular character actors in the business. Villainy was provided by young Michael Dante and veteran Michael Pate. If you read the credits, you discovered former "B" stars Jack Perrin, Buddy Roosevelt and Kermit Maynard. A treat for any fan. Roosevelt had been in several Scott westerns over the years.

Westbound told the story of a U. S. Army Officer (Scott) assigned to select a stage route from California over which the gold from the California mines could be shipped to mints in the East. Of course, there were those who

With Jay C. Flippen (left) and Frank Faylen in *7th Cavalry* (Columbia-1956).

7th Cavalry (Columbia-1956) with Donald Curtis (center).

A tense moment in *The Tall T* (Columbia-1957) with Richard Boone.

would rather "divert" the gold for other uses. It was a "typical" Scott western—as good as the best, better than most.

So long, Jack Warner.

1960 and another era drew to a close. In one fell swoop, we said goodbye to Columbia, to Scott-Brown and to the finest series of westerns ever put on film.

Randolph Scott's association with Columbia Pictures dated back to 1933 and covered some twenty motion pictures. His association with Harry Joe Brown dated back to 1941's *Western Union* (Fox). Mr. Stanley and Mr. Livingston weren't the only ones who benefited from a fortuitous meeting. Randolph Scott and Columbia both grew over the years. Today Columbia Pictures is one of the biggest and finest motion picture companies in the industry. Today, Randolph Scott is remembered as the best western actor to ever throw a leg across a saddle.

1960. The picture was Ranown's *Comanche Station*. It marked the final effort of director Budd Boetticher in a Randolph Scott film. In the six years he had been associated with Randolph Scott, Boetticher had directed a series of seven films that will rank at or near the top of all-time best westerns, and established Boetticher as an all-time director of fine, quality action films. *Comanche Station* was photographed in Eastmancolor. Eastmancolor fell somewhere between the richness of Technicolor and the blue-orangeness of Ansco Color (WarnerColor, MetroColor, Deluxe) and Trucolor. It was a warm color. It was used for a time by most majors including MGM, United Artists, Columbia and Universal. *Comanche Station* was also filmed in CinemaScope. The cast featured Nancy Gates, Claude Akins and Skip Homeier who, ten years earlier, had killed Gregory Peck in Henry King's classic, *The Gunfighter* (Fox-1950).

Comanche Station told the story of Jefferson Cody (Scott) a man searching for his wife who had been captured by the Comanches. Scott finds and rescues another woman, a Mrs. Lowe (Gates). On the way back to her ranch, they meet three outlaws who know there is a $5000 reward for the return of Mrs. Lowe and decide they want the money. They also want to kill Scott for past deeds and claim her as their "bonus" for rescuing her. Scott prevents this and returns her safely to her husband. Refusing any reward, the end of the film finds Scott again riding off in search of his wife. The viewer is left with the feeling that he will search for the rest of his life if necessary.

A man of action—Randolph Scott in *The Tall T* (Columbia-1957).

CHAPTER XIV

RIDE THE HIGH COUNTRY

Randolph Scott intended to retire from motion pictures after *Comanche Station*. It had been his ninety-ninth film in a career that had spanned over three decades. He didn't need the money. His popularity showed every sign of continuing for another three decades unabated. It is quite possible he was just tired. He was 62 and had ridden a lot of trails, although, with his trim body and handsome visage, he looked a lot younger. *Comanche Station* was good-bye. However, fate was to intervene.

1961 saw no output from Randolph Scott. It was the only year since 1928 that he had made no films.

In 1962, Sam Peckinpah was a relatively unknown director and screenwriter. MGM was producing a film entitled *Ride The High Country*. It was to be produced by Richard Lyons and the screenplay was written by N. B. Stone Jr. MGM wanted Peckinpah to direct. It would be filmed in CinemaScope and MetroColor. What made this film different from any of the other dozen or so western films in production at that time was the cast. The stars were Randolph Scott and Joel McCrea.

Despite the fact they had careers that were very similar and followed parallel patterns (both were in westerns exclusively in their later years), they had never appeared together in a picture (excepting C. B. DeMille's *Dynamite* in 1929, in which both young actors vied for the same part. The part went to McCrea and Scott had a bit in the picture.) The appearance of both was enough to whet the appetite of any red-blooded western fan. These guys, along with John Wayne, were the Kings.

Released in May of 1962, *Ride The High Country* held many firsts for Scott. It was his first film for the famous Metro-Goldwyn-Mayer Studios. It was his first time to work with this producer, director, writer and co-star. The old gang was gone. Excepting some of the supporting players, everyone

Two giants—Randolph Scott and Joel McCrea—as they appeared together for the only time in the classic *Ride The High Country* (MGM-1962).

Randy had reason to smile in this scene from MGM's *Ride The High Country* as the curtain came down on a splendid career that spanned thirty-four years.

and everything was new or different. Even the story was totally different than any either actor had appeared in in the past. It didn't take an absolute genius to figure out what was happening. Two of the greatest cowboy stars of all time were saying goodbye. And doing it with truth and style.

When MGM first released *Ride The High Country*, it was doubtful they realized what they had. It didn't get the promotion of some of the company's other efforts. Perhaps it didn't need it. It had a pre-sold audience for McCrea and Scott. If not another soul saw it, that would make the film profitable. What MGM had, and finally realized, was one of the most respected westerns of that or any time. Also one of the saddest and most poignant, for it told the story of a time that had passed away and would never be again. The film was a box-office smash.

Sam Peckinpah, in his pre-*Wild Bunch* and violence days, directed the film with feeling. The cast, besides Scott and McCrea, included Mariette Hartley (in her first film), Ronald Starr, Edgar Buchanan (in a splendid performance), R. G. Armstrong, L. Q. Jones, John Anderson and James Drury.

The story of *Ride The High Country* was a very simple one. It told the story of ex-marshal Steve Judd (McCrea) who is asked by a banker friend to protect a gold shipment for him. Judd asks his old friend Gil Westrum (Scott), another ex-lawman who is now, in his later years, a carnival sharp-shooter, to help him. Westrum agrees. McCrea also picks a young gunsel (Ronald Starr) to help. They get two more volunteers who really want the gold for themselves.

Scott sides with the ones who want to steal the gold. He has known the frustration and disappointment and lean years of being ignored and forgotten, just for being old, after being an honest and good lawman for so many years. McCrea, on the other hand, still clings to his integrity and fully intends to do the job he promised he would do.

Along the way, they pick up a girl (Mariette Hartley) and her father (R. G. Armstrong) who are fleeing from a wild and murderous family who are out to revenge themselves because Miss Hartley has jilted one of them, a ruffian named Billy. To make matters worse, she falls in love with Starr.

The highjacking attempt by Scott and Starr proves unsuccessful. McCrea, however, is willing to let Scott ride away for old times sake.

With Robert Burton in *The Tall T* (Columbia-1957).

A friendly moment with fine character actor, Arthur Hunnicutt in *The Tall T* (Columbia-1957).

No doubt watching a Randolph Scott film was a horse-lovers dream as in *Shoot-out At Medicine Bend* (WB-1957).

With Dani Crayne and James Garner in *Shoot-out At Medicine Bend* (WB-1957).

Shoot-out At Medicine Bend (WB-1957).

Decision At Sundown (Columbia-1957) with John Litel, Vaughn Taylor and Noah Beery Jr.

Later, McCrea is jumped by the wild family and Scott turns back to help him.

In the battle, the gold is saved, but McCrea is badly wounded. He asks his old friend to safely deliver the gold. Scott promises to do so and McCrea dies.

Ride The High Country is eloquent in its simplicity. It had a story to tell and told it. The story was, of course, fiction, but it is highly likely it was played out in reality many times at the close of what we have come to know as the "western era." William K. Everson, renown film historian, wrote: "*Ride The High Country* was not only one of the best westerns of the sixties, but one of the best from any period."

Exceptional scene from *Decision At Sundown* (Columbia-1957).

Decision At Sundown with Noah Beery Jr. (Center) (Columbia-1957).

Decision At Sundown (Columbia-1957) with Noah Beery Jr.

Buchanan Rides Alone (Columbia-1958) with Peter Whitney (left rear), Craig Stevens (holding horse), Roy Jenson and Joe DeSantis.

A purposeful Randolph Scott in *Buchanan Rides Alone* (Columbia-1958).

EPILOGUE

EXIT RANDOLPH SCOTT

A vibrant and youthful 64-year-old Randolph Scott quit films forever after *Ride the High Country*. The year was 1962. He had made 100 films in the span of 34 years and he simply had other things he wanted to do with his life. It would be a couple of years before we realized he wasn't coming back, and there would be a pang of regret that he'd stopped making movies in what we considered the prime of his career. But gone he was — with our thanks for a job well done.

On March 2, 1987, at the age of 89, Randolph Scott passed peacefully from this life. People the world over felt a deep sense of personal loss. This wasn't just anybody. This was Randy Scott. Our grief was real.

Randolph Scott's films continue to give us joy, and they will do so for many generations to come. He epitomized the word *gentleman*. To the legion of fans and admirers he left behind, he was the quintessential gentleman.

Randolph Scott. Actor. Gentleman. We shall not likely see his kind again.

IN MEMORIAM

George Randolph Scott

January 23, 1898–March 2, 1987

Ride Lonesome (Columbia-1959) with Karen Steele and Pernell Roberts.

Ride Lonesome (Columbia-1959) with James Best (left), Karen Steele and Pernell Roberts.

Ride Lonesome (Columbia-1959) with Karen Steele.

Westbound (WB-1959) with Virginia Mayo.

Westbound (WB-1959) with Virginia Mayo.

Westbound (WB-1959) with Karen Steele and Michael Dante.

THE SONG

"WHATEVER HAPPENED TO RANDOLPH SCOTT"
Words and Music by Don Reid and Harold Reid.
Recorded on Mercury Records by The Statler Brothers.
Published and Copyrighted by American Cowboy Music Company.
Used by permission.

The Statler Brothers today. From left: Jimmy Fortune, Harold Reid, Phil Balsley and Don Reid.

In 1973, The Statler Brothers, Harold Reid, Lew Dewitt, Phil Balsley and Don Reid, did what they do so well, recorded a song that told about a bit of Americana. It was titled "Whatever Happened to Randolph Scott". It made us all stop and wonder what had happened to the heroes we had grown up with in the thirties and forties. It made me wonder what DID happen to Randolph Scott. That was the reason for this book. The Statlers have continued right along, recording songs that can only be classified as pure Americana. And for their troubles they have found fans by the legion and won more awards than they probably have space for. It couldn't have happened to nicer people.

The group remained intact from it's inception in the early 1960s until mid-1982, when, for reasons of health, Lew Dewitt retired and was replaced by Jimmy Fortune. Today, they remain one of the most popular, and certainly most loved group of singers anywhere.

Lew Dewitt

202

What Ever Happened To Randolph Scott
Words and Music by Don Reid and Harold Reid

Ev'rybody knows when you go to the show,
    you can't take the kids along.
You gotta read the paper and know the code
    of G, PG and R and X.
And you gotta know what the movie's about before
    you even go.
Tex Ritter's gone and Disney's dead and the screen
    is filled with sex!

Whatever happened to Randolph Scott ridin' the trail alone?
Whatever happened to Gene and Tex and Roy and Rex, the Durango Kid?
Oh whatever happened to Randolph Scott, his horse plain as could be?
Whatever happened to Randolph Scott has happened to the best of me!

Ev'rybody's trying to make a comment about our doubts and fears.
True Grit's the only movie I've really understood in years.
You gotta take your analyst along to see if it's fit to see.
Whatever happened to Randolph Scott has happened to the industry.

Whatever happened to Johnny Mack Brown and Allan Rocky Lane?
Whatever happened to Lash Larue, I'd love to see them again.
Whatever happened to Smiley Burnette, Tim Holt and Gene Autry?
Whatever happened to all of these has happened to the best of me.

Whatever happend to Randolph Scott has happened to the industry.

Selected Articles and News Items

The following reviews are reprinted courtesy of the New York Times. Copyright 1931/32/33/34/35/36/37/38/39/40/41/42/43/44/45/46/47/48/49/50/51/52/ 53/54/62 by the New York Times Company. Reprinted by permission.

A Vacation to Fame

by INEZ WALLACE

OCIETY forms the background for many a Hollywood picture, but can Society succeed in Hollywood? Specifically, can a gentleman succeed in Hollywood? Here's one who did. He's Randolph Scott (the Randolphs of Virginia) with a social background which covers the solid South. He was secretly married last March to Mrs. Mariona Dupont Somerville, sportswoman and a member of the famed Dupont family of Delaware. Earlier in the season, Mrs. Vincent Astor, describing Scott's popularity in the film capital said, "There is no Hollywood. There is only Randolph Scott."

Scott was born at his father's country place, near Orange, Virginia. None of his family had ever been on the stage, although two of his four sisters studied in Europe for musical careers. His mother (so tiny he calls her "The Half Pint") decided when he was ten that he should go to Woodbury Forest, a preparatory school near Orange.

He had acquired three years of knowledge and a height of nearly six feet, though still only thirteen years old, when he returned one spring to his mother's home in Charlotte, North Carolina. America had entered the war and soldiers were leaving for the battlefields of France.

Young Randolph remembered the stories of how his grandfather Scott had been only fourteen when he marched off to war with "Stonewall" Jackson — and decided to go with them. He told a white lie about his age, and enlisted at Fort Caswell, N. C. The boy's father had given his consent. But they had reckoned without "The Half Pint." When she learned what was happening she promptly followed Randy to New York and caught up with him just as

RANDOLPH SCOTT --- HE WENT TO HOLLYWOOD FOR A LARK

he was about to embark for France.

It looked like the six foot, thirteen-year-old soldier was going back to school.

"But Mother, there are so many *little* men enlisting," he pleaded, "I'd feel ashamed staying home. Don't tell them I'm thirteen. You'll ruin me."

There were other boyish arguments, and at last his mother gave in. She would not interfere. She kissed her boy goodby, and turned to leave. Randy caught her arm. "Let's say a prayer like we used to, mother," he said, "only this time you follow *me*." And before the eyes of soldiers hurrying to board ship, the lanky Southern boy and his tiny mother knelt on the ground and said a prayer together.

With the curiosity of boyhood, Randy lingered on in France after the Armistice was signed, and landed, somewhat mysteriously, in a French training school for soldiers. It required the assistance of Newton D. Baker, the Secretary of War, to have him returned to America.

Scott's next "war" was on the football team of Georgia Tech where he was studying textile manufacturing. He played for one season, and sustained injuries which kept him from future activity on the gridiron.

He completed his education in the Universities of North Carolina and Virginia but scarcely had he settled down to work as an engineer with his father, when a chum suggested a month's vacation in California.

"I never intended to be an actor," Scott says, "but one day we were playing golf with Howard Hughes, just after he had produced 'Hell's Angels.' As a lark he got us both jobs as extras. Maybe it was the uniform I wore that first day, but I decided that, if one could become an officer merely by applying to the wardrobe department, I'd do the rest of my fighting in the movies."

His real fighting in Hollywood, however, was still ahead of him.

It was late one night, toward the end of his month vacation, that the break came that was to decide his future. Cecil B. De Mille was at the Cocoanut Grove. So was Randolph Scott — six feet three and a half now and wearing tails. De Mille noticed him and decided he could use him as an English army officer in a picture. Randy was called to the De Mille

table and told to report for work next morning. He arrived at the studio early, and was ushered into De Mille's presence. "I can use you in this picture," De Mille told him, "and I will, if you want me to. But it would be an injustice to you. You need training in the theater. Go get that and then come in here through the *front* door."

Randy wired his dad that he was joining the Pasadena Players for stage experience. Then he cashed in his return railroad ticket for room rent, and began the hardest fight of his career — a struggle for existence. Work with the Pasadena Players was spasmodic and poorly paid. Randy cooked his own meals — did his laundry at night — slept in a bed that was inches too short for him — and wrote glowing letters to his folks. Then one day a friend of his family came to Hollywood on a visit, dropped in on Randy unexpectedly, and found him washing clothes to wear the next day. The family heard about that.

Millionaire Howard Hughes also

Many Happy Returns

by FOUGASSE *and* McCULLOUGH

"THAT PEDAL WAS THE ACCELERATOR!"

Don't forget that to the crazy driver in front you may be the crazy driver behind. It isn't your fault if all the other road users are completely daft, but it *is* your fault if you aren't prepared for them to be so.

dropped unannounced into Scott's furnished room with kitchenette attached. Randy was exhausted after a day's search for work, and was trying to stretch out his six feet three and a half in a six-foot bed. Not long afterward a bed made-to-order for Randy's measurements arrived at the rooming house — a gift from Mr. Hughes. A card attached to it read: "Here's one bed that you won't kick the foot off."

After that, whenever he sought a new rooming house he would wait until his landlady came to "money palaver" on room rent. Then he would interject, "But I have my own bed" — and usually he got a discount. Today, in the large, beautiful house he now occupies, there are many beds, but only one for Randy.

After eight months he left the Pasadena Community Playhouse Group to play the juvenile lead in "Under a Virginia Moon" at the Hollywood Vine Street Theater. This engagement eventually landed him the romantic lead in "The Broken Wing" at the El Capitan Theater in Hollywood, and it was while he was appearing in that rôle that he was signed by the movies to do "westerns." "Roberta" was his first "straight" rôle of importance. "So Red the Rose" and "Follow the Fleet" followed, and the fan letters began to come in.

When his father died recently, after a heart attack, Mr. Zukor held up production on a picture named, ironically, "—And Sudden Death," so that Randy might attend the funeral in North Carolina — an unheard-of gesture in Hollywood.

Over long distance, his mother had said, "Randy, you have just been home — let me handle things here."

"I'm leaving in five minutes, mother," he answered. His sister met him gravely in the hall when he arrived, and replied to his unasked question, "It's 'The Half Pint.' She's cracked up entirely — the doctor's with her now."

In that silent room the doctor and his patient faced Randolph Scott, no longer a movie star but his mother's boy come home. "Oh, Randy," she sobbed, "your father is gone. We have no head of the family now."

"I'm the head of the family now, mother," he told her. "You're still only a half pint, and I've got to look after you."

The Dallas Morning News
September 27, 1953

★

Randolph Scott
In Cup Matches

—————— By Harry Gage ——————

Randolph Scott, the North Carolina cowboy movie veteran who is a scratch golfer on any of the California courses, has been added to the Texas Cup Matches program for an exhibition.

SCOTT

Scott's acceptance to an invitation to take part in the added attraction for the charity matches at Dallas Country Club on Oct. 24 and 25 was announced Saturday by Bill Castleman, president of the Dallas Golf Association, sponsors of the event.

Joining the Charlotte horse-opera star for the special event will be Ben Hogan, who gave his services to the charity cause last year, and possibly Governor Shivers and Bob Hope. DGA officials aren't sure they can get the Governor or Hope, but Hogan promised last year he'd return if it could be worked into his schedule.

The sponsors are sure of one thing, however, and that is if they can make up a foursome of Hogan, Scott, Hope and Shivers, they'd have an attraction that would pack Dallas Country Club to capacity.

As it now shapes up, the Texas PGA squad may boast some of the top names of the pro circuit.

Byron Nelson, of course, will captain the pro team again. He was offered, and accepted, the captaincy for 1953 at the conclusion of the matches at Lakewood Country Club last year.

ednesday

Randolph Scott Here For Brief Visit

After spending Tuesday in Dallas with his mother, Mrs. George B. Scott of Charleston, Va., Randolph Scott, screen star, left at 1:30 a.m. Wednesday on the westbound American Airlines plane for Hollywood to resume his picture work. The actor had some business matters to discuss with his mother, who has been visiting in Atlanta, Ga., so he arranged to meet her here at the half-way point. Mother and son spent the day together in their suite at the Adolphus Hotel going over their business affairs, with a trip to the beauty parlor for Mrs. Scott, and some joint sight-seeing on the side. She will return to her home in Charleston Wednesday. Mr. Scott's latest film, soon to be released, is "High, Wide and Handsome" in which Irene Dunne is costarred with him, and Dorothy Lamour has a featured role.

The Dallas Times Herald
May 26, 1937

UARY 28, 1938

Randolph Scott,
Movie Actor, in
Dallas Briefly

Randolph Scott, who is portraying a Texan of the cattle-driving days in a motion picture being produced by Paramount, was in Dallas Sunday nights between planes.

Scott has been working with the company on location at Cotulla, LaSalle County. He was on his way to the West Coast Sunday night and will rejoin the company at Laredo this week.

The picture being made is "The Texan," in which Scott has the role of Curt Jordan, trail driver. The story is built around the movement of cattle over the Chisholm Trail.

The Dallas Times Herald
February 28, 1938

Randolph Scott, the 79-year-old retired actor, was released from a hospital in Rochester, Minn., where he had been undergoing tests supervised by the Mayo Clinic, after a 10-day stay. Mr. Scott, who said he was returning to Beverly Hills, Calif., had a birthday while hospitalized. He received dozens of cards and notes, he said, and was "very touched and moved."

●

New York Times News Service
January 29, 1979

Whatever happened to Randolph Scott?

By JOSEPH MASTRANGELO
The Washington Post

If the Statler Brothers, who made a song titled "Whatever Happened to Randolph Scott" famous a few years ago, had bothered to look, they might have found the durable (he's 80) and wealthy (worth something between $50 million and $100 million) cowboy star in his Hollywood Boulevard office supervising his holdings in real estate, gas, oil wells and securities.

"On weekends," he advised cheerfully, "you can find me puttering around my garden in my Beverly Hills home."

Scott himself gave his age as 80 although the Biographical Dictionary of Film lists his birth date as 1903.

Born Randolph Crane in Glen, Va., Scott was always known in Hollywood as "the gentleman from Virginia."

When his first marriage (to heiress Marianna Somerville Dupont) ended in divorce, Scott moved in to "batch" it with his still-close friend Cary Grant.

He married actress Pat Stillman in 1944 and the couple adopted two children.

Scott was always athletic — he says he still shoots "under my age" when he plays golf twice a week or so — and with his rangy 6-foot-2, 185-pound frame, he made the perfect cowboy.

He was in Hollywood for his health in 1929 and met a young fellow named Howard Hughes on the golf course. Hughes got him into his first movie, a silent one called "Far Call."

He made more than 100 movies during his career that spanned 33 years, including 39 "big-budget" westerns. For four successive years, 1950 to 1955, he was among the 10 top box-office stars.

Actor Lee Marvin once recounted a typical Scott-on-the-set story:

"There was a flaming stagecoach in one scene, racing along while the cameras rolled in the driver's seat. Holding the reins sat the stunt man while 20 yards away, sitting in a canvas chair, sat Scott, all dressed in his cowboy outfit, with legs crossed, reading the Wall Street Journal."

When Scott left show biz, he said, "I retired, but I was not going to relax so I got off my fanny and got busy.

DALLAS TIMES HERALD, Wednesday, August 2, 1978,

REVIEWS

Skylarking.

SKY BRIDE, based on a story by Joseph L. Mankiewicz, Agnes Brand Leahy and Grover Jones; directed by Stephen Roberts; produced by Paramount Publix. At the Times Square Paramount and the Brooklyn Paramount.

Speed Condon..................Richard Arlen
Alec Dugan.......................Jack Oakie
Ruth Dunning.................Virginia Bruce
Willie...........................Robert Coogan
Jim Carmichael.............Charles Starrett
Mrs. Smith...............Louise Closser Hale
Eddie............................Tom Douglas
Bill Adams....................Harold Goodwin

Notwithstanding the efficient acting of Jack Oakie and Richard Arlen, several humorous sequences and a rather effective climactic incident, "Sky Bride," the present pictorial attraction at the Paramount, falls short of being good entertainment. It is too argumentative, and several of the flying scenes are unnecessarily lengthy.

The main idea in this film is to depict the remorse of an aviator who is the cause of another flier's death. Speed Condon, one of a trio that goes from town to town thrilling the inhabitants and taking passengers for a ride in the clouds, is a crack pilot who delights in skylarking, and one day his joking results in a crash in which his friend, Eddie, is killed.

Mr. Oakie portrays Alec Dugan, the barker for this flying circus. It seems as though the intrepid fliers defeat their purpose of making money through being too venturesome when in the air.

After the accident Condon leaves his friends and resolves never to go in the air again. Through some miracle Dugan discovers where Condon is working, and he strives to make him go up in a plane. Several good, hard blows are exchanged between Condon and Dugan and also between Condon and a conceited flier they encounter in an aircraft works. Condon is willing to work on the engines, but still refuses to fly.

Louise Closser Hale impersonates Eddie's mother, who does not learn of her son's death until long after the tragedy. Bobby Coogan appears as the dead flier's nephew, Willie. This child has a penchant for trying out improvised parachutes, and one day he is taken up unwittingly on the undercarriage of one of the flying machines.

Condon goes to the rescue in another plane, and while he signals to the aviator piloting the craft to which the boy is hanging, the makeshift parachute gives way bit by bit. Condon then attaches his control wires and climbs on top of his machine and succeeds in holding on to the boy's legs. Condon soon finds himself away from his machine and clinging to Willie. A fraction of a second later they both drop, but are saved by Condon's parachute.

This last melodramatic bit is quite exciting. The girl in the case, Ruth Dunning, is played by Virginia Bruce.

Leo Carrillo, Tamara Geva, Evelyn Hoey and others are to be seen in a stage revue called "Here We Are."

M. H.

Ap 23, 1932.

THE SCREEN
By MORDAUNT HALL.

Cecil De Mille's First Talker.

DYNAMITE, with Conrad Nagel, Kay Johnson, Charles Bickford, Julia Faye, Joe Mc-Crea, Muriel McCormac, Robert Edeson, William Holden, Henry Stockbridge, Leslie Fenton, Barton Hepburn, Ernest Hilliard, June Nash, Nancy Dover, Neely Edwards, Jerry Zier, Rita Leroy, Tyler Brooke and others, an original screen story by Jeanie Macpherson directed by Cecil B. De Mille; "Bermuda Bound," a stage production, devised by Chester Hale, with Teddy Joyce, "The Runaway Four" and others. At the Capitol.

In "Dynamite," Cecil B. De Mille's first entry in the talking picture field, this producer evidently is undaunted by the vocal angle of his film, for he pursues much the same tactics he did in his silent contributions. As in the past, he proves himself to be a master of technical detail and a director who is able to elicit from his players thoroughly competent performances. Nevertheless, this offering is an astonishing mixture, with artificiality vying with realism and comedy hanging on the heels of grim melodrama.

Even in the work of the performers, there are moments when they are human beings and then, at times, they become nothing more than Mr. De Mille's puppets. The dialogue is a potpourri of brightness and banality and it was no wonder that the audience in the Capitol yesterday afternoon found humor in scenes that were intended to be serious.

Most of this film holds one's attention, but toward the end the incidents become a trifle too bizarre for one's peace of mind.

Both Mr. De Mille as the director and Miss Jeanie Macpherson as the author need a restraining hand to guide them, for the result of this audacious adventure becomes a hodge-podge, with characters behaving strangely and conversing in movie epigrams, whether they are at a country club, enjoying the queer series of sporting events, or in danger of death in a coal mine cave-in. The chatter that threads its way through this photoplay can be judged by the avowal of the miner husband of the society woman that he loves her from the top of her silly head to the soles of her feet, and adding that he would like to crown her with a pickaxe. When three persons are presumed to be within a few minutes of death one of the men, a polo player, turns to the girl and asks what she's worrying about!

It all begins with Hagon Derk, a coal miner, being sentenced to death for murder. Then it darts to a scene depicting Cynthia Crothers, a society girl, being told that unless she is married and living with her husband on her twenty-third birthday, she will not inherit her grandfather's substantial fortune. Matters become further entangled through the fact that Cynthia is in love with Roger Towne, who "could not set a date for his wedding to Cynthia, because his present wife would not set a date for her divorce."

But that is not all, for Marcia Towne, Roger's wife, is willing to go to Reno to start divorce proceedings if she receives $50,000 down and $150,000 when the divorce is granted. Cynthia finds herself in a dilemma, being close to her twenty-third birthday. She notices the picture of Derk in a newspaper and is seized by a sudden inspiration. She goes to the jail and there asks Derk whether he will marry her if she pays him $10,000. Derk, a strong character, consents to do so, as he needs the money to save his motherless little girl from being sent to an orphanage.

The next turn in the events is the confession by a young man that he committed the murder for which Derk is sentenced to be hanged, and word is sent to the prison warden at the last minute that Derk is innocent.

Thus Cynthia finds herself with a hale and healthy husband, but a coal miner instead of a society polo player. Derk invades a party and lets the drunken and excited persons know what he thinks of them. A parrot is heard by Derk to say, "I'm a good girl," and Derk turns to the bird and declares, "You're the only one here!"

Derk goes to Cynthia's boudoir later in the evening and flings the package of $10,000 at her and leaves. But the following day Cynthia, having been reminded that she must be living with her husband to inherit the legacy, drives to the mining community and finds Derk. The car in which she motors up to his humble abode is no flivver, but one of the most costly vehicles. She is arrayed in her Fifth Avenue finery, and Derk is ashamed of his rich wife. She, however, has an opportunity to win the hearts of the miners' wives, but, after a thundering browbeating from Derk, she calls up Roger and asks him to come down and rescue her from her unfortunate alliance.

The story might have finished then, but Mr. DeMille and Miss Macpherson evidently thought it advisable to have some dynamite brought into the narrative. Hence the scenes down in a mine. Roger goes there with Cynthia, just to tell Derk that he is going to run away with his (Derk's) wife. But fate and Mr. DeMille will otherwise.

Kay Johnson shows herself to be an accomplished actress in her impersonation of Cynthia. Charles Bickford gives a splendid performance as Derk. Conrad Nagel, as Roger Towne, does not act up to his usual standard, especially in speaking his lines, all of which is probably the result of direction and the lines given to him.

_____
Δ1929

Life in New York.

WOMEN MEN MARRY, based on a story by John Francis Natteford; directed by Charles Hutchison; a Headline production. At the Warners' Beacon.

Dolly Moulton..............Natalie Moorhead
Rose Bradley...................Sally Blane
Steve Bradley.............Randolph Scott
Fred Moulton..............Kenneth Harlan
John Graham...............Craufurd Kent
Pierre Renault...............Jean Del Val
Jimmy.....................James Aubrey

After a chance look at "Women Men Marry," an ordinary sentimentalist would likely decide to remain single—or, at least, never to leave Montgomery, Ala. For New York changes one rapidly. There is something about it which inspires musicians to make love in penthouse studios and leads business men to give away diamond bracelets. It does things to husbands, too, or perhaps the wives are responsible. Once ordinary Southern boys, they soon begin carrying guns; or, as they say in the gangster films, packing rods.

The Beacon Theatre is probably not the best place in which to see "Women Men Marry." Its audiences live up that way, some of them in penthouses, and they know their actions are not quite so ornate. Possibly it is a matter for regret. At all events, when the picture gets to Montgomery it should prove more satisfactory. There is a general feeling that New York is a sinister sort of place, and "Women Men Marry" takes considerable pains to prove it. The department publicizing the city's Summer resort properties should see the proprietors.

The story is of a young Southern couple who come North (symbolically through a snow storm) to live. They meet old friends, and while the men work, the less recent New York lady leads the newcomer into temptation and bridge games with high stakes. There are many near social disasters before the big business man is shot and wounded, and considerable agitation afterward. But he recovers; they do in New York. At the end one couple starts happily to a new post in Europe, where it is hoped the atmosphere may be more like Montgomery.

Randolph Scott and Sally Blane take the parts of the couple who learn about the ways of the city, and Natalie Moorhead and Kenneth Harlan those who already have done so. Craufurd Kent is the donor of bracelets and victim of the assassin's fire. And so is New York.   L. N.

Jl 13, 1931.

THE SCREEN

A Rich Man's Ruse.

A SUCCESSFUL CALAMITY, an adaptation of a play by Clare Kummer; directed by John Adolfi; produced by Warner Brothers. At the Roxy Theatre.

Henry Wilton...............George Arliss
Emmie Wilton...............Mary Astor
Peggy Wilton...............Evalyn Knapp
Connors...................Grant Mitchell
Partington................David Torrence
Eddie Wilton..............William Janney
George Struthers..........Hardie Albright
John Belden...............Hale Hamilton
Pietro Rafaelo............Fortunio Bonanova
Larry.....................Randolph Scott
Mary......................Nola Luxford
Curtis....................Murray Kinnell
Lawrence..................Richard Tucker
Pauline...................Barbara Leonard
Valet.....................Harold Minjur
Barney Davis..............Leon Waycoff

By MORDAUNT HALL.

George Arliss is the principal figure in a film version of "A Successful Calamity," a play by Clare Kummer, which was presented in the Winter of 1917 with William Gillette and Estelle Winwood in the leading rôles. It is a light, breezy, improbable tale, which, although it hardly affords the English actor any major opportunity, makes a pleasing diversion.

The pictorial conception of this stage work is modernized, but otherwise the story remains virtually the same as the original work, and its amusing incidents evidently appealed to a Roxy audience yesterday afternoon.

In it Mr. Arliss appears as Henry Wilton, a financial wizard who at the outset is being thanked by a President of the United States for his work in European countries. Although only the back of the head of the impersonator of the Chief Executive is shown, the image nevertheless reminds one of President Hoover.

After leaving the White House, Mr. Wilton is besieged by reporters and photographers, and finally on reaching New York, where he arrives a day sooner than he was expected, he learns that his wife is giving a musicale, his son is playing polo and his daughter is playing bridge. Subsequently, he finds that during his prolonged absence a huge wing has been built on his country home, but what makes him a trifle uneasy is the change made in the drawing room. No longer are there any comfortable chairs, and the walls, decorated in a modernistic fashion, are painful to his eyes. The cheer of a wood fire is denied him, electricity being used instead.

Connors, Wilton's loyal butler, has moved some of his master's favorite chairs into his (Connor's) room, and the financier chooses to sit there to avoid the offending bizarre furnishings.

Wilton soon discovers that he has no real home life, for his wife, son and daughter are occupied night after night in one long round of dinners, bridge parties and dances. He feels that something ought to be done about it, and profiting by remarks uttered by Connors, who says that only the poor stay at home, he decides to tell his wife that he has been ruined. She at once is sympathetic, but she is his second wife and much younger than her husband, and she wonders if she can put up with poverty.

The son and daughter are eager to help their father by seeking employment. To supply a sort of plot to this narrative, there is the idea of a man named Partington breaking his word to Wilton by refusing to let him have the Seaboard Chemical stock at the price agreed upon. Partington, through young Wilton, is the first outsider to hear of Wilton's supposed financial difficulties. This ends in the wily Wilton making another million out of Partington and in the old man confessing to his wife and son and daughter that he is not ruined, but merely wants the occasional peace and quiet of a home.

There are times in this picture when Mr. Arliss reminds one of his interpretation in "Old English," and on other occasions his actions and utterances recall his performance in "The Millionaire."

Mary Astor is graceful and charming as Mrs. Wilton. Evalyn Knapp does well as Wilton's daughter, and Randolph Scott is acceptable as the son. Other players who do good work are Grant Mitchell, as Connors; David Torrence, as Partington; Fortunio Bonanova, as a musician; Hale Hamilton, as Wilton's partner, and Hardie Albright, as a suitor for the hand of Wilton's daughter.

On the stage program is Frank Cambria's production, "Treasure Cruise," with the Roxyettes, Charles Carver, Joseph Griffin, Mitzi Mayfair, Karavaieff and several others. This piece is divided into four scenes—"Spanish Main," "Neptune's Daughters," "Pirate's Cove" and "Treasure Chest."

S, 1932

Malicious Gossip.

HOT SATURDAY, based on a novel by Harvey Fergusson; directed by William Seiter; produced by Paramount Publix. At the Times Square Paramount and the Brooklyn Paramount.

Romer Sheffield...........Cary Grant
Ruth Brock................Nancy Carroll
Bill Fadden...............Randolph Scott
Conny Billop..............Edward Woods
Eva Randolph..............Lillian Bond
Harry Brock...............William Collier Sr.
Mrs. Brock................Jane Darwell
Camille...................Rita La Roy
Annie Brock...............Rose Coughlan
Edward W. Randolph........Oscar Apfel
Aunt Minnie...............Jessie Arnold
Archie....................Grady Sutton

Small-town tongues are wagging at the Paramount and small-town eyes are watching that Brock girl from behind drawn shades. "Hot Saturday," which is from Harvey Fergusson's novel, describes the evolution of an idle bit of gossip in an average American community with considerable freshness and candor, and in the main manages to survive a meandering script and some uneventful writing. Nancy Carroll, as the girl caught in the net of malicious gossip, gives a lifelike portrayal; and she is acutely touching in the final episodes as she searches frantically for some one who will understand and believe her. The dénouement is unintentionally ambiguous, and a rather startling conclusion at that;

for the girl runs off with the notorious libertine to a marriage in New York which, if one is to believe all the things people say about Romer Sheffield, will be merely theoretical.

The title suggests the social activities of the young people on their day off, the dancing, cheap liquor and furtive amour with which they escape once a week from their routine labors. Some may raise the criticism that the behavior in "Hot Saturday" is more typical of the years immediately prior to 1926—the year the novel appeared—than of the present.

Ruth Brock, on this particular "hot Saturday," accompanies the crowd to Sheffield's place in the country. Her young man, resenting Sheffield's attentions to the girl, quarrels with her. When she is left alone in the millionaire's house for a few hours and arrives home in his car, the gossip-mongers go to work with a relish. The accumulation of outraged virtues results in Ruth's dismissal from the bank and a violent scene at home. Even her gentle, understanding sweetheart of school days turns against her.

Edward Woods, as the malicious and resentful escort, gives the most satisfactory performance in support of Miss Carroll. Cary Grant is a nonchalant young libertine as Sheffield, and Randolph Scott is solidly virtuous as the boyhood sweetheart.

N 5, 1932.

Kate Smith's Picture.

HELLO, EVERYBODY, based on a story by Fannie Hurst; directed by William A. Seiter; a Paramount production. At the Paramount.

Kate Smith	Kate Smith
Hunt Blake	Randolph Scott
Lily Smith	Sally Blane
Mrs. Smith	Julia Swayne Gordon
Bobby Smith	Jerry Tucker
Bettina Smith	Marguerite Campbell
Mr. Parker	William Davidson
Mr. Blair	George Barbier
Mr. Lindie	Paul Kruger
Jed	Charles Grapewin
Ettie	Fern Emmett
Joe	Irving Bacon
Kate's Radio Manager	Ted Collins
Mr. Thompson	Frank Darien
Mr. Sinclair Eldridge	Edwards Davis
Horton	Russell Simpson

The cinema glorification of Kate Smith is taking place at the Paramount. In an admirable effort to prevent any misunderstanding, the producers have cast the radio singer as herself and have named the picture after her familiar greeting, "Hello, Everybody." The story is one of Fannie Hurst's literary efforts. It is a rustic tale picturing Miss Smith as a simple lass from the farmlands who knits sweaters between broadcasts and is more interested in the health of her chickens than in the shekels that come her way in the city.

The picture is obviously designed for those special admirers who never tire of hearing Miss Smith describe the moon coming over the mountain. As such it is completely successful. The old songs are in it and some new ones. Miss Smith gives an amiable portrait of Miss Smith, happily avoiding the more strenuous phases of dramatic expression. Here Kate Smith leads the embattled farmers to victory over the power trust.

On the sentimental side of "Hello, Everybody," its lyric heroine is made to illustrate the idea that nobody really loves a fat girl. Although Kate loses her heart to a dashing young man from the city, she gallantly resigns when she discovers he is really interested in her more attractive sister. Thereafter she pours out her heart in her songs and lives vicariously in the happiness of others. Randolph Scott and Sally Blane portray the young lovers of the story.

On the Stage.

Willie and Eugene Howard are the stage headliners. Willie gives his familiar impersonations of the stars of the stage and screen, and he is painfully funny as a member of a hillbilly act and later in a German musical quartet.

Donald Novis sings some of the popular songs and Melissa Mason contributes a round of eccentric dances. Rubinoff is on hand with an Irving Berlin medley and the Berry Brothers repeat their amusing piano and dance routine.

A. D. S.

Ja 30, 1933

A Zane Grey Story.

HERITAGE OF THE DESERT, based on a novel by Zane Grey; directed by Henry Hathaway; a Paramount production. At the Seventh Avenue Roxy.

Jack Hare	Randolph Scott
Judy	Sally Blane
Adam Naab	J. Farrell MacDonald
Judson Holderness	David Landau
Snap Naab	Gordon Westcott
Lefty	Guinn Williams
Windy	Vincent Barnett

A drama of the sagebrush and cactus country is being enacted on the screen of the Seventh Avenue Roxy this week, with the wistful "moo" of cows and the "baa-baa" of sheep for atmosphere. The difficulty with this microphonic edition of "Heritage of the Desert" is that something of the windiness of those open spaces has been permitted to filter into the script. The men who want the land through which the canyon runs stand around threatening the men who are reluctant to surrender it. The conferences that lead up to a big free-for-all fight are as numerous as those preceding a championship bout, and it is not until late in the story that the bad man begins to prove his reputation.

After that, things do begin to happen. Judson Holderness, who had originally offered $40,000 for the property, brings the price down to $5,000 and announces the cut in a note attached to the body of old Adam Naab's son. The answer still bein "No," Holderness captures the hero, Randolph Scott, with the intention of shipping his corpse back with an announcement of a further reduction in real estate values. But Mr. Scott is in love with old Naab's pretty ward, played by Sally Blane, and that makes a lot of difference. With a heroic disregard for the inconvenience of a bullet in the back, Mr. Scott manages to convince the rascal that the land is not for sale. But "Heritage of the Desert," although the horses are fleet and the villains boastful, is only mildly entertaining.

———

On the Stage.

Dave Schooler and his musicians serve as a genial background for a variety entertainment on the Roxy stage. Ralph Kirbery, billed as "The Dream Singer," runs through some of the popular tunes of the day, and Zelda Santley is an amusing item with her impersonations of well-known entertainers.

The Gae Foster girls contribute some energetic chorus work. A dog act, an acrobatic duo and a dance turn by the Harris Twins and Loretta complete the program on the stage.

A. D. S.

———

Mr 11, 1933

An Imaginative Killer.

MURDERS IN THE ZOO, based on a story by Philip Wylie and Seton I. Miller; directed by Edward Sutherland; a Paramount production. At the Paramount.

Peter Yates	Charles Ruggles
Eric Gorman	Lionel Atwill
Jerry Evans	Gail Patrick
Dr. Woodford	Randolph Scott
Roger Hewitt	John Lodge
Evelyn Gorman	Kathleen Burke
Professor Evans	Harry Beresford
Dan	Edward McWade

Just as it seemed that the cinema's experiments in sadism were ended for the season, the Paramount disclosed a particularly gruesome specimen. In the opening scenes of "Murders in the Zoo" an irate husband is shown in the act of destroying his wife's lover in an Indian jungle. Having sewed the wretch's lips together with thread, following what he declares to be a symbolic Oriental custom, Eric Gorman, zoologist, leaves the fellow to perish miserably among the pythons and tigers. This murderous sportsman then returns to America with his latest batch of wild fauna, keeping a weather eye on the activities of his erratic wife. Soon she is engaged in an informal romance with another unsuspecting youth. The film thereafter describes the somewhat ghastly manner in which Gorman arranges for his wife to expiate her infidelities in the crocodile pool and for her new lover to be bitten by a mamba's fangs.

It happens that the director has been almost too effective in dramatizing these cheerless events, and one is thankful for the generous footage given to Charles Ruggles as a timid and bibulous press agent for the zoo. Those who demand their leaven of romance even in horror pictures are likely to find "Murders in the Zoo" inadequate in this direction. Randolph Scott, as the zoo's toxicologist, and Gail Patrick, as the curator's lovely daughter, enjoy their romantic moments between murders, but their affair is sketchily written.

Lionel Atwill as the insanely jealous husband is almost too convincing for comfort, and Kathleen Burke as the wife suggests the domestic terrors of her life capably. Judged by its ability to chill and terrify, this film is a successful melodrama.

On the Stage.

The Paramount stage show offers a hilarious variety of comedians. Bob Hope and his assistant stooges set a fast and funny pace for the program. Patsy Kelly reproduces her excellent comedy sketch from "Flying Colors"—the bon voyage number. Carl Randall and Barbara Newberry, tap dancers, and Ruth Petty are also in evidence.

The lunatic band supervised by Milt and Frank Britton brings the curtain down on a rowdily humorous finale.

A. D. S.

———

Ap 3, 1933

THE SCREEN

Allan Dinehart, Carole Lombard and H. B. Warner in a Film Dealing With Evil Spirits and Fake Mediums.

SUPERNATURAL, based on a story by
Garnett Weston; directed by Victor
Halperin; a Paramount production. At
the Paramount.

Roma Courtney	Carole Lombard
Grant Wilson	Randolph Scott
Ruth Rogen	Vivienne Osborne
Paul Bavian	Allan Dinehart
Dr. Houston	H. B. Warner
Madame Gourjan	Beryl Mercer
Robert Hammond	William Farnum

By MORDAUNT HALL

Notwithstanding the incredibility of many of its main incidents, "Supernatural," the present picture at the Paramount, succeeds in awakening no little interest in its spooky doings. It not only depicts the various tricks of a charlatan spiritualist but also undertakes through camera wizardry to show the spirit of a dead murderess entering the body of a wholesome girl and causing her to behave like a savage.

The story, which owes its origin to one written by Garnett Weston, is worked out shrewdly and the scenes are for the most part pictured in a fashion suited to the eerie happenings. At the outset one is reminded that Confucius issued a warning to treat all supernatural beings with respect, but to keep aloof from them. Mohammed and the New Testament also are quoted and to put the spectator in a receptive mood there are wind and rain and dirgelike music.

Allan Dinehart plays the crooked spiritualist, Paul Bavian, who is to be congratulated on the thoroughness of his methods to extort money from a wealthy girl named Roma Courtney. Bavian had been on intimate terms with Ruth Rogen, who, after killing three of her lovers, expiates her crimes in the electric chair. It is the theory of a Dr. Houston that the spirits of dead evildoers continue to commit crimes through other flesh and blood mediums. He has more than a mere suspicion that Ruth Rogen's spirit will be running amuck and that susceptible women had better keep out of its way.

It is not disclosing any great secret to say that Bavian has an easy way of getting rid of those who

Allan Dinehart as He Appears in "Supernatural."

thwart him. A little poison in a ring, a handshake and they die. This sinister faker writes to Roma telling her that he has heard from the spirit of her brother, who recently died, and that he (Bavian) was requested to summon her. This missive subsequently leads to Roma and others visiting Bavian's apartment, where the crook pretends to go into a trance and in an artful manner impresses the girl.

Subsequently one beholds the wraith of Ruth Rogen governing Roma's actions and the beautiful girl is transformed temporarily into a wild person, who seeks to strangle Bavian. Her attack on the so-called spiritualist is not especially convincing, unless one is to presume that the evil spirit gives her superhuman strength.

Mr. Dinehart does very well by his rôle. Miss Lombard's portrayal also is praiseworthy. Vivienne Osborne makes the most of the part of Ruth Rogen and Randolph Scott is pleasing as Roma's sweetheart. H. B. Warner is natural as Dr. Houston, but William Farnum overacts the rôle of an individual known as Robert Hammond. Beryl Mercer is effective as Bavian's landlady.

On the Stage.

What with dancing, singing and acrobatic performers, the stage program, which is known as "Spring Varieties," is quite a lively entertainment, with humor furnished by the indefatigable Al Trahan.

Among others who contribute to this show are Jane Friman, Betty Jane Cooper and the Lathrop Brothers, the California Collegians and Gertrude Hoffman Girls.

Ap 22, 1933

THE SCREEN

His Foster Mother.

BROKEN DREAMS, based on a story by
Olga Printzlau; directed by Robert Vignola; a Monogram production. At Loew's
Ziegfeld Theatre.

Dr Robert Morley	Randolph Scott
Martha Morley	Martha Sleeper
Pop Miller	Joseph Cawthorn
Mom Miller	Beryl Mercer
Billy Morley	Buster Phelps
Grace	Charlotte Merriam
Hopkins	Sydney Bracy

The report that "Broken Dreams," which began a two-day engagement at Loew's Ziegfeld yesterday, is an independent cinema enterprise should not be misconstrued. One of the things it is not independent of is a routine reliance on the formulae for assembling a routine tear-jerker.

There is in "Broken Dreams" a child actor who is required to weep when they take his dog away; to weep when they separate him from his supposed father and mother; to struggle with the man who is trying to kiss his beautiful foster-mother, and to be hurled to the floor with sufficient force to render him unconscious; to lie pathetically still while those who love him shuffle and sniffle unhappily around his bed, and to murmur "Mama" in his delirium and thereby reveal to his daddy that he really loves his foster-mother, a circumstance which prevents the threatened dissolution of the happy home. Buster Phelps is the lad who plays this part, and his performance is probably no more irritating, and certainly no less, than the average of its type.　A. D. S.

N 21, 1933

THE LAST ROUND-UP, based on Zane Grey's novel "The Border Legion"; directed by Henry Hathaway; a Paramount production. At the Criterion.

Jim Cleve	Randolph Scott
Joan Randall	Barbara Fritchie
Jack Kells	Monte Blue
Sam Gulden	Fred Kohler
Bunko McGee	Fuzzy Knight
Judge Savin	Richard Carle
Charley Benson	Barton MacLane
Sheriff	Charles B. Middleton
Shrimp	Frank Rice
Rush	Dick Rush

By MORDAUNT HALL.

It is a gruff, murdering and thieving tale of the old days in the Far West that has burst into the Criterion under the title of "The Last Round-Up." It hails from Zane Grey's novel, "The Border Legion," and the song from which it has acquired its new title is rendered during the course of the narrative.

The Border Legion does not apply to a law-abiding lot of fellows, but to a band of desperadoes who made things hum in various places. The sympathy in the story is on the wrong side of the fence and toward the end it seems imminent that Jack Kells, the bandit leader, is going to shed a few tears. His loyal lieutenant has stopped a bullet and there are only three members of the legion left. Kells, however, does not weep, for another piece of lead comes his way and it is only a question of a minute or so before the head marauder himself topples from the saddle in death.

Up to that time Kells had led a charmed life, for he rides in the face of gunfire and is unharmed when the citizens of one place have the effrontery to use dynamite. Although he has killed many a man and feathered his nest with loot, those responsible for this pictorial production seem to feel that he is entitled to a hero's grave. The real heroic character of the tale is sidetracked. He is Jim Cleve, a handsome fellow who does not seem to be long on brains. Jim, however, has the satisfaction in the end of living and riding off with that fair creature, Joan Randall, a pianist, who at one time thought Kells to be quite a charming chap.

Among the drinkers in the film is Judge Savin, who is no skinflint, being always willing to stand a round. He also presides in court and winks at hangings. Judge Savin is acted by Richard Carle, who years and years ago used to chant, "For I picked a lemon in the Garden of Love, where they say only peaches grow."

Monte Blue personates the dauntless Kells. Sam Gulden, the scarface of those days, comes to life in the form of the stalwart Fred Kohler. Joan is acted by the gray-eyed Barbara Fritchie and Randolph Scott appears as Cleve.

But riding's the thing in this piece of gunplay.

My 10, 1934

The Oregon Trail.

WAGON WHEELS, based on a story by Zane Grey; directed by Charles Barton; a Paramount production. At the Mayfair.

Clint Belmet	Randolph Scott
Nancy Wellington	Gail Patrick
Sonny Wellington	Billy Lee
Hetty Masters	Leila Bennett
Abby Masters	Jan Duggan
Murdock	Monte Blue
Jim Burch	Raymond Hatton
Bill O'Meary	Olin Howland
Couch	J. P. McGowan
Jed	James A. Marcus
Mrs. Jed	Helen Hunt
Masters	James B. Kenton
Ebe	Alfred Delcambre

Another story—or is it the same one?—of the covered wagon days had its shy première at the Mayfair last night. The picture, produced by Paramount and based on Zane Grey's novel, "Fighting Caravans," is called "Wagon Wheels" and, while it rates a better classification than "horse opera," has not quite the epic sweep that its producers intended it should have.

It treats of the Oregon trail, the first band of settlers, their relentless march across a hostile country; of an intrepid mother and her young son; of the stalwart young scout; of a half-breed fur trader; of marauding redskins. Having so many colorful ingredients, the story must, of necessity, produce an aura of romantic adventure. But the glow is short-lived and, in retrospect, the film is a pallid reflection of the history it attempts to relive.

Ever since "The Covered Wagon," picture-makers have attempted to find new uses for the picturesque story of our Western colonization. A few have succeeded—"Cimarron" notably—because the producers managed to subordinate the sideplot of romance to the essentially dramatic story of the immigrant train and its cumbersome march to empire.

"Wagon Wheels" fails to join this honored list through its neglect of that principle. Too much is made of the romance between Clint Belmet (Randolph Scott) and Nancy Wellington (Gail Patrick). The film loses dignity, too, through the stock introduction of the renegade fur trader who incites the Indians to attack the train in an attempt to preserve, for a few more years, the trapping country. In its emphasis upon these phases the picture lapses into pure horse opera.

The film does possess much that is interesting and entertaining. The regrets are mostly for what it might have been. Mr. Scott and Miss Patrick do well enough, but the honors belong to young Billy Lee, as the 4-year-old son, and to Jan Duggan—the Mrs. Pepperday of "The Old-Fashioned Way"—as a romantic spinster. F. S. N.

O 4, 1934

THE SCREEN

Out Green Valley Way.

HOME ON THE RANGE, based on Zane Grey's "Code of the West" and adapted by Charles Logue, with the screen play by Ethel Doherty and Grant Garrett; directed by Arthur Jacobson and produced for Paramount by Harold Hurley. At the Criterion.

Jack	Jackie Coogan
Tom Hatfield	Randolph Scott
Georgie	Evelyn Brent
Thurman	Dean Jagger
Beady	Addison Richards
Cracker	Fuzzy Knight

By ANDRE SENNWALD.

Tom Hatfield, who knew a rat when he saw one, walked into Beady's office and drew a bead on him before Beady ever seed him. "We're plain folks out this-a-way," says Tom, easy like, twirling his six-shooter. "Now I got every chamber in this here gun loaded up. I'm agoin' to shoot four bullets careless, and then I'm agoin' to put the last two through the dirtiest coyote in Green Valley, and you're it. That is, unless you open up that there safe and sign over the deed of the ranch that you stole off'n us Hatfields, and while that safe is open maybe you better pay back that money that your boys took off'n me." Beady had slits where his eyes oughter been. "You'll hang for this," he says. "Not while there's honest men in Green Valley," says Tom, cool as brass. "Now git!"

Outside of the colloquy between Tom Hatfield and Beady, and perhaps the drag-'em-out slugging match behind the fence, "Home on the Range" is a Western only by courtesy. The shooting-irons might just as well be toy pistols for all the good that the new film at the Criterion makes of them. The narrative progresses by fits and starts, with depressing interims during which you have the suspicion that the scenarists are just behind the camera working up something for the next scene. Jackie Coogan, a mighty braw lad now, ought not to be judged by his performance in "Home on the Range," which seems to be a strictly makeshift Western. Since the film bears the Paramount label, we must conceal our disappointment behind the reflection that Mr. Zukor probably didn't set much store by it anyway.

F 13, 1935

ROBERTA, screen play by Jane Murfin and Sam Mintz, with additional dialogue by Allan Scott and Glenn Tryon; music by Jerome Kern, book and lyrics by Otto Harbach with additional lyrics by Dorothy Fields and Jimmy McHugh; directed by William A. Seiter; produced for RKO Radio by Pandro S. Berman. At the Radio City Music Hall.

Stephanie	Irene Dunne
Huck	Fred Astaire
Scharwenka	Ginger Rogers
John	Randolph Scott
Roberta	Helen Westley
Ladislaw	Victor Varconi
Sophie	Claire Dodd
Voyda	Luis Alberni
Lord Delves	Ferdinand Munier
Albert	Torben Meyer
Professor	Adrian Rosley
Fernando	Bodil Rosing

By ANDRE SENNWALD.

With the excellent help of Professor Astaire, the Kubla Kahns at RKO Radio have erected a bright and shimmering pleasure dome in "Roberta," which was unveiled with appropriate cheering at the Radio City Music Hall yesterday. The work is a model for urbanity in the musical films and Mr. Astaire, the debonair master of light comedy and the dance, is its chief ornament. To watch him skipping on effortless cat's feet across a dance floor is to experience one of the major delights of the contemporary cinema. For Mr. Astaire's dancing is not only an esthetic excitement, but also comedy of a unique and lofty order. In one of the best episodes in "Roberta" he engages in a pantomimic dance with Miss Ginger Rogers which is quite as eloquently comic as an acrimonious love scene out of Noel Coward.

But "Roberta" contains additional splendors and delights, even if the agile professor does create the illusion that he is always several miles ahead of his interference. Jerome Kern's songs, some of them borrowed from the stage edition and others composed for the occasion, are distinguished both for their literacy and their romantic wit. After being bombarded by the loud speakers these many months, you may imagine that you are just a bit weary of having smoke blown in your eyes, but that superb lyric is still able to capture your attention. For the liquid sentimental songs like "Lovely to Look At," "Yesterday" and "Touch of Your Hand" there is the cool soprano of Irene Dunne. For the pattering humor of "Let's Begin," "Hard to Handle" and "I Won't Dance" there are the extraordinarily pleasing song-and-dance duets of Mr. Astaire and Miss Rogers.

Does a gentleman dare confess the full extent of his enjoyment at the dazzling fashions which Ernard Newman has devised for the photoplay? Well, even a lumberjack can see that they are the height of chic and allure. "Roberta" spends a good deal of its time in a Parisian dressmaking establishment and in the finale it blossoms out with a ravishing fashion show. Doubtless this was originally intended to ensnare the enthusiasms of the ladies. But since Mr. Kern has put it gayly to music and Mr. Astaire has been persuaded to act as master of ceremonies, the gentlemen may be pardoned for enjoying it enormously.

The libretto, which proved a definite handicap to "Roberta" on the stage, has been visibly brightened by the dialogue polishers in the studio. It is still the fable of the All-American gridiron hero who journeys to Paris with a collegiate band and, owing to the demise of his aunt, finds himself the proprietor of the most fashionable shop in the city. This time it is Randolph Scott who loves his co-partner, Miss Dunne, an expatriate Russian princess. That perennial vixen, Miss Claire Dodd, manages with her usual success to interrupt the romance. Meanwhile Mr. Astaire is enjoying himself hugely at the expense of Miss Rogers, who strives to conceal her American ancestry behind an unsteady Gallic accent. Helen Westley, that grand actress, also participates as the kindly and aging Roberta who founded the shop.

Now that Charles Laughton and "Ruggles of Red Gap" have set the 1935 standard for screen comedy, Mr. Astaire and "Roberta" have dashed right along and established a model for lavishness, grace and humor in the musical film. If there is a flaw in the photoplay, it is the unfortunate circumstance that Mr. Astaire and his excellent partner, Miss Rogers, cannot be dancing during every minute of it. Anyway, the title is "Roberta" and the place is the Music Hall. . . . The Leonidoff pageant on the stage, "Cavalcade of Color," presents a Rhapsody in White, a Tango in Scarlet and a Lament in Blue.

Mr 8, 1935

Fred Astaire appearing in the film version of "Roberta."

SHE, adapted from Sir H. Rider Haggard's novel; screen play by Ruth Ross, with additional dialogue by Dudley Nichols; directed by Irving Pichel and Lansing G. Holden; produced by Merian C. Cooper for RKO Radio Pictures. At the Radio City Music Hall.

She, ruler of Kor .... Helen Gahagan
Leo Vincey .... Randolph Scott
Tanya Dugmore .... Helen Mack
Holly .... Nigel Bruce
Billali .... Gustav von Seyffertitz
John Vincey .... Samuel Hinds
Amahagger Chief .... Noble Johnson
Dugmore .... Lumsden Hare

H. Rider Haggard's "She," which was published about fifty years ago and is reported to have fired the imaginations of between one and two million juvenile readers, has been converted by RKO Radio into a gaudy, spectacular and generally fantastic photoplay which is likely to find its greatest favor with the younger generation. The adult reaction, we fear, will be decidedly lukewarm.

At the risk of being considered illiterate, the department must confess to having missed the Haggard novels in its youth and consequently has had to rely, for purposes of comparison, upon the memories of a few gray-haired individuals in the city room who grew both excited and reminiscent at the mention of She, the ruler of the land of Kor, who stood in the Flame of Life and gained immortality.

On their testimony, the Music Hall's new film appears to parallel the novel rather closely, barring, perhaps, the fact that it places Kor somewhere north of Manchuria, while Sir Rider had it in Africa. But otherwise it still is the same old "She," with the handsome English scientist trekking into the unknown to investigate the five-century-old legend about a lost kingdom, a white woman ruler and a flame of eternal youth.

It is one of the film's disappointments that the events leading up to the scientist's discovery of Kor are much more exciting than those within the grim-walled city. The desertion of the native guides, the finding of a saber-toothed tiger frozen in the ice; an avalanche, capture by a fierce-looking tribe of cavemen—this sort of thing is bound to make one look forward to all kinds of excitement when the high priest, Billali—who is Gustav von Seyffertitz in a tin hat—conducts the captives into Kor.

And then the picture fades into a series of eye-filling spectacles so dear to the heart of Hollywood: huge sets, jammed with massive gongs, Roman centurions and Egyptian dancing girls; weird incantations, incense, ceremonial dances and curt orders in a barbaric tongue (additional dialogue by Dudley Nichols); the haughty queen who has been in love with the English scientist—or with his great-great-great-grandfather — for 500 years, and the trader's daughter who is only mortal, but loves the young man in a non-eternal way; the scene in which the girl is to be sacrificed, the rescue, the fight, the chase, the escape. . . . It must have been a familiar pattern even when Haggard used it fifty years ago and RKO Radio hasn't done much except produce it on grander scale than ever before.

Conceding that Helen Gahagan, in her film début, is an impressive She and that Randolph Scott, Nigel Bruce and Helen Mack lend their respective talents and beauty to the tale, the photoplay still cannot be accounted much more than a King Kong edition of "lost kingdom" melodramas. If it belongs anywhere, it is in the children's branch of the film library.

F. S. N.

J 26, 1935

Helen Gahagan in "She," at the Radio City Music Hall.

THE SCREEN

King Vidor's Screen Version of the Stark Young Novel 'So Red the Rose' at the Paramount.

SO RED THE ROSE, as adapted by Laurence Stallings, Maxwell Anderson and Edwin Justus Mayer from Stark Young's novel, "So Red the Rose"; directed by King Vidor; produced for Paramount by Douglas MacLean. At the Paramount.

Vallette Bedford	Margaret Sullavan
Malcolm Bedford	Walter Connolly
Duncan Bedford	Randolph Scott
Sally Bedford	Janet Beecher
Mary Cherry	Elizabeth Patterson
Middleton Bedford	Dickie Moore
Edward Bedford	Harry Ellerbe
George Pendleton	Robert Cummings
George McGehee	Charles Starrett
Yankee Boy	Johnny Downs
William Veal	Daniel Haynes
Cato	Clarence Muse
Major Rushton	James Burke
Confederate Sergeant	Warner Richmond
Charles Tolliver	Alfred Delcambre

By ANDRE SENNWALD.

The cinema goes into well-bred mourning for Stark Young's aristocrats of the old South in the beautifully photographed screen production of "So Red the Rose," at the Paramount Theatre. The film scarcely possesses the significance that we might have anticipated from the distinguished collaboration of King Vidor as director and Maxwell Anderson, Laurence Stallings and Edwin Justus Mayer as screenplaywrights. But it is a well-made sentimental drama and it celebrates the last days of the planter aristocracy with a warmth, skill and romantic fervor that should delight Mr. Young.

It is difficult in this turbulent day to subscribe to the film's point of view or to share its rage against the uncouth legions of Mr. Lincoln as they dash about the lovely Southern landscape putting crazy notions in the heads of the plantation slaves. By presenting the alien forces which destroyed this civilization as cruel and vulgar intrusions instead of inevitable realities, "So Red the Rose" cheats itself of contemporary meaning.

In its reworking of Mr. Young's best-selling novel, the photoplay becomes the tragedy of degeneration in a proud Louisiana family during the war between the States. Beginning with scenes of indolent luxury at the columned mansion where most of the action takes place, it ends on desolation, humbled pride and the remnants of a house in mourning for the men it

Margaret Sullavan, who is seen in "So Red the Rose."

has sacrificed in a doomed cause. Only briefly does Mr. Vidor bring the war actually in focus: Mrs. Bedford searching for her slain son on the field at Shiloh, or a clash of horsemen at night on the plantation.

Several scenes are in Mr. Vidor's best style. There is the highly effective bit in which Randolph Scott goes off to war, walking into the camera with gradually increasing tempo until at last hysteria has gripped him and he is running madly. There is also the shrewdly emotional climax when the lovers, separated by a stream and a bridge, rush toward each other, a scene that is reminiscent of the reunion of the lovers in Mr. Vidor's "The Big Parade." But the film has its moments of unconscious irony that shatter the mood it is trying to evoke, such moments as the enthusiastic cheering of the slaves when their master goes off to fight their liberators, and Margaret Sullavan's absurdly sentimental appeal to the slaves later on when they are primed for rebellion.

Walter Connolly gives one of his most satisfying performances as the head of the family, the rum-sodden aristocrat who goes off to war in a cocked hat. There is a fine bit by Robert Cummings (who, incidentally, possesses the only convincing accent in the film), as the chivalric young Texan. Margaret Sullavan is prettily effective as the young belle of the household and there is good work by Randolph Scott, Clarence Muse, Elizabeth Patterson and Janet Beecher

N 28, 1935

THE SCREEN

'Follow the Fleet,' the Season's Best Musical Comedy, Opens at the Radio City Music Hall.

FOLLOW THE FLEET, adapted from "Shore Leave," a play by Hubert Osborne; screen play by Dwight Taylor and Allan Scott; music and lyrics by Irving Berlin; directed by Mark Sandrich; produced by Pandro S. Berman for RKO Radio. At the Radio City Music Hall.

"Bake"	Fred Astaire
Sherry	Ginger Rogers
Bilge	Randolph Scott
Connie	Harriet Hilliard
Iris	Astrid Allwyn
Dopey	Ray Mayer
Captain Hickey	Harry Beresford
Lieutenant Williams	Addison Randall
Nolan	Russell Hicks
Sullivan	Brooks Benedict
Kitty	Lucille Ball
Trio—Betty Grable, Joy Hodges and Jeanne Grey.	

By FRANK S. NUGENT.

We don't expect to hear another word from the Radio City Music Hall for at least two weeks, and if there's any justice for the Rockefellers, it may be three. Ginger Rogers and Fred Astaire checked into the theatre yesterday in "Follow the Fleet," and even though it is not the best of their series it still is good enough to take the head of this year's class in song and dance entertainment. If you are one of those outlanders who never have seen the screen's première dancing team in action, now is a propitious time to complete your education; if you have enjoyed them before, it should be assurance enough to hear that they tap as gayly, waltz as beautifully and disagree as merrily as ever.

With Irving Berlin's score as a rhythmic accompaniment and with a considerably altered edition of Hubert Osborne's play, "Shore Leave" (1922), as a convenient excuse, "Follow the Fleet" reduces itself, and quite pleasantly, to a generous series of attractive song and dance numbers linked almost imperceptibly by the most nebulous of plots. This, of course, is the way with all the Rogers-Astaire pictures, and we mention it only for the record—not because we expect any one to consider it a serious criticism of the film.

Breaking away from the mistaken-identity formula followed in "Top Hat" and in "The Gay Divorcée," their new photoplay treats Mr. Astaire as an out-and-out sailor who joined the navy because his vaudeville dancing partner—Miss Rogers, naturally—refused to marry him. When Sailor Astaire gets shore leave he sets out to make Miss Rogers change her mind. Beyond that we really have only the vaguest idea of the story. There was something about his shipmate, Randolph Scott, being blind to the charms of Harriet Hilliard and showing preference for Astrid Allwyn, and there was some added business about a benefit show to keep Miss Hilliard's schooner from being sold down the river, or wherever mortgaged vessels go.

Memory is stronger of Mr. Astaire's comic chantey about the men who joined the navy to see the world and only saw the sea. There was one particularly Cole Porterish rhyme about a taxi and the Black Sea and the Pacific not being terrific. We have no difficulty recalling the Astaire-Rogers competition for the dancing trophy offered by the Paradise dance hall, or Mr. Astaire's seamanlike tap dance drill with a group of his shipmates, or his and Miss Rogers's whirling, perfectly balanced and liquid ballroom routine which serves as the picture's rhythmic finale. All these mean so much more than the story itself—but you probably know that of old.

Mr. Berlin, who contributed a full catalogue of song hits to "Top Hat" last year, was not at his best when he composed the battery of tunes for the current picture. Melodious they are, but not quite up to the high standard he set with "Cheek to Cheek," "Isn't This a Lovely Day?" and others. His "Let's Face the Music and Dance" is quite the best thing in the new show, and we have no quarrel with "I'd Rather Lead a Band," "All My Eggs in One Basket," "We Saw the Sea" and "Let Yourself Go." No quarrel, but no rhapsodies, either.

Perhaps the major flaw—and it is really a minor one, considering the severity with which we rate our favorite musical comedy team—is the film's failure to include a few comedians to help carry the picture along when Rogers and Astaire are not in there dancing. Edward Everett Horton would have helped, and so would Eric Blore or Erik Rhodes. Comedy, rather than the minor romance of Mr. Scott and Miss Hilliard, would have been a more satisfactory order of the day. We still feel an admiral's salute is due Miss Rogers and Mr. Astaire, with a general broadside of approval for Mr. Berlin, Miss Hilliard, Mr. Scott and Miss Allwyn.

Ginger Rogers, who is appearing in "Follow the Fleet."

F 21, 1936

AND SUDDEN DEATH, from a story by Theodore Reeves and Madeleine Ruthven; screen play by Joseph Moncure March; directed by Charles Barton; produced by A. M. Botsford for Paramount.

Lieut. James Knox	Randolph Scott
Betty Winslow	Frances Drake
Jackie Winslow	Tom Brown
Bobby Sanborn	Billy Lee
Steve Bartlett	Fuzzy Knight
"Bangs"	Terry Walker
District Attorney	Porter Hall
Mike Andrews	Charles Quigley
J. R. Winslow	John Hyams
Sergeant Sanborn	Joseph Sawyer
Counsel for the Defense	Oscar Apfel
Sergeant Maloney	Don Rowan
Mr. Tweets	Jimmy Conlin
Dodie Sloan	Maidel Turner
Archie Sloan	Charlie Arnt
Nurse	Wilma Francis
Meggs	Herbert Evans

There is something faintly reminiscent of J. C. Furnas's treatise about dismemberment on the highways in the first reel or two of

"And Sudden Death." But once the new film at the Rialto takes up the screen play concocted by Joseph Moncure March, it becomes enmeshed in hackneyed melodramatic situations. A certain heavy handedness of direction causes several of the film's more violent scenes, such as the one in which a scatterbrained juvenile sends his car crashing into the guard rail of a bridge and hurtling down the embankment into the river, to lose much of their effectiveness.

As a crusade against reckless driving the film lacks conviction, chiefly because it broaches a vital subject with typical Hollywood timidity. Lieutenant James Knox, the crusading traffic officer, never should have become acquainted socially with Betty Winslow—young, beautiful and wealthy, but a potential murderess when seated behind the wheel of her high-powered roadster. But meet they do, and the impetuous Betty is, by the power of romance, transformed into a speed-conscious motorist. Her irresponsible brother, Jackie, continues to mix Scotch and soda with gasoline, however. The result is, of course, that on one of his escapades, Jackie's car crashes into a bus loaded with children. And following in the self-sacrificing footsteps of Ann Harding, Betty assumes responsibility for the accident.

Betty's is a noble gesture, but there ought to be a law prohibiting heroines from shielding juveniles like Jackie, who frankly admits, "I have a yellow streak a mile wide down my back," after his sister is sentenced to prison. Tom Brown succeeds admirably in making Jackie a thoroughly disagreeable character. There also are competent performances by Randolph Scott as Lieutenant Knox, Frances Drake as Betty and Joseph Sawyer as the motorcycle officer whose son is killed in the bus crash. But the real acting honors must go to Porter Hall as the District Attorney and to Jimmy Conlin, who appears briefly as a disgruntled owner of a suburban cottage.
                                    T. M. P.

J 18, 1936.

THE LAST OF THE MOHICANS, based on the novel by James Fenimore Cooper; screen play by Philip Dunne from an adaptation by John Balderstone. Paul Perez and Daniel Moore; directed by George B. Seitz; produced by Edward Small for Reliance Pictures; released by United Artists.

Hawkeye	Randolph Scott
Alice Munro	Binnie Barnes
Cora Munro	Heather Angel
Colonel Munro	Hugh Buckler
Major Duncan Heyward	Henry Wilcoxon
Magua	Bruce Cabot
Chingachgook	Robert Barrat
Uncas	Philip Reed
Captain Winthrop	Willard Robertson
David Gamut	Frank McGlynn Sr.

It may seem captious, perhaps, to quibble over details in the telescoping of so ponderous an item as "The Last of the Mohicans" into a mere hour or so of screen entertainment, especially now that the shores of Horican are bestrewn with Summer hotels and the adjacent wooded valleys criss-crossed with three-lane concrete trails blazed with such ideographs as 9A and 9B. But we left the Rivoli yesterday with the feeling that Reliance Pictures had played fast and loose with the favorite fictional character of our youth.

To one who has stalked through leafy forest wearing a makeshift approximation of the squirrel-pelt cap of lean old Hawkeye, the long rifle, pausing stealthily to sight down the glittering barrel of his trusty Killdeer in the direction of the skulking figment of a Huron, the mere suggestion that the noted scout of the Leatherstocking Tales might soften even for a moment under the blandishments of a woman is clear heresy.

And that, you erstwhile cronies of wrinkled old Chingachgook, you sage counselors of impetuous and ill-fated young Uncas, is what Director George Seitz and a whole caboodle of writers and adapters dare to suggest.

They have, of course, done a grand job of bringing the high spots of the story to the screen, even if it did require technical aid from Boy Scouts to teach the modern Redskins how to whoop and holler in the accepted James Fenimore Cooper manner. Bruce Cabot's Magua is as evil a Huron as ever you pictured him and his misdeeds during and subsequent to the eventful journey from Fort Edward to Fort William Henry of Duncan Heyward and the colonel's daughters, Alice and Cora Munro, are even more ghastly than those the original text cited. The massacre of Fort William Henry is by far the bloodiest, scalpingest morsel of cinematic imagery ever produced, and we were consequently about ready to overlook the elisions made necessary in fitting the novel to the screen when Hollywood permitted Hawkeye to fall in love. Only that stolid Sagamore, Chingachgook, thinks to voice his, and our, disapproval. "Hawkeye's heart like water," he says.

Henceforth Hollywood keeps control, blending a love motif into the famed shooting contest between Duncan and Hawkeye and going so far, we are told (we covered our eyes when the disheartening incident seemed inevitable) as to permit Alice and Hawkeye to kiss at the picture's finale.

Randolph Scott, we must admit, is our Hawkeye to the life, despite his newfound failing for a pretty face, something you must admit about Binnie Barnes. Robert Barrat is an agile, if not sufficiently wrinkled, Chingachgook, and Henry Wilcoxon endows Major Heyward with characteristics that neither we nor James Fenimore Cooper ever thought of. Uncas, the last of the Mohicans, played by Philip Reed, is one of the story's two forgotten men. The other, played by Frank McGlynn Sr., is the gaunt psalm-singer, David Gamut, whose appearance is so brief that he is never properly introduced to the audience.
                                    J. T. M.

S 3, 1936

GO WEST, YOUNG MAN, based on the play "Personal Appearance," by Lawrence Riley, screen play by Mae West; directed by Henry Hathaway; produced by Emanuel Cohen for Paramount. At the Paramount Theatre.

Mavis Arden	Mae West
Morgan	Warren William
Bud	Radolph Scott
Harrigan	Lyle Talbot
Mrs. Struthers	Alice Brady
Gladys	Isabel Jewell
Aunt Kate	Elizabeth Patterson
Joyce	Margaret Perry
Professor Rigby	Etienne Girardot
Clyde	Maynard Holmes
French maid	Alice Ardell
Nicodemus	Nicodemus

The suasively undulating Mae West is back on the Paramount screen with a new and engagingly robustious exposition of her theory that "a thrill a day keeps the chill away." This time the medium is that eminently successful Broadway spoof of a Hollywood glamour girl, "Personal Appearance," which Miss West has wrought, with slight alterations, into something she modestly has caused to be titled, "Go West, Young Man."

Generally speaking, "Personal Appearance" has lost little in Miss West's edition. The mobility of the camera permits the screen audience a glimpse or so of the susceptible screen idol, Mavis Arden, actually engaged in one of her saccharine personal appearances. It also brings into being, in the person of Lyle Talbot, the unseen telephone lover of the play.

At the finish, the stage Miss Arden's Parthian shot at the triumphant figure of the press agent who managed to queer her incipient love affairs one by one goes back to the doghouse. In its place is substituted a fadeout betrothal to that same press agent, because the screen permits its departing heroines to hold no grudges.

These are the chief changes in story structure. But the salty idiom and the haughty malapropisms that punctuated the stage piece have been retained wherever they could be got by the censors, and there is something to be said for Miss West's presentation of these features. Apart from that incessant swaying of hers (it is some one's idea, probably her own, that it represents the epitome of eroticism) her treatment of the rôle of the prurient lady of the screen is what the casting directors call a natural. She never allows Mavis Arden to delude any but herself and a few star-struck youngsters.

As is customary when Hollywood makes a special effort, the supporting cast is uniformly excellent. If special mentions must be made, they should be made of the work of Isabel Jewell, Alice Brady, Elizabeth Patterson and Randolph Scott. Warren William, as the press agent, is, of course, deserving of the most special mention of all. He is the only player who has ever come close to stealing a picture from Mae West.

Also on the Paramount bill, and worthy of note because it marks the invasion of a new field by one of the screen's most popular figures, is the first color version of Popeye. Here Popeye meets, and worsts, the tinted teratoids of the island stronghold of Sinbad the Sailor, and finally subdues Sinbad himself after a generous helping of really verdant spinach.   J. T. M.

N 19, 1936, 31:3

HIGH, WIDE AND HANDSOME, based on a story and screen play by Oscar Hammerstein 2d, with additional dialogue by George O'Neill; music by Jerome Kern, with lyrics by Mr. Hammerstein; directed by Rouben Mamoulian; produced by Arthur Hornblow Jr. for Paramount. At the Astor.

Sally Watterson	Irene Dunne
Peter Cortlandt	Randolph Scott
Molly	Dorothy Lamour
Doc Watterson	Raymond Walburn
Red Scanlon	Charles Bickford
Grandma Cortlandt	Elizabeth Patterson

IRENE DUNNE

Mac	William Frawley
Varesi	Akim Tamiroff
Samuel	Ben Blue
Walter Brennan	Alan Hale
Stark	Irving Pichel
Dr. Lippincott	Lucien Littlefield
Mrs. Lippincott	Helen Lowell
Boy	Tommy Bupp
Thompson	Russell Hopton
Shorty	Billy Bletcher
Zeke Smith	Stanley Andrews
Gabby Johnson	Frank Sully
Wash Miller	Jack Clifford
Stackpole	James Burke
Seamstress	Claire MacDowell

By FRANK S. NUGENT

Another colorful chapter of American history—the discovery of the Pennsylvania oil fields and the bitter struggle for their control—has been set to music and retold in vividly cinematic terms by Paramount's "High, Wide and Handsome," which had its première at the Astor last night and seems destined to continue for months on a two-a-day basis. A richly produced, spectacular and melodious show, it moves easily into the ranks of the season's best and probably is as good an all-around entertainment as we are likely to find on Broadway this Summer.

Produced by Arthur Hornblow Jr., directed by Rouben Mamoulian, with a book and score by Oscar Hammerstein 2d and Jerome Kern, and with Irene Dunne and Randolph Scott at the head of a completely satisfying cast, the picture—like "Showboat" and "San Francisco"—defies ready classification. Musical romance is closer to it than "operetta," yet has too tinkling a connotation to be applied to a rugged and virile historical saga. "Symphonic drama" is the phrase fastened to it by Hollywood's Idwal Jones, and that may describe it best, although it has a slightly esthetic sound.

Clearly, "High, Wide and Handsome" is not a gingerbread concoction with an overlayer of romantic whipped cream, but a beef and brawn pasty leavened by the Irene Dunne-Dorothy Lamour caroling. Against it, "Showboat" was an effeminate piece, nostalgic and sentimental. To have treated the oil wars that way would have been too much of a refinement. The dramatic product, like the natural, has an honest crudity which Kern and Hammerstein have tapped in their score, which the astute Mr. Mamoulian has let run unmolested through his film. When Miss Dunne sings a sweet ballad to the contrapuntal grunting of a hungry sow she sets the tone for the picture.

Oil comes to the film's Titusville soon after the descent thereon of Doc Watterson's medicine show, which, unfortunately, was burned to its wagontrees, leaving—not so unfortunately—the lovely Sally Watterson on the figurative doorstep of Peter Cortlandt, the young Pennsylvania farmer who had rigged up a derrick and drill and had some fool's notion that rock-oil could be used to light the lamps of China. Hastily identifying Miss Dunne as Sally and Mr. Scott as Peter Cortlandt, we will skip their inevitable nuptials, except to note that the Cortlandt gusher comes in on their wedding day.

With that as the gentle beginning, the picture gallops post-haste into the oil rush of 1859 and the decision of the railroad crowd, led by the burly Alan Hale, to freeze out the Pennsylvania farmers by increasing freight costs to the refineries until there will be no profit in their black gold. Against this worthy ruggedly individualistic notion young Cortlandt advances another: construction of a pipe line across the State to carry Titusville's oil to the refineries. With that the war begins, pipemen and farmers against railroad hirelings and truckmen with bullwhips, and with carnival interludes, a domestic break, and a rousing battle at the finish when Sally's circus arrives like the United States Marines to put the pipe line through.

I said it was a spectacular show. It also is picturesque, folksy, brimful of Americana. The songs have that quality, too; almost seem to have been plucked from the minstrelsy of the pre-Civil War years rather than coined this season. "High, Wide and Handsome" (the rousing theme song) and "The Things I Want" (sung by Miss Lamour on the shantyboat) are a shade on the contemporary side. But "The Folks Who Live on the Hill" is pure ballad and quite lovely, and "Allegheny Al" might have been sung anywhere up and down the Monongahela.

Mr. Mamoulian's direction has solved again, as it did in last year's "The Gay Desperado," the problem of interweaving song and story gracefully, effectively. Miss Dunne's voice is as delightful as she is, and Mr. Scott's portrayal of Cortlandt is resolute and consistently natural. Elsewhere in the picture's broad and amiable panel you will encounter Elizabeth Patterson as a perfect Grandma Cortlandt, Raymond Walburn as that amiable Wizard Oil peddler, Doc Watterson; William Frawley as his irrepressible Indian brave; Akim Tamiroff (who steals so many scenes he should be arrested for kleptomania) as a gambler, and Ben Blue as an addlepated hired man. In sum, the story material was there and Producer Hornblow was fortunate enough to find a company to treat it properly. The Astor has the best show in town.

Jl 22, 1937.

At the Roxy

REBECCA OF SUNNYBROOK FARM, from a screen play by Karl Tunberg and Don Ettlinger suggested by the Kate Douglas Wiggin story; music and lyrics by Mack Gordon and Harry Revel, Lew Pollack and Sidney D. Mitchell, Sam Pokrass and Jack Yellen, Raymond Scott, Mr. Pollack and Mr. Mitchell; directed by Allan Dwan; produced by Raymond Griffith for Twentieth Century-Fox.

Rebecca Winstead	Shirley Temple
Anthony Kent	Randolph Scott
Orville Smithers	Jack Haley
Gwen Warren	Gloria Stuart
Lola Lee	Phyllis Brooks
Aunt Miranda Wilkins	Helen Westley
Homer Busby	Slim Summerville
Aloysius	Bill Robinson
Raymond Scott Quintet	Themselves
Purvis	Alan Dinehart
Dr. Hill	J. Edward Bromberg
Peters Sisters	Themselves
Receptionist	Dixie Dunbar
Mug	Paul Hurst
Henry Kipper	William Demarest
Melba	Ruth Gillette
Cyrus Bartlett	Paul Harvey
Jake Singer	Clarence Hummel Wilson
Radio Announcers	
Sam Hayes, Garry Breckner, Carroll Nye	
Hamilton Montmarcy	Franklin Pangborn
The Rev. Turner	William Wagner
Mrs. Turner	Elly Malyon
Florabelle	Mary McCarty

Sentimental rediscoverers of Kate Douglas Wiggin may be somewhat taken aback to learn that "Rebecca of Sunnybrook Farm," at the Roxy, opens in a radio station, where Shirley is trying out for a job. Now, don't rush us please: we know the Wiggin masterpiece appeared first in 1903 (we looked it up) and that for all we know it contains potential depths of nostalgia which the Twentieth Century-Fox version has miserably failed to recapture. But at the same time, we are honor bound to report that Mrs. Wiggin's poison is Miss Temple's meat: the greatest trouper of them all is still in there, at the officially certified age of 8, putting over the show for American childhood, not to mention Mr. Zanuck and the stockholders.

We are quite serious about this: any actress who can dominate a Zanuck musical (leaving Mrs. Wiggin out, for the nonce) with Jack Haley, Gloria Stuart, Phyllis Brooks, Helen Westley, Slim Summerville, Bill Robinson, et cetera, can dominate the world. We go even further: we venture to predict for Miss Temple a great future, and that includes singing, dancing, straight dramatic acting, or all three combined, if her fancy runs that way. When it comes to sheer histrionism, we consider her greater than Garbo, Rainer, Hepburn, the Barrymore family (its heirs and assigns) Ginger Rogers and Gypsy Rose—pardon us—Louise Hovick. And Shirley will get you, too, if you don't watch out.

It would be presumptuous of us to try to repeat the Wiggin story, where Mr. Zanuck himself has failed. It's enough for us that Shirley has put her hair up—when most leading ladies are taking it down—and that she succeeds in panicking the networks (and us) with a corn flakes program, when her rather stern but basically soft Aunt Miranda thinks she is snug in bed. Incidentally, though it's supposed to be her first night on the air, her biggest success is a reminiscent medley of previous Temple successes, which she delivers as glibly as Ethel Merman.

However, that was all right with us, because by that time we had ceased to think of her as Rebecca, at all. She was just Shirley to us, and so far as we are concerned, Sunnybrook Farm could go peddle its produce.

B. R. C.

Mr 26, 1938,

THE TE-ANS, from a screen play by Bertram Millhauser, Paul Sloane and William Wister Haines, based on a story by Emerson Hough; directed by James Hogan; produced for Paramount by Lucien Hubbard. At the Paramount.

Ivy Preston..................Joan Bennett
Kirk Jordan.................Randolph Scott
Granna....................May Robson
Chuckawalla............Walter Brennan
Alan Sanford.............Robert Cummings
Isiah Middlebrack............Robert Barrat
Lt David Nichols.........Harvey Stephens
Uncle Dud................Francis Ford
Cal Tuttle................Raymond Hatton
Sam Boss................Clarence Wilson
Slim.....................Jack Moore
Juan Rodrigues...........Chris Martin
Rosita Rodriguez...........Anna Demetrio
General Corbett..........Richard Tucker
Sergeant Grady.............Ed Gargan
Henry.....................Otis Harlan
Chairman................Spencer Charters
Corporal Thompson.......Archie Twitchell
Sergeant Cahill............William Haade

By FRANK S. NUGENT

As time and Paramount goes on, our national history becomes increasingly simplified. Behind each great event—be it the War of 1812, the Pony express, the creation of Standard Oil—lurks a dazzling ingenue and a square-jawed leading man. "The Texans," which accompanied Gene Krupa's band into the Paramount yesterday, adds still another chapter: Texans during the Civil War reconstruction, the opening of the Chisholm Trail, the transcontinental railroad, the formation of the Ku Klux Klan—all neatly abridged to suit the modest co-starring dimensions of the very ingenuous Joan Bennett, the very square-jawed Randolph Scott.

It's not the sort of picture we dare take seriously, muc has we would like to for the glory of the Lone Star State and Adolph Zukor. Theoretically it's "epic," that convenient Hollywood word for any Class A picture filmed on location, but practically it is just another romance with unjustified pretensions to importance. The material might have been there, but a commonplace cast, bad direction and a fairly silly script have stripped it of dignity, reduced it to the mildly entertaining level of a large-scale horse opera.

The scene, as noted before, is Texas after the Civil War when the carpet-baggers have begun their land-grabbing radis, their confiscatory taxation program, their ruthless persecution of all Confederate sympathizers. When they lexy a tax of a dollar a head on all cattle, Mr. Scott rides to Miss Bennett's rescue with the plan to smuggle every white-faced steer on the Boca Grande ranch across the Mexican border and thence north to the Kansas terminus of the railroad. It is an overland trek of 1,500 miles, through Indian country, and with the wretched carpet-baggers in pursuit.

James Hogan, who directed it, makes the usual capital of stampeding steers, of dust storms, blizzards, Indian raids, and the inevitable charge of the blue-coated cavalry. He has not the same success with such concomitant business as the grudging love story, his comic relief and, ultimately, with the sequence which establishes Mr. Scott's responsibility for the continuation of the railroad. (It seems the line would have been discontinued if his

Walter Brennan

10,000 head of cattle hadn't arrived just when they did.)

Mr. Scott stomps through his part, Miss Bennett braves fire, blizzard, flood and mud without mussing a finger-wave, and May Robson and Walter Brennan—the latter especially—do their troupers' best to invest their character roles with a degree of honesty and color. Our feeling is that Paramount muffed an opportunity, even though it has achieved a moderately entertaining show.

Jl 28 1938.

THE ROAD TO RENO, screen play by Roy Chansior and Adele Comandini, dialogue by Brian Marlowe, directed by S. Sylvan Simon for Universal Pictures. At the Globe.

Steve Fortness.............Randolph Scott
Linda Halliday.............Hope Hampton
Sylvia Shane................Glenda Farrell
Aunt Minerva.............Helen Broderick
Walter Crawford............Alan Marshal
Salty....................David Oliver
Linda's Attorney.............Ted Osborn
Sylvia's Attorney........Samuel S. Hinds
Mike.....................Charles Murphy
The Judge................Spencer Charters
Mrs. Brumleigh.............Dorothy Farley
Hannah..................Mira McKinney
Woman Bailiff...............Renie Riano

What this country needs and has needed for years now, it seems to us, is a good inexpensive Western which nevertheless recognizes certain basic facts of the West as we know it at present—Reno, for instance. We have always said that if producers would just forget Indians and buffalos for awhile and concentrate on something modern like divorcees, they could stop worrying about Movie Quiz contests, Bingo and giveaways of that nature. And a picture like "The Road ot Reno," at the Globe, in which the sombreros are secondary to the business at hand—call it romance, sex, or whatever you will—goes far toward corroborating our thesis.

Besides being an amusingly indoors slant on the Great Outdoors, "The Road to Reno" is distinguished by the presence in its cast of a former star of silent films, who not only can talk—and fascinate both Randolph Scott and Alan Marshal in the process—but who sings: we refer to Miss Hope Hampton. The story is that Hope (who is Spring eternal) goes out to Nevada for a divorce and then decides that she loves her first—or was it her second?—husband. It's that thin, but there is a certain, as we said before, slant in the way it is told.

For instance, when Randolph, Hope's Western incumbent, tries to win her back by showing up Alan, her Eastern suitor, Alan is up before he is, as fresh as a daisy, outswims him in the icy lake, sticks on the "outlaw" horse the boys had saddled for him as long as any

bronco buster could. And still Hope decides to stick with Randolph. In addition to the novel script (obviously indebted to that famous Reno scene in "The Women") and Miss Hampton's winsome warblings, the direction, by S. Sylvan Simon—who would rather meet a technical problem than a pieman—is worthy of mention.   B. R. C.

O 3, 1938.

JESSE JAMES, from a screen play by Nunnally Johnson based on historical data assembled by Rosalind Shaffer and Jo Frances James; directed by Henry King; produced by Darryl F. Zanuck for Twentieth Century-Fox. At the Roxy.

Jesse James ....Tyrone Power
Frank James ....Henry Fonda
Zerelda (Zee) ....Nancy Kelly
Will Wright ....Randolph Scott
Major Rufus Cobb ....Henry Hull
Jailer ....Slim Summerville
Mr. Runyan ....J. Edward Bromberg
Barshee ....Brian Donlevy
Bob Ford ....John Carradine
McCoy ....Donald Meek
Jesse James Jr. ....John Russell
Mrs. Samuels ....Jane Darwell
Charles Ford ....Charles Tannen
Mrs. Bob Ford ....Claire Du Brey
Clarke ....William Robertson
Hank ....Harold Goodwin
Pinkie ....Ernest Whitman
Deputy ....Eddy Waller
Bill ....Paul Burns
Minister ....Spencer Charters
Tom Colson ....Arthur Aylesworth
Doctor ....Charles Middleton
Heywood ....Charles Halton
Roy ....George Chandler
Farmer ....Harry Tyler
Boy's Mother ....Virginia Brissac
Judge Rankin ....Ed Le Saint
Judge Mathews ....John Elliott
Old Marshal ....Erville Alderson
Farmer Boy ....George Breakston
One of James Gang ....Lon Chaney Jr.

It certainly isn't Jesse James, as even Jo Frances James, a granddaughter of the great outlaw and a technical advisor on his film biography, ruefully admitted this week in an Associated Press interview, but "Jesse James," at the Roxy, is still the best screen entertainment of the year (as of Friday, Jan. 13). Handsomely produced by the Messrs. Darryl Zanuck and Nunnally Johnson, stirringly directed by Henry King, beautifully acted by its cast—notably Henry Hull, Henry Fonda, and even its stars, Tyrone Power—and buoyed by a brilliantly and slyly humorous screen play by the versatile Mr. Johnson, it becomes an authentic American panorama, enriched by dialogue, characterization, and incidents imported directly from the Missouri hills.

In order to make Jesse, the train robber and bank bandit, romantically presentable at Seventh Avenue and Fiftieth Street (and the job undoubtedly was a tough one) the ingenious Johnson script presents him as a handsome Quixote, hopelessly jousting with a public utility —a career with which any stanch American who has ever launched an individual campaign against the gas, telephone, or electric light companies, can sympathize. In Jesse's case the enemy was the "St. Louis Midland Railroad"—an industrial octopus which stole his farm and caused the death of his aged mother while he himself was a fugitive in the hills for resisting the trend of the times. (And a beautiful scene it is, thanks to Mr. King's

direction, in which the James brothers rout the strong-arm squad of the railroad barons).

Henry Fonda, as the tobacco-chewing Frank James, is a beautiful characterization, but our favorite is Henry Hull, as the small-town editor and friend of the James clan, whose dictated editorials are priceless gems of frontier humor. "Shoot 'em down like dogs" is his favorite phrase, and his enemies include lawyers, railroad presidents (in the revengeful person of Donald Meek), dentists, and anybody who tends to upset the order of uncivilized existence. "It's lawyers that are ruining everything" declaims Mr. Hull, while his assistant furiously sets the type. His office, meanwhile, is the spot in which Mr. Power meets Nancy Kelly, while posses vainly scour the hills.

The principal beauty of "Jesse James" (aside from Technicolor) is its Nunnally Johnson dialogue, and its individual scenes: the rout of the railroad gorillas, the train and bank hold-ups—especially the politeness of the railroad bandits—the marriage scene, in which the James boys interrupt Sabbath service in a country church-house and discover a sociological friend in the pastor: ("I had given up preaching and was making an honest living off the land till the railroad stole my farm"), and the acting, including that of Tyrone Power, who makes out an excellent melodramatic case against himself as Jesse, although, as far as we are concerned, the verdict is still "Not Guilty."

B. R. C.

Ja 14, 1939

At the Roxy

SUSANNAH OF THE MOUNTIES, screen play by Robert Ellis and Helen Logan from a story by Fidel La Barba and Walter Ferris based on a book by Muriel Denison; directed by William A. Seiter; produced by Darryl F. Zanuck for Twentieth Century-Fox.

Susannah Sheldon ....Shirley Temple
Monty Montague (Inspector Angus),
                          Randolph Scott
Vicky Standing ....Margaret Lockwood
Little Chief ....Martin Good Rider
Pat O'Hannegan....J. Farrell MacDonald
Chief Big Eagle .....Maurice Moscovich
Supt. Andrew Standing.....Moroni Olsen
Wolf Pelt....................Victor Jory
Harlan Chambers.........Lester Matthews
Randall................Leyland Hodgson
Doctor...................Herbert Evans
Williams...................Jack Luden
Sergeant MacGregor.........Charles Irwin
Corporal Piggott............John Sutton
Chief....................Chief Big Tree

The presence of Mistress Shirley Temple on the Rhine and in the Far East might go a long way toward solving the current problems of the British Foreign Office. For the history of British imperial diplomacy, as Twentieth Century-Fox gives it to us, chapter by chapter, becomes ever more conspicuously the lengthened shadow of Mistress Temple. It was Mistress Temple who quieted the rebellious Hindus in "Wee Willie Winkie," and practically won the Boer War with her ministrations to the wounded in "The Little Princess."

And now it seems it was Mistress Temple who quelled the big

Blackfoot Indian uprising in the Canadian Dominion, by taking her childish appeal for peace directly to Big Chief Maurice Moscovich in "Susannah of the Mounties" (at the Roxy). Inspector Randolph Scott, who found her in the wreckage of a wagon train massacre and adopted her, was already tied to the stake, with the dry brush piled about his feet, but the savage heart of Chief Moscovich melted at her pretty plea. Randolph was released; the war ended; everybody was happy. It was as simple as that.

Old Temple fans who, at the first mention of Blackfeet, eagerly expected Bill Robinson to come tap-stepping in, were disappointed, but Shirley obliges with her usual dances, in the course of teaching Randolph how to fascinate Margaret Lockwood, the Colonel's daughter. She also does a war dance with Little Chief, an adolescent brave by the name of Martin Good Rider, and even does a little Shirley Temple song, wilderness or no wilderness. The early Canadian Northwest Mounted Police certainly wore tricky uniforms, though. Except for the fact that they are on the screen, people at the Roxy might almost mistake them for ushers.

B. R. C.

Je 24, 1939.

FRONTIER MARSHAL, screen play by Sam Hellman based on the book by Stuart N. Lake; directed by Allan Dwan; produced by Sol M. Wurtzel for Twentieth Century-Fox.

Wyatt Earp	Randolph Scott
Sarah Allen	Nancy Kelly
Doc Holliday	Cesar Romero
Jerry	Binnie Barnes
Ben Carter	John Carradine
Dan Blackmore	Edward Norris
Eddie Foy	Eddie Foy Jr.
Town Marshal	Ward Bond
Pringle	Lon Chaney Jr.
Buck Newton	Tom Tyler
Pete	Chris-Pin Martin
Curly Bill	Joe Sawyer
Proprietor Bella Union Cafe	Del Henderson
Mayor Henderson	Harry Hayden
Pablo	Ventura Ybarra
Prospector	Si Jenks
Dance Hall Girl	Gloria Roy
Mother	Margaret Brayton
Customer	Pat O'Malley
Indian Joe	Charles Stevens
Curly Bill's Men	Harry Woods
	Dick Alexander

The story of Wyatt Earp, who brought the law to Tombstone, Ariz., belongs to frontier folklore, to have touched it at all, and not to have made a great Western out of it, would have been a cinematic crime even lower than horse-stealing. But in the case of "Frontier Marshal" at the Roxy, nobody can say that Sol M. Wurtzel has not been faithful to the great tradition. With a grand cast, and an excellent job of directing by Allan Dwan, Mr. Earp's screen biography becomes entirely worthy of its fabulous subject.

From Randolph Scott, who walks through the role of Wyatt with his customary sang-froid, to Eddie Foy Jr., in the role of his own famous father, the players fit their parts with such perfection that it is hard to know whether to credit the acting or the casting director. In the case of Binnie Barnes, as a be-spangled dance hall drab in love with the romantic, melancholy killer, Doc Holliday (with his taste for sable suitings and his resemblance to Cesar Romero), the praise undoubtedly belongs to both. Uncompromisingly blond, hard and harsh-voiced, Miss Barnes is a miracle of rightness.

Equally felicitous, albeit in soberer guise, is Nancy Kelly as the Good Woman who has followed the dark-browed, diseased, idealistic killer to the hell-holes of Tombstone with adoring eyes. Eddie Foy Jr., in one of his Dad's old costumes, is delightful, and John Carradine, with that pulmonary picturesqueness of his, is too mean to live in his role as the major menace, whose outlaw dance hall is plowed under to make way for a savings bank before Earp gets through with the town. In short, "Frontier Marshal" is a cracking good Western, and in the movies there's nothing much better than that. B. R. C.

J 29, 1939.

20,000 MEN A YEAR, screen play by Lou Breslow and Owen Francis from a story by Frank Wead; directed by Alfred E. Green; produced by Sol M. Wurtzel for Twentieth Century-Fox. At the Roxy.

Brad Reynolds	Randolph Scott
Jim Howell	Preston Foster
Ann Rogers	Margaret Lindsay
Joan Marshall	Mary Healy
Tommy Howell	Robert Shaw
Skip Rogers	George Ernest
Mrs Allen	Jane Darwell
Al Williams	Kane Richmond
Walt Dorgan	Maxie Rosenbloom
Crandall	Douglas Wood
Harold Chong	Ben Young
Gerald Grant	Paul Stanton
Wally Richards	Tom Seidel
Dunk	Edward Gargan
Joe Hungerford	Harry Tyler
Irving Glassman	Sidney Miller
Chief Pilot Lawson	Edwin Stanley

By FRANK S. NUGENT

Never more than a sleeper jump behind the times, the screen has hurried around to the Roxy with a melodramatic salute to the aviation training program instituted not so long ago by the Civil Aeronautics Authority. "20,000 Men a Year," which is a statistical reference to the number of civil pilots the CAA hopes to be turning out, is pat both as to title and in its reply to the worried Midwestern school teacher who tells the college flying instructor she has no objection to planes but thinks her kid brother is too young to be learning to fly one.

The answer to that, in the customarily-suspect logic of the aviation melodrama, is the creation of a situation in which the kid brother has to fly a plane out of a mountain canyon and bring it down safely, in spite of its damaged landing gear, with the injured instructor and unconscious student pilot aboard. That, of course, convinces the school marm of her error, but wouldn't everyone have been just as happy if the CAA had never

Maxie Rosenbloom

come to the campus and there had been no first crack-up to bring on the need for a mercy flight? (Just a rhetorical question, naturally.)

At any rate the film has its moments, especially those involving Maxie Rosenbloom as the mechanic with a vacuum where his brain ought to be. The flying sequences are exciting to watch and Randolph Scott, Preston Foster, Robert Shaw, Margaret Lindsay and George Ernest have played it competently enough. That seems to entitle it to a rating of "fair" and a pair of wings from the CAA.

O 28, 1939.

MY FAVORITE WIFE; screen play by Samuel and Bella Spewack; based on a story by Samuel and Bella Spewack and Leo McCarey; directed by Garson Kanin; a Leo McCarey production, released through RKO-Radio. At the Radio City Music Hall.

Ellen ....Irene Dunne
Nick ....Cary Grant
Burkett ....Randolph Scott
Bianca ....Gail Patrick
Ma ....Ann Shoemaker
Tim ....Scotty Beckett
Chinch ....Mary Lou Harrington
Hotel Clerk...............Donald MacBride
Johnson ....Hugh O'Connell
Judge ....Granville Bates
Dr. Kohlmar................Pedro de Cordoba

By BOSLEY CROWTHER

This is briefly to report the discovery of a new island yesterday—a little island of joy at Fiftieth Street West and Sixth Avenue North, where Leo McCarey's "My Favorite Wife" floated into the ken of audiences at the Radio City Music Hall. Let's hoist a flag and claim it for King Comus, for this is the sort of refuge we all can find pleasure in these days—a frankly fanciful farce, a rondo of refined ribaldries and an altogether delightful picture with Cary Grant and Irene Dunne chasing each other around most charmingly in it.

Do you remember "The Awful Truth" (which was also a McCarey picture)? Do you remember Mr. Grant and Miss Dunne as the interlocutorially divided lovers, whose immediate return to domesticity was prevented by nothing much more substantial than Miss Dunne's tantalizing contrariness? Then you know pretty well what to expect in "My Favorite Wife," only more of it. Mr. McCarey is, without compare, a master of the technique of the prolonged and amorous tease; and with an actress such as Miss Dunne through whom to apply it—she with her luxurious and mocking laughter, her roving eyes and come-hither glances—mere man is powerless before it. So obviously Mr. Grant, a normally susceptible male, is thrown about, bewildered and helpless, like an iron filing, when he comes within the magnetic field of Miss Dunne's allure.

For a story, Mr. McCarey and his writers, the comical Spewacks, have followed the old line of most resistance. This time it is Mr. Grant who is firmly attached to some one else when his first wife, Miss Dunne, returns from what every one believed was a watery grave. How to break away is his first problem, and then secondly how to clear his mind of the horrid suspicions which arise when he discovers that his wife really spent seven years cast away on a desert island with Randolph Scott. Poor Mr. Grant has his torments, which are finally assuaged only after another one of those particularly tantalizing chez-nous scenes with Miss Dunne. That man McCarey is a sadist

Irene Dunne, who is seen in "My Favorite Wife," at Music Hall.

But to make it agreeable he has provided a particularly Spewacky script, full of lively wit and flashy back-talk which is clipped and stylized for speed. (The direction of Garson Kanin is spotty, and there is evidence of faults in editing—but who cares?) And the remaining cast is excellent—Gail Patrick as the second and neglected wife, who spends most of her time in negligee; Donald MacBride, as a darkly suspicious hotel manager, and Granville Bates as an acid, contemptuous and fuddle-brained judge.

In fact, Mr. Bates deserves a separate mention for his masterpiece of comic creation. Such a terrifying jurist you never saw. "Where did you go to school?" he inquires sharply of Mr. Grant. "Harvard," replies the latter. A black look, a lift of the eyebrows, then a casual "I'm a Yale man myself" leaves no doubt of Mr. Bates's sentiments. "My Favorite Wife" owes a lot to him.

Also on the bill at the Music Hall is an interesting short entitled "Cavalcade of Academy Awards," which swiftly reviews the recipients of "Oscars" over the last twelve years. It is in the nature of an industry advertisement, but has a quaint reminiscent appeal.

My 31, 1940.

WHEN THE DALTONS RODE; original screen play by Harold Shumate, based on the story "When the Daltons Rode," by Emmett Dalton and Jack Jungmeyer Sr., directed by George Marshall for Universal Pictures. At Loew's State.

Tod Jackson ....Randolph Scott
Julie King....................Kay Francis
Grat Dalton ....Brian Donlevy
Caleb Winters...........George Bancroft
Bob Dalton...........Broderick Crawford
Ben Dalton....................Stuart Erwin
Ozark ....Andy Devine
Emmett Dalton...........Frank Albertson
Ma Dalton ....Mary Gordon
Rigby ....Harry Stephens
Sheriff ....Edgar Deering
Wilson ....Quen Ramsey
Nancy ....Dorothy Grainger
Photographer ....Bob McKenzie
Hannah ....Fay McKenzie
Suzy ....June Wilkins
Judge Swain ....Walter Soderling

By BOSLEY CROWTHER

Of one thing you may be sure: Universal will never make a sequel to "When the Daltons Rode." No, sir, friends, you'll never see a "Return of Bob Dalton," for coincidence, or "The Daltons Ride Again"—not within the realm of reason, anyhow. For the climax of this titanic Western, which blasted its way into Loew's State and eleven other theatres in the metropolitan area yesterday, results in such wholesale tribal slaughter, such a complete patrilineal blackout of the clan, that "When the Daltons Rode" is decisively the last of the Daltons. We have long wanted to see one of these shootin' pictures in which the final scene is a smoking ruin with everybody dead. This one comes mighty close to being it. At the fade-out there are only a few pious and inconsequential folk, like Randolph Scott and Kay Francis, standing around. The Dalton gang is no more.

But, boy, while those buckos are living, they certainly do put on a show! Like the James brothers before them—or, at least, like the Twentieth Century-Fox Jameses—they start out a law-abiding family of Kansas farmers, back about 1891. But when the inevitable railroad "land grabbers" try to move in on them, when one of the boys accidentally kills a villain and it looks like the end of a rope for him, the brothers automatically constitute themselves a fraternity of fighting fiends, go marauding around the country robbing banks and sticking up trains and eventually go down in a furious battle with their backs against the walls of Coffeyville, Kan.

We wouldn't like to suggest that this is the true saga of the famous Dalton gang. Neither would we highly recommend the romantic byplay of Miss Francis nor the ineffectual intervention of Mr. Scott in the plot. But we will say that Brian Donlevy, Broderick Crawford, Andy Devine and others of the gang make some fine desperados; the picture itself is straight, fast Western fare, and for folks who like plenty of shootin', here is your gunpowder.

Ag 23, 1940.

WESTERN UNION; screen play by Robert Carson, based on the novel by Zane Grey; directed by Fritz Lang and filmed in Technicolor for Twentieth Century-Fox. At the Roxy.
Richard Blake .... Robert Young
Vance Shaw .... Randolph Scott
Edward Creighton .... Dean Jagger
Sue Creighton .... Virginia Gilmore
Doc Murdoch .... John Carradine
Herman .... Slim Summerville
Homer .... Chill Wills
Jack Slade .... Barton MacLane
Governor .... Russell Hicks
Charlie .... Victor Kilian
Pat Grogan .... Minor Watson
Herb .... George Chandler
Chief Spotted Horse ...... Chief Big Tree
Indian Leader .... Chief Thundercloud
Porky .... Dick Rich
Barber .... Irving Bacon

Randolph Scott, in "Western Union"

By BOSLEY CROWTHER

Telegraphic communication is a great and wonderful thing, and the temptation for a film producer to wax grandiloquent about it might be understood. But it is our pleasure—and relief—to report this morning that Twentieth Century-Fox has not risen blindly to the bait, and that Director Fritz Lang's "Western Union," which was delivered yesterday to the Roxy, is more a bang-up outdoor action picture than an epic of the singing wires, that it derives much more eloquence from the six-gun than it does from the sounding key.

One can readily imagine what certain directors might have done with this story of the heroic laying of the first telegraph wire across the country. Without trying, one can vision the accumulation of prolonged door-die clichés which might have been dragged into it, one can hear the crescendo of symbolic sounds which might solemnly have represented the electric flight of words across the land. But Mr. Lang and his lavish producers have this time avoided the trap. They have brought within the frame of a straightaway "Western" adventure tale as much of the excitement and significance of the project as one could fairly desire.

Never having read the novel by Zane Grey from which the picture is derived, we wouldn't know how much of the film's effectiveness is due to it. But apparently Mr. Lang has borrowed a firmly-constructed fiction about the scout for the Western Union party which strung the cross-continent wire back in 1861, and then has kept it spinning with plenty of action and colorful incident. We will not divulge the story, which hangs upon a neat surprise twist, but suffice it to say that its plotting involves Indian fights, a fiery ambush and a climactic pistol duel quite as suspenseful as the memorable conclusion of "Stagecoach."

This much, however, we do say: a large share of the film's excitement is attributable to the excellent Technicolor in which it is magnificently dressed. Breath-taking shots of vast stretches of prairie across which the construction gang is seen drawing its tiny wire; brilliant scenes in which Indians and bearded pioneers blend in artistic contrast assist in making it one of the finest color films ever seen.

So, too, are the actors' performances of superior quality. Randolph Scott, who is getting to look and act more and more like William S. Hart, herein shapes one of the truest and most appreciable characters of his career as the party's scout. Dean Jagger is the cool and determined chief engineer of the wire-laying gang—a portrait of the real Edward Creighton which does that gentleman worthy justice. And Robert Young as a "dude from the East," Slim Summerville as a terrified cook, Chill Wills as a leather-skinned lineman and Virginia Gilmore as the unobtrusive "love interest" are just four of a generally excellent cast.

Any way you take it, "Western Union" is spectacular screen entertainment — a "Western," you might say, with the proper cinematic unity.

———

F 7, 1941.

BELLE STARR; screen play by Lamar Trotti; based on a story by Niven Busch and Cameron Rogers; directed by Irving Cummings for Twentieth Century-Fox.
Sam Starr .... Randolph Scott
Belle Starr .... Gene Tierney
Major Thomas Crail .... Dana Andrews
Ed Shirley .... John Shepperd
Sara .... Elizabeth Patterson
Blue Duck .... Chill Wills
Mammy Lou .... Louise Beavers
Jasper Tench .... Olin Howland
Sergeant .... Paul Burns
John Cole .... Joseph Sawyer
Jim Cole .... Joseph Downing
Colonel Thornton .... Howard Hickman
Colonel Bright .... Charles Trowbridge
Sergeant .... James Flavin
Mr. Wilkins .... Edward Fielding
Carpetbagger .... Charles Middleton
Bride .... Elena Verdugo

To the panel of neurotic unreconstructed rebels spawned in the aftermath of the Civil War, Twentieth Century-Fox has added the portrait of a gun-toting lady in "Belle Starr," now at the Roxy. And a stange melange of Technicolored fuss - and - feathers they have made of it. As has become almost habitual by now in films of post-war desperadoes, Hollywood has turned the tables on history. Instead of a female thug she turns out to be a sort of border Joan of Arc fighting bravely for the lost cause of the Confederacy. There are sources also which deny that the original killer was the immaculately manicured glamour girl that Gene Tierney is, but no matter—this is merely a sidelight on a pompously operatic fiction that becomes rousingly active only when it tires of weeping in its own beard.

For it matters not so much what has been done to history as what has been done to the film. Continually it tries to flavor its outright bunkum with real emotion and out of a Wild West junket it has tried to squeeze the liebestod Romeo and Juliet. Sam Starr, or rather Randolph Scott as the renegade who smelled blood and went from bad to worse, is a fine swashbuckler in action but absurd when he begins to listen to his nobler self. As for Miss Tierney, her youth and fancy finishing school background betray her. As Belle, she never shot a man, much less loved one.

Here and there the film comes to life in some fine heroics as rebels and Union soldiery pursue each other across the moonlit hills, or in Chill Wills's performance as a grizzled bandit side-kick, but too often are there the embarrassing moments when Sam and his headstrong mate pledge their love, capped by the scene in which he returns the wedding ring to the dead hand of his ambushed wife. And that is the failure of a film which already falls in a stale tradition. This Belle Starr was never a scourge and legend in the West. She is a cantankerous school child fighting over jacks and marbles, not life and death. When you're playing at bokum it's best not to fudge. You get caught too easily.

T. S.

N 1, 1941

Elisabeth Bergner Returns in 'Paris Calling,' the Globe's New Melodrama—'Treat 'Em Rough' Is Seen at the Rialto

PARIS CALLING; from an original screen play by Benjamin Glazer and Charles S. Kaufman; directed by Edwin Marlin and produced by Mr. Glazer for Universal. At the Globe.

Marianne	Elisabeth Bergner
Nick	Randolph Scott
Benoit	Basil Rathbone
Colette	Gale Sondergaard
Schwabe	Lee J. Cobb
Lantz	Charles Arnt
Mouche	Edward Ciannelli
Madame Jannetier	Elisabeth Risdon
Butler	George Ranavent
Prof. Marceau	William Edmunds
McAvoy	Patric O'Malley
Waiter	George Metaxa
Chief of Underground	Paul Leyssac
Wolfgang Schmitt	Gene Garrick
Paul	Paul Bryar
Gruber	Otto Reichow
Gestapo Agent	Adolph Milar
Charlie	Marion Murray
Marie	Grace Lenard
Simone	Yvette Bentley
Renee	Marcia Ralston

Elisabeth Bergner, in "Paris Calling."

The fall of France left in its wake the shattered bits of a hundred dramas. It also left, like other historical catastrophes, an emotional vacuum into which a film producer enters at his own peril. Certainly it seems too early to loot the heart-breaking tragedy of France for such a flimsily concocted adventure as "Paris Calling," now at the Globe. Although Elisabeth Bergner, who makes her American film debut in it, has a deep and pathetic charm and can create a mood with a single gesture, her talents might well have been spent on more rewarding material. For "Paris Calling," though moments of excitement break through its uninspired direction, its generally poor performances and its fantastic implausibilities of plot, resembles a graceless frivolity on the edge of doom.

Perhaps in a less extravagant tale, the anxieties and hopes of the French underground rebels would have seemed truer. The film begins well as it shows the conversion of a wealthy young Parisienne who flees from the city only to return to its empty streets after she has seen the refugee roads bombed and strafed by the Nazis. From that point the scenarists become totally irresponsible. The lady from Paris joins the French counter-espionage, falls in love with an American aviator who trots through the German lines with the greatest of ease, shoots a former lover turned traitor and is finally rescued by the commandos in a scene like the last sequence of a twelve-part serial.

It is all mechanically contrived melodrama, and neither the direction nor most of the performances have made it seem less so. Miss Bergner, with her lost and frightened look, her small, haunted voice, is always more believable than her lines. And Lee Cobb, as a Gestapo chieftain, creates a ruthless, three-dimensional man rather than a puppet brute. But they cannot inject much life into a faltering adventure. This message from Paris is weak and thin.   T. S.

Ja 19, 1942, 21:2

'To Shores of Tripoli,' Colorful but Implausible Film About a Recruit in the U. S. Marine Corps, Is Presented at Roxy

TO THE SHORES OF TRIPOLI, screen play by Lamar Trotti; from an original story by Steve Fisher; directed by Bruce Humberstone; produced by Darryl F. Zanuck for Twentieth Century-Fox. At the Roxy.

Chris Winters	John Payne
Mary Carter	Maureen O'Hara
Sergeant Dixie Smith	Randolph Scott
Helene Hunt	Nancy Kelly
Johnny Dent	William Tracy
Okay Jones	Maxie Rosenbloom
Mouthy	Henry Morgan
Butch	Edmund MacDonald
Major Wilson	Russell Hicks
Captain Winters	Minor Watson
Bill	Ted North
Joe Sutton	Basil Walker
Swifty	Charles Tannen
Tom Hall	Alan Hale Jr.
Susie	Margaret Early
Barber	Frank Orth
Blonde	Iris Adrian

By BOSLEY CROWTHER

In all the accustomed panoply of a "big" Technicolored service film, Twentieth Century-Fox and Darryl F. Zanuck have dressed up a routine wiseguy yarn, and are presenting it to the American public as a glowing tribute to the United States Marine. There is plenty of martial music in it, some handsome shots of "leathernecks" at training drills and a few stimulating glimpses of our real battle fleet at sea. But aside from the music and

Randolph Scott, in "To the Shores of Tripoli."

parading, which is barely a token display, this new color-poster at the Roxy, "To the Shores of Tripoli," is just another Rover Boy fable about a fresh young pup who hears stern duty's call.

This is the more disappointing, in view of the contemporary facts, because Mr. Zanuck had a subject dear to the nation's heart. A literal, unglamorized portrayal of the training of a United States Marine —in a bare dramatic framework— would be a thrilling picture today. Furthermore, Mr. Zanuck had available the ready-made "set" of the Marine Corps base at San Diego and its personnel as background for his film.

Yet what has he shown? Without exception, it is a compound of familiar cliches. An impudent lad, fresh out of Culver, joins the Marines for no purpose save to mark time until a "soft job" in Washington is tossed his way. He tangles with the tough drill-sergeant, who was his father's "top kick" in the First World War. He pursues, in a most saucy fashion, a commissioned Navy nurse, who falls for him. He saves the sergeant's life during target practice after the sergeant has risked demotion for his sake. And finally, just as he is leaving for that soft job in Washington, comes word of the raid on Pearl Harbor, and he makes a highly unmilitary return to the corps.

If this film is a fair estimation of Marine discipline and tradition, then wire Congress. For, with typical cinematic license, it assumes that one arrogant kid, protected by a sergeant's strange sentiment, could violate every rule in the book. Further, it does not lay emphasis upon a genuine esprit de corps. Contrary to military nature, the Marines fall in around a self-willed lad.

As the latter, John Payne is trim and flippant, and he expresses contempt quite charmingly. Randolph Scott makes a doughty drill-sergeant, despite the humiliating restrictions the script impels. Maureen O'Hara is very beautiful and delightfully accommodating as the Navy nurse, while William Tracy and Maxie Rosenbloom are very minor as comic recruits.

No doubt a great many persons will take pleasure in "To the Shores of Tripoli." The music is highly infectious, and the color reveals some quickening sights. As straight cinematic fiction, it is an adroit artificial job. But it is very hard to recognize in it the United States Marines. Wait until the Navy sees it. Oh, boy!

Mr 26, 1942.

At the Capitol

THE SPOILERS; screen play by Lawrence Hazard and Tom Reed, from the novel by Rex Beach; directed by Ray Enright; produced by Frank Lloyd for Universal Pictures. A Charles K. Feldman Group production.

Cherry Malotte	Marlene Dietrich
Alexander McNamara	Randolph Scott
Roy Glennister	John Wayne
Helen Chester	Margaret Lindsay
Al Dextry	Harry Carey
Bronco Kid	Richard Barthelmess
Banty	George Cleveland
Judge Stillman	Samuel S. Hinds
Flapjack	Russell Simpson
Wheaton	William Farnum
Idabelle	Marietta Canty
Mr. Skinner	Jack Norton
Clark	Ray Bennett
Bennett	Forrest Taylor
Deputy	Art Miles
Deputy	Charles McMurphy
Struve	Charles Halton
Marshall	Bud Osborne
Galloway	Drew Demorest
Poet	Robert W. Service

Bring out the arnica, folks—those he-men are back. Having pinched the muscles of John Wayne and Randolph Scott and found them solid, Ray Enright has leaped to a safe perch on a camera boom and let them slug it out for Marlene Dietrich's well-manicured hand in "The Spoilers," now raising ructions at the Capitol. He has tossed overboard the Marquis of Queensberry rules and let the blows fall where they may. Certainly, after some of the feeble fisticuffs we have seen of late, Mr. Enright has brought forth a lulu of a fight. Out of the Rex Beach extravaganza of tough men and headstrong women in the Klondike gold rush he has created a brawling bedlam of battles fought along distinctly primeval lines of etiquette. If the Messrs. Wayne and Scott aren't recuperating in a quiet hospital room right now, this corner has been badly deceived.

Naturally, a row of the dimensions that Mr. Enright has sent hurtling across tables, balconies and through windows in the last reel of "The Spoilers" requires some sort of excuse. It has been doubly provided. Not only does Mr. Scott, that smooth-talking villain, try to rook Mr. Wayne of the Midas Gold Mine, but also he makes a few impolitic gestures in the direction of Miss Dietrich, who understands an impolitic gesture when she sees one. As Cherry Malotte, a lady saloonkeeper, Miss Dietrich carries on in the rough-cut diamond tradition of Mae West and wears beruffled costumes about as concealing as the fins on a fish. In short, Miss Dietrich has left behind the subtle nuance, the languorous murmurings of love. In "The Spoilers" she introduces the subject with a dozen hard-boiled eggs and a quart of brandy. A hearty belle, Miss Dietrich.

That, of course, is the only approach to tender communion that such calloused rowdies as Mr. Wayne or Mr. Scott could understand, and Cherry Malotte knew it. No doubt that was the reason why they returned so often after jail breaks, train wrecks and free-for-all battles over a jumped claim. But Cherry, good woman, remained true to one man. She turned down Bronco Kid, otherwise Richard Barthelmess, who used to win the girl himself regularly not so many years ago, and when a frail young lady in the person of Margaret Lindsay momentarily threatened the theft of Mr. Wayne, Cherry shed only one tear before going on the warpath.

Perhaps Cherry's complex affections seem a bit amusing at this distance, and thank Mr. Enright and Miss Dietrich's witty playing for keeping them so. Sprinkled with double entendres nearly as frankly cut as Miss Dietrich's gowns, the author and producer have kept their tongues firmly in their cheeks, even when stout Mr. Wayne and Mr. Scott begin tearing up the set. It's a lovely brawl.

T. S.

My 22, 1942

At Loew's Criterion

PITTSBURGH, screen play by Kenneth Gamet and Tom Reed, with additional dialogue by John Twist; from an original story by George Owen and Tom Reed; directed by Lewis Seiler; a Charles K. Feldman Production presented by Universal.

Josie Winters	Marlene Dietrich
Cash Evans	Randolph Scott
Pittsburgh Markham	John Wayne
Doc Powers	John Craven
Shannon Prentiss	Louise Allbritton
Shorty	Shemp Howard
Joe Malneck	Thomas Gomez
Dr. Grazlich	Ludwig Stossel
Morgan Prentiss	Samuel S. Hinds
Mine Operator	Paul Fix
Johnny	William Haade
Butler	Charles Coleman
Barney	Nestor Paiva

Having survived their clout-fests in "The Spoilers," John Wayne and Randolph Scott are again throwing their mitts high, wide and handsome for the sake of ideals and the woman—again, naturally, Marlene Dietrich. Against the brawling background of "Pittsburgh," now at the Criterion, they are repeating most of the shennanigans considered de rigeur in dramas about up-and-coming tycoons. As a pair of coal-mine lunkies who paw their way to the top, quarrel over noble principles, and finally are reunited by the war emergency, patriotism, and a stout speech for unity by Miss Dietrich, their story makes "Pittsburgh" another lusty and totally synthetic film.

Perhaps you'll recognize the characters beneath those coal-smudged faces. Mr. Wayne is the hammer-fisted boy with the big ideas, and generally rides roughshod over all opposition, male or female, until he gets his comeuppance—but good. As his partner, Mr. Scott is just as tough but he sees things differently; he believes in giving his coal-miners a living wage, the public some of the benefits of his profits through hospitals and research institutes, and he believes in giving a lady an even break. As the lady who gets that break, after an ill-starred attachment for Mr. Wayne, Miss Dietrich emerges as a phoney countess, a rough-and-ready girl who's waiting for love on a white horse but keeps busy meanwhile.

The fact that the three build a gargantuan coal and steel combine, only to see it fail through Mr. Wayne's antagonistic ways, and finally rise chastened to the top when war production requires their talents, merely proves that patriotism can make good men out of bad. "Pittsburgh" also proves that you can put an old design on a new chassis and it will still run. With the three stars in usual form, scientist-narrator who reminisces throughout the film, "Pittsburgh" is just another chance on the popular box-office sweepstakes and it may hit a modest jackpot. But it is routine entertainment at best.

On the same bill at the Criterion, the Office of War Information offers its short subject "Point Rationing," a cartoon which will be placed on other Broadway screens today. As its title indicates, it is an explanation of the use of the new ration books for which everyone has been registering during the past three days. It also tells why rationing is necessary, and it tells it lucidly, quickly, and interestingly. It should be a timely and genuinely helpful item for those confused by the rows of numbers in their ration books.

T. S.

F 25, 1943

'The Desperadoes,' a Western Drama in Technicolor, With Glenn Ford, at Criterion— 'Tahiti Honey' at the Palace

THE DESPERADOES, screen play by Robert Carson, from an original story by Max Brand; directed by Charles Vidor; produced by Harry Joe Brown for Columbia Pictures. At Loew's Criterion.
Steve Upton...............Randolph Scott
Cheyenne Rogers............Glenn Ford
Countess Maletta...........Claire Trevor
Allison MacLeod............Evelyn Keyes
Willie MacLeod............Edgar Buchanan
Judge Cameron...........Raymond Walburn
Nitro Rankin.............Guinn Williams
Stanley Clanton..............Porter Hall
Sundown................Joan Woodbury
Jack Lester...............Bernard Nedell

By BOSLEY CROWTHER

A straightaway, sock-'em-and-shoot-'em Western — filmed in bright Technicolor, that's all—is Columbia's "The Desperadoes," which came to Loew's Criterion yesterday. Most of the old familiar characters of Western fiction are scattered about therein and most of the old familiar clichés (and anachronisms) are shamelessly indulged. There's the bold and incipient young outlaw who comes riding into a Utah town, presumably to commit a holdup but actually to lose his heart to the local scoundrel's little gal. There's the lean and soft-spoken sheriff who realizes the kid is good at heart, and so helps him to evade the villains who try to pin a robbery and a couple of murders on him. There's also the local fancy-lady (who also has a heart of purest gold) and the inevitable banker-swindler (played, of course, by Porter Hall).

Columbia has put it all together in the usual horse-opera style, with a couple of barroom battles and a big stampede to kick up some dust. And it has also worked in some colored scenery to fill if not dazzle the eye. Glenn Ford plays the regenerate outlaw like a clean-cut, collegiate lad and Randolph Scott plays the sheriff in his customary constabulary way. Claire Trevor is the spangled lady, Evelyn Keyes is the innocent flower and Edgar Buchanan plays her rascally papa with the only genuine flavor in the film.

One little point we would mention to indicate the sort of picture this is. The time of the story is set down as 1863. Yet in one scene a casual reference is made to Custer's Last Stand. For the information of the authors, Custer's Last Stand happened in 1876.

Glenn Ford, in "The Desperadoes"

My 13, 1943

BOMBARDIER—Screen play by John Twist, from a story by Mr. Twist and Martin Rackin; directed by Richard Wallace; produced by Robert Fellows for RKO Radio Pictures, Inc. At Loew's Criterion.
Major Chick Davis............Pat O'Brien
Captain Buck Oliver.......Randolph Scott
Burt Hughes................Anne Shirley
Tom Hughes.................Eddie Albert
Jim Carter'................Walter Reed
Joe Connors................Robert Ryan
Sergeant Dixon...........Barton MacLane
Jap Officer................Leonard Strong
Chito Rafferty............Richard Martin
Paul Harris................Russell Wade
Captain Rand..............James Newill
Chaplain Craig.............John Miljan
Instructor................Charles Russell

By BOSLEY CROWTHER

That rah-rah Rover-Boy spirit which vitiates so many Hollywood war films is the first and most distasteful defect in RKO's "Bombardier," a film about the lads who man the bombsights, which came to Loew's Criterion yesterday. Second fault is the rambling story, which is a compound of many clichés, and third fault is the blistering climax, which is heroics in the worst bombastic style. Those are the major imperfections. There are others of a minor degree. Added all together in one picture they leave little or no room for good.

For this is one of those pictures having to do with an aerial-bomber school which vaguely goes through the business of showing how bombardiers are trained. It is one of those pictures in which the trainees are hearty, clear-eyed lads who are always pulling one another out of grave predicaments. And whenever, by force of circumstance over which he has no control, one of the trainees is "washed out," he always gulps and takes it bravely like a man.

It is also one of those pictures in which there is a big feud. Major Pat O'Brien champions the bombsight and the role of the bombardier. Captain Randolph Scott believes the pilot is the all-important man in a bombing plane. They jaw over this point interminably. They also tussle gingerly over a girl, who happens to be 'Anne Shirley, the owner of the training field. However, a brassy young trainee steals her right out from under both of their chins.

The big climax comes when everybody who was at the training school (everybody, that is, except Miss Shirley) makes a bombing raid on Japan. Then Mr. Scott, whose plane is shot down in the van with its load of fire bombs, turns himself (upon the ground) into a bonfire to light the target so his chums can drop their "eggs." Naturally he is killed, and Mr. O'Brien sheds a tear o'er the fallen hero's pyre. In death, Mr. Scott clutches a letter from Miss Shirley saying, etc., etc.

In concept, in manner of presentation and in performance this is a cheap, fictitious film. RKO, John Twist and Richard Wallace, the writer and director, should hang their heads in shame.

Jl 2, 1943

'Corvette K-225' Thrilling Film of Heroic Service by British and Canadians to Defend Convoys, at Loew's Criterion

CORVETTE K-225, original story and screen play by Lieut. John Rhodes Sturdy, directed by Richard Rosson, produced by Howard Hawks for Universal. At Loew's Criterion.
Lieut. Commdr. MacClain....Randolph Scott
Sub-Lieut. Cartwright........James Brown
Joyce Cartwright..............Ella Raines
Stone.......................Noah Beery Jr.
Stokey O'Mera.............Barry Fitzgerald
First Officer..............John Frederick
Convoy Commander........Holmes Herbert
Walsh.......................Andy Devine
Crickett....................Fuzzy Knight
Smithy.....................Thomas Gomez
Lieut. Rawlins...............David Bruce
Admiral.....................Richard Lane
Evans.......................Walter Sande
Merchant Ship Captain......Oscar O'Shea
Gardner.....................James Flavin
Jones.......................Murray Alper
Shephard..................Robert Mitchum
Wardroom Steward........Gene O'Donnell
Bailey.......................John Diggs
Lieut. LeBlanc...........Edmund MacDonald

By BOSLEY CROWTHER

Out in the trackless sea-lanes where the roving U-boats wait to catch our wallowing transports carrying materials of war overseas, a tremendous heroic service has been done by the fabulous fleet of tiny escort warships of the British and Canadian navies known as corvettes. These rakish deep-sea terriers, 900 tons of fire-power and caprice, shepherd the slow-moving convoys and guard them from lurking perils. It is the story of one of these vessels and her sturdy Canadian crew on an eastward Atlantic crossing from Halifax to the British Isles which is told with tremendous excitement and a pounding sense of the sea in Universal's latest war film, "Corvette K-225," which came to Loew's Criterion yesterday.

In a virtually documentary treatment of life aboard the K-225, Producer Howard Hawks and Richard Rosson, director of the film, have realized the physical strain and torment of work in a rampant corvette. They have pictured with indubitable fidelity the discomforts of an escort vessel's crew—the eternal tossing and rolling of the ship in a moderate sea; her plunging and gyrating in the grip of a North Atlantic gale, with tons of sea water pouring over her, battering and soaking every man.

Also, they have caught the terrible tension of men ever on the alert for the sudden attack of the enemy—either a screaming rain of bombs from the sky or the dark and more deadly torpedo of a submarine prowling beneath the sea. They have whipped up some bris-

Randolph Scott, in "Corvette K-225."

tling excitement when attacks of both natures come, especially when the corvette is blasting the insides of the ocean with "ash cans." And they have evidenced the courage and tenacity, the unspoken magnificence, of the men who endure such service. They have turned out a tough, manly film.

Much of the flavor of the picture may be thankfully credited to the fact that most of its backgrounds and some action were photographed aboard corvettes. Director Rosson and a camera crew spent several months at sea, combing the North Atlantic with the little ships on convoy patrol, and the lash of salt spray and howling sea winds fairly beat in the audience's face. The experience obviously tempered Mr. Rosson's regard for his film, and he has kept the whole thing within a pattern which is impressive and credible.

Randolph Scott gives a beautiful performance as the skipper of the corvette—a restrained and authoritative master, you can tell by the cut of his jib. James Brown is boyish and stubborn as a youngster who learns to stand his watch, and Ella Raines plays his sister prettily in the on-shore preamble of the film. John Frederick, David Bruce and Edmund MacDonald are rugged and dependable ship's officers, and Barry Fitzgerald, Fuzzy Knight, Thomas Gomez and Noah Beery Jr. stand out among those who man this lively little vessel and sing "Bless 'Em All" in the mess-deck off watch.

This film lacks the scope and compassion of Noel Coward's "In Which We Serve." But, in its purely graphic marshaling of sea warfare, it compares most favorably with that film.

O 21, 1943

'Gung Ho!' a Lurid Action Film About the Makin Island Raid, With Randolph Scott, Opens at the Criterion Theatre

GUNG HO!, screen play by Lucien Hubbard, based on the factual story, "Gung Ho," by Capt. W. S. Le Francois, USMC; additional dialogue by Joseph Hoffman; directed by Ray Enright; produced by Walter Wanger for Universal Pictures. At Loew's Criterion.
Colonel Thorwald..........Randolph Scott
Kathleen Corrigan.......Grace McDonald
John Harrison.............Alan Curtis
Kurt Richter.............Noah Beery Jr.
Lieut. Cristoforos........J. Carrol Naish
Larry O'Ryan.............David Bruce
Kozzarowski.................Peter Coe
Lieut. Roland Browning..Louis Jean Heydt
Pigiron...................Rob Mitchum
Capt. Dunphy.............Richard Lane
Rube Tedrow..............Rod Cameron
Transport..................Sam Levene
Commander Blade..........Milburn Stone
Frankie Montana..........Harold Landon
Buddy Andrews.............John James

By BOSLEY CROWTHER

The famous stab of Colonel Carlson's Raiders at Makin Island on Aug. 17, 1942, was a "natural" for playing in the movies. It possessed all the elements of suspense, of sudden and concentrated action and of heroic accomplishment against odds. It also possessed the further virtue of being a carefully

J. Carrol Naish in "Gung Ho!"

calculated affair in which personal ingenuity was encouraged — a feature upon which Hollywood dotes. So it is not in the least sur-

prising that Walter Wanger and Director Ray Enright have found inspiration in it for a sizzling war film entitled "Gung Ho!" if—as one might suspect at moments—they have gilded the lily just a bit, if they have touched up the desperado aspects with a dash of Hollywood coloring here and there, it is not necessarily misleading. The raid on Makin Island, we've been told, was almost as boldly theatrical as this new film at Loew's Criterion.

"Gung ho," you may know is a watchword which, in Chinese, means "work together" and which was adopted by Col. Evans Carlson as the slogan of his Marine Raiders. It signifies rigid self-discipline and the willing sacrifice of the individual for the group. And it is the "gung ho" spirit which the authors have endeavored to make the theme of this film, the spirit of a tight organization carrying out a perilous task.

That theme comes through essentially, for "Gung Ho!" punctiliously shows how a group of individuals mold into one big fighting unit in battle heat. Without naming actual names of officers, the story tells generally how the Second Marine Raider Battalion was picked and trained for the Makin Island raid, how the 200 final participants were transported thither in submarines, how they hit the island like a bombshell and fought the length and breadth of it for hours and hours. Some of the details are fictitious, such as a bombing from Jap planes while in the sub and a ruse which draws the enemy to his own destruction, but in the main the outline is exact. Capt. W. S. Le Francois wrote the story and he was there, so he certainly should know.

Without any subtleties or shadings, the performances are all rugged and good, particulary J. Carrol Naish's counterparting of Captain Le Francois. Randolph Scott makes a tough, reliable colonel, and Harold Landon, Bob Mitchum, Rod Cameron and Sam Levene are convincing as "leathernecks." Mr. Enright has directed for good tension and pyrotechnic display, the settings are true and the fighting on the island is as hot and lurid as any that we've seen. As a matter of fact, the stabbing and the sticking go on ad nauseam. "Gung Ho!" is for folks with strong stomachs and a taste for the sub-machine gun.

Ja 26, 1944

At the Palace

BELLE OF THE YUKON; written for the screen by James Edward Grant; from a story by Houston Branch; produced and directed by William Seiter; presented by International Pictures and released by RKO-Radio; music and lyrics by Johnny Burke and Jimmy Van Heusen. At the Palace.

Honest John Calhoun	Randolph Scott
Belle DeValle	Gypsy Rose Lee
Lettie Candless	Dinah Shore
Sam Slade	Bob Burns
"Pop" Candless	Charles Winninger
Steve	William Marshall
Mervyn	Guinn (Big Boy) Williams
George	Robert Armstrong
Viola	Florence Bates
The Professor	Victor Kilian
C. V. Atterbury	Edward Fielding

With "Belle of the Yukon," Gypsy Rose Lee makes her return to films in a vehicle chromatically as pretty as a new Easter bonnet and one which makes just about as much sense. For the Palace's new offering, which begins with the assertion that it is to be taken with tongue in cheek, follows its own ruling too carefully. It takes neither itself nor the audience too seriously, with the result that this serio-comic musical about confidence men, double-dealing and young love in the Klondike of the gold rush era never quite makes up its mind whether to be satiric or just plain musical narrative. And, sad to state, Miss Lee's lines are only sedately visible and not the least bit aural.

Perhaps it is not quite equitable to blame Miss Lee entirely. Randolph Scott, Dinah Shore, Bob Burns, Charles Winninger and William Marshall also are involved as principals in this complex tale. And, as such, they, as well as William Seiter, who produced and directed, are equally responsible. Perhaps, too, the producers meant the musical numbers to be the film's main attraction. It is certainly hard to tell. It is conceivable, however, that the plot having to do with the efforts of Honest John Calhoun to go straight in a fancy dance hall in Malamute and his attendant involvement with his old flame and première chanteuse, Belle, didn't seem quite enough. So, other developments—a romance between Dinah Shore and a piano player, a bank robbery and a few mistaken identities—have been included in the labyrinthine scenario. Fortunately, the right parties shake the shackles of the law and the plot to live happily ever after.

Miss Lee sings one number provocatively, while Miss Shore does well by several, the best of which are "Sleigh Ride in July" and "Like Someone in Love," both of which have had a vogue on the radio. Randolph Scott gives a literal portrayal of "Honest John," while the comedy, which is not inspired, is handled by Bob Burns, Charles Winninger and Guinn (Big Boy) Williams. Despite its Technicolor glitter, "Belle of the Yukon" yields few nuggets. It's fool's gold, after all.   A. W.

Mr 30, 1945.

At the Palace

CHINA SKY, adapted by Brenda Weisberg and Joseph Hoffman from the Pearl S. Buck novel; directed by Ray Enright; produced by Maurice Geraghty for RKO-Radio Pictures.

Dr. Gray Thompson	Randolph Scott
Dr. Sara Durand	Ruth Warrick
Louise Thompson	Ellen Drew
Chen Ta	Anthony Quinn
Siu Mei	Carol Thurston
Colonel Yasuda	Richard Loo
Little Goat	Ducky Louie
Dr. Kim	Philip Ahn
Chung	Benson Fong
Charlie	Chin Kuang Chow

Whatever its merits as a novel, Pearl Buck's "China Sky" turns up on the screen of the Palace as a regulation marital triangle drama with a dash of old-fashioned melodrama thrown in — in a most literal sense—for full measure. The valiant struggle fo the Chinese is projected here merely as background, or atmosphere, and it is impossible to believe that RKO used more than the title of Mrs. Buck's book in fashioning this picture. In a remote little hill village serving as a supply base for the bold guerilla leader, Shen Ta, a pair of heroic American doctors—Randolph Scott and Ruth Warrick—work medical wonders around the clock, patching up villagers after each Jap bombing. Theirs is an idyllic association until Dr. Scott goes home on a fund-raising mission and returns with a wife, a beautiful, selfish, rich girl, who immediately becomes jealous of Dr. Warrick and—need a routine plot be further exposed?

As Chen Ta, Anthony Quinn sounds more Latin than Chinese. And, in a climactic flourish of action filled with the spirit of "head 'em off at Eagle Pass," Chen Ta and warriors charge down from their mountain hide-away to rescue the village from a force of Jap paratroopers. No, it is hard indeed to believe that the scenarists paid much attention to Mrs. Buck's narrative. Mr. Scott and Miss Warrick are competent, and Ellen Drew is satisfactory as the nasty wife. The Chinese characters are the typical, self-effacing types to be found on the screen and who probably would be looked upon as curios in Chungking. RKO undoubtedly meant will in producing this film as an expression of American friendhip for China, but it seems to us that this is a case where 10,000 words would have been better than one picture.

T. M. P.

My 25, 1945

At the Globe

CAPTAIN KIDD, screen play by Norman Reilly Raine, from an original story by Robert N. Lee; directed by Rowland V. Lee; produced by Benedict Bogeaus for United Artists release.

Capt. William Kidd	Charles Laughton
Adam Mercy	Randolph Scott
Lady Anne Falconer	Barbara Britton
Cary Shadwell	Reginald Owen
Orange Povey	John Carradine
Lorenzo	Gilbert Roland
Boyle	Sheldon Leonard
Blades	Abner Biberman
King William III	Henry Daniell
Bart Blivens	John Qualen
Lord Albemarle	Ian Keith
Rawson	William Farnum

It seems only yesterday that Charles Laughton, crisp and overbearing, was treading the quarterdeck of the Bounty, berating a mutinous Clark Gable. Well, sir, the salt is still in Mr. Laughton's veins and speech, to judge by "Captain Kidd," which hove to at the Globe yesterday. As Mr. Laughton puts it, once he comes aboard H. M. S. Adventure Galley, "it's good to feel the roll of a stout ship again." And it's very likely that the boys, both young and old, will be glad he put to sea again. For, as the fabulous pirate, Mr. Laughton makes sovereign use of the picture's title role, being as much the posturing comedian as the blood-thirsty buccaneer. Swashbuckling, naturally, is the word for this cruise, but there's also an uncommon lot of talk and much potential excitement is missing. The good ship Adventure Galley is becalmed pretty often.

Writers Norman Reilly Raine and Robert N. Lee have parlayed fact and fancy to bring Laughton from piracy to his eventual end on London's Execution Dock. He is a spuriously sanctimonious rascal, who, commissioned by King William III to protect honest shipping off Madagascar, turns the tables to rob the craft he is sent to protect. And, his covey of cutthroats, recruited from Newgate Prison, run into all the standard adventures, from treasure buried by moonlight, swordplay and sinking galleons to the beauteous damsel, saved in the nick of time by the standard hero.

Randolph Scott is properly convincing and dashing as that grim and well-born hero, who finally brings Captain Kidd to justice. John Carradine and Gilbert Roland, as Kidd's henchmen, take to their roles as to the manner born, while Reginald Owen plays Kidd's "gentleman's gentleman" with taste and quiet efficiency. Rowland V. Lee has directed the Benedict Bogeaus production leisurely and with meticulous regard for seventeenth-century decor and manners. "Captain Kidd," however, is strictly Charles Laughton's vehicle. The rest of the crew are merely along for the ride. A. W.

N 23, 1945

At the Globe

ABILENE TOWN, screen play by Harold Shumate; from the novel, "Trail Town" by Ernest Haycox; directed by Edwin L. Marin; produced by Jules Levey and released through United Artists.

Dan Mitchell	Randolph Scott
Rita	Ann Dvorak
Bravo Trimble	Edgar Buchanan
Sherry Balder	Rhonda Fleming
Henry Dreiser	Lloyd Bridges
Ed Balder	Howard Freeman
Charlie Fair	Richard Hale
Jet Younger	Jack Lambert
Big Annie	Helen Boice
Ryker	Dick Curtis
Hannaberry	Eddie Waller
Doug Neil	Hank Patterson
Hazelhurst	Earl Schenck

Since the conversion to law and order of practically every lawless hamlet in the Old West now is in Hollywood's archives, it was but a matter of time before Abilene's lusty story was considered cinematically. And, in "Abilene Town," which came to the Globe on Saturday, Jules Levey, the producer, has fixed his camera sights on that Kansas crossroads and has come up with a Western that may or may not be history but that certainly should satisfy lovers of that genre. True, it is basically horse opera in which the music isn't stinted, but it is turned out with flavor and pace, and the shooting and fighting are unrestrained.

Ernest Haycox, as noted a chronicler of the Old West as any (i.e., "Stagecoach"), is responsible for the yarn, which in the main treats of the homesteaders' struggles to settle the prairie at Abilene and the dying attempts of the cattlemen to keep the trail and range free at that terminal. In the course of this saga Edwin L. Marin, the director, apparently a man averse to nuance, has seen to it that the action is loud and plentiful.

There are no new twists. His marshal singlehandedly holds off all the hard hombres. But his cattle stampede with the noise of an earthquake, wheat farmers' homes are razed in crackling conflagrations and bad men bite the dust with a thump. And when the grim hero engages in a titanic donnybrook with the villain, the socks in the jaw have resonance. If the ultimate battle between the peaceful citizens and the drovers on Abilene's Texas Street never does come off, Harold Shumate, the scenarist, can be forgiven for paraphrasing poetry in having the marshal, Randolph Scott, say, "that's the way a tough street dies, not with a roar but with a whine." The audience will agree that the fireworks, up to this point, have been adequate.

Mr. Scott makes a tough and convincing peace officer, whose duties also include dalliance with two lovely ladies. Ann Dvorak, as the saloon prima donna who wins him, is properly seductive and adept at romance and the handling of a couple of ditties that are closer to Broadway than Kansas of the 'Seventies. Rhonda Fleming, as the other lady, and Edgar Buchanan, as a timorous and bumbling sheriff, head the featured cast. "Abilene Town" may be cut from a familiar pattern but it is guaranteed to keep the customers awake. A. W.

Mr 4, 1946

Desperadoes Busy Again

BADMAN'S TERRITORY, screen play by Jack Natteford and Luci Ward; directed by Tim Whelan; produced by Nat Holt for RKO Radio Pictures. At the Victoria.

Mark Rowley	Randolph Scott
Henryette Alcott	Ann Richards
Coyote	George (Gabby) Hayes
Colonel Farewell	Ray Collins
John Rowley	James Warren
Bill Hampton	Morgan Conway
Meg	Virginia Sale
Hank McGee	John Halloran
Doc Grant	Andrew Tombes
Ben Wade	Richard Hale
Hodge	Harry Holman
Chief Tahlequah	Chief Thundercloud
Jesse James	Lawrence Tierney
Frank James	Tom Tyler
Bob Dalton	Steve Brodie
Grat Dalton	Phil Warren
Bill Dalton	William Moss
Sam Bass	Nestor Paiva
Belle Starr	Isabel Jewell

The James Boys, the Dalton Brothers, Belle Starr, Sam Bass and a dozen or more less-celebrated desperadoes of the wild and lawless West of yore all contribute a fair share of shootin' an' brawlin' in "Badman's Territory," the lumbering-action melodrama which arrived yesterday at the Victoria. All of the boys scowl and growl in what has now become traditional fashion, and they conveniently spur their overworked horses and whip out their six-shooters to divert attention from what little story the picture has to offer over its ninety-eight-minute course.

The action takes place in a strip of territory called Quinto, which is outside the law and presumably the last bandit stronghold in the Southwest. But its isolation is threatened by a crusading petticoat editor who bravely defies threats and advertising boycotts in her newspaper campaign to make Quinto part of the Oklahoma territory. That's only one of the plots, however. There is another tale about a Sheriff from Texas who rides into Quinto after the James Boys and, before he knows it, is himself being framed on a shooting and horse-stealing charge by a wicked and politically ambitious United States marshal.

Randolph Scott is the rangy, tight-lipped Texan; Ann Richards is the courageous lady and George (Gabby) Hayes is the customary old whiskered, rum-sodden character, who really isn't quite as bad as his reputation. They and all the others in the long cast—long, that is, for a Western—do the prescribed things in the prescribed manner. In fact, the only thing unusual about "Badman's Territory" is its inordinate length. Westerns seem to have a lot more life when told rapidly and concisely. T. M. P.

My 31, 1946,

CHRISTMAS EVE: screen play by Laurence Stallings; from original stories by Mr. Stallings and Richard H Landau; directed by Edwin L. Marin; produced by Benedict Bogeaus and released through United Artists.

Mario .... George Raft
Michael .... George Brent
Aunt Matilda .... Ann Harding
Jonathan .... Randolph Scott
Ann .... Joan Blondell
Claire .... Virginia Field
Jean .... Dolores Moran
Phillip .... Reginald Denny
Judge Alston .... Clarence Kolb
F. B. I. Agent .... John Litel
Harriet .... Molly Lamont
Doctor .... Douglass Dumbrille
Psychologist .... Carl Harbord
Butler .... Dennis Hoey
Gimlet .... Joe Sawyer
Reichman .... Konstantin Shayne
Hood .... Walter Sande

"Christmas Eve," a film package which has rushed that festive season and which came to the Broadway Theatre yesterday, seems to have been filled with all manner of things. But none of the slightly-scrambled contents has the elements of surprise or imagination. For this episodic potpourri about a rich, aged eccentric maiden lady about to be declared mentally unfit, and her three errant wards, tries hard to emulate the pattern of such successful episodic yarns as "Tales of Manhattan" and only succeeds in being transparent, plodding and occasionally confusing.

The Messrs. Laurence Stallings and Richard H. Landau, who were responsible for the writing, certainly had a fairly intriguing framework in the idea of a sentimental grande dame's desire to be reunited with and defended by her missing "sons" on Christmas eve. But her adopted family are

a trio who are hardly the types to convince any doubting surrogate. One is a wastrel, who has affixed his John Hancock to a small fortune in rubber checks, another is a racketeer who is avoiding the FBI and doing quite handsomely down in South America, and the third is an improvident bronco buster not averse to firewater. Told in flashback their activities are unfolded in a rather abrupt and sometimes implausible fashion.

Of the headliners in the cast none is precisely convincing. Ann Harding, as the harried spinster, comes closest to the mark, although there is more than a vestige of flamboyance in her portrayal. Merely adequate, however, are George Raft, as the racketeer who disposes of a Nazi bigwig before coming home; George Brent, the playboy who helps unmask Reginald Denny, a conniving relative, and Randolph Scott, the cow-

boy who manages to become involved in a baby-adoption racket en route to the Christmas rendezvous. And merely adequate, too, are Virginia Field, Joan Blondell and Dolores Moran, as their respective girl friends. Clarence Kolb, the bewildered surrogate called to judge on the old lady's fitness, delivers what seemed the film's most illuminating line when he declares heatedly, "I'm beginning to think you all need guardians."
A. W

N 28, 1947

TRAIL STREET, screen play by Norman Houston and Gene Lewis, based on the novel by William Corcoran; directed by Ray Enright; produced by Nat Holt for RKO-Radio Pictures. At the Palace.

"Bat" Masterson .... Randolph Scott
Allen .... Robert Ryan
Ruby .... Anne Jeffreys
Billy .... George "Gabby" Hayes
Susan .... Madge Meredith
Maury .... Steve Brodie
Carmody .... Billy House
Hannah .... Virginia Sale
Larkin .... Harry Woods
Slim .... Phil Warren
Mayor .... Harry Harvey
Jason .... Jason Robards

It would take more thumbing through the records than the present occasion justifies to determine how many westerns have already been made about the frontier marshal, "Bat" Masterson, and his way with bad men and bad towns. But we'd venture to say that the number runs to several score, at least, and that "Trail Street," the latest in the series is no be,tter nor worse than most of the rest. It is just another pistol drama in which the good marshal, played by Randolph Scott, cleans out a nest of cowboy villains who are making life miserable on the Kansas farms.

Everything takes place on schedule, including a pious romance between a farm agent, Robert Ryan, and a local girl, Madge Meredith. Even the routine introduction of "Gabby" Hayes for comedy relief is as cut and dried as a cowhide. It's at the Palace. Any questions? Class Dismissed.
B. C.

Ap 10, 1947

GUNFIGHTERS, screen play by Alan LeMay from the Zane Grey novel. "Twin Sombreros"; directed by George Waggner; produced by Harry Joe Brown for Columbia Pictures.

Brazos Kane .... Randolph Scott
Bess Banner .... Barbara Britton
Jane Banner .... Dorothy Hart
Bard Macey .... Bruce Cabot
Inskip .... Charley Grapewin
Jose .... Steven Geray
Ben Orcutt .... Forrest Tucker
Sheriff Kiscaden .... Charles Kemper
Deputy Bill Yount .... Grant Withers
Johnny O'Neil .... John Miles
Banner .... Griff Barnett

All you Western fans—and there must be a lot of them, or else they wouldn't make so many of these things—can safely flock this week to the Victoria, where "Gunfighters" had its opening yesterday, for your gun-totin', hard-ridin', rootin'-tootin' action. All the rest of you movie fans can safely dispense with the proceedings.

The current re-hash of everything Hollywood has ever filmed about those sturdier frontier days is from a Zane Grey novel and has a silent, steely-eyed Randolph Scott as the star. That's probably enough in the way of explanation, but for the more precise readers it's got to do with a one-man army (Mr. Scott), who cleans up a whole county run by a cattle operator who's trying to squeeze out the smaller ranchers. Lots of people are killed but, of course, avenged by

the hero in the last gasps of the final reel.

Outside of the fact that the film is too long, the sound track is often blurry and a pair of twin girls (Barbara Britton and Dorothy Hart) confuse things immensely, it is average fare for the inveterate Western addicts. The picture is filmed in Cinecolor, which is not to be construed as a recommendation.
E. J. B.

JI 25, 1947

Neighborhood Tragedy

HOME SWEET HOMICIDE, screen play by F. Hugh Herbert from the novel by Craig Rice; directed by Lloyd Bacon and produced by Louis D. Lighton for Twentieth Century-Fox. At the Roxy.

Dinah Carstairs .... Peggy Ann Garner
Bill Smith .... Randolph Scott
Marian Carstairs .... Lynn Bari
Archie Carstairs .... Dean Stockwell
April Carstairs .... Connie Marshall
Sergeant O'Hare .... James Gleason
Polly Walker .... Anabel Shaw
Jo-Ella Holbrook .... Barbara Whiting
Mr. Sanford .... John Shepperd
Mr. Cherington .... Stanley Logan
Luke .... Olin Howlin

By BOSLEY CROWTHER

What must have seemed to its author and to the people at Twentieth Century-Fox a pip of a comedy idea — namely, to have the clever kids of a lady mystery novelist solve a murder that happens next door—falls far shy of building to a picture of any rich or original sort in the Roxy's current attraction, "Home Sweet Homicide." As a matter of fact, this forced exhibit of precocity in the young is just a catch-penny grown-up contortion of the acumen of kids.

Allowing that children naturally would be very much concerned about a neighborhood case of murder—especially a litter of tots raised in a home where mystery fiction is the breath of domestic life—it is doubtful, indeed, that they would view it so coolly as the kids do in this film or with such absolute conformance to fictional patterns of juvenile types. It is doubtful, too, that their devices for reaching a solution of the crime would be so bleakly unoriginal and unsuspenseful as the ones used herein.

Plainly, Peggy Ann Garner, Connie Marshall and Dean Stockwell, playing the kids, are much more natural and attractive than the things they have to do and say, and Lynn Bari and Randolph Scott, as major grown-ups, are consistently lacking adult ease. James Gleason, as a baffled detective, is amusing but right out of stock. As for Lloyd Bacon, the director — let's charge him with exploiting the young.

On the stage at the Roxy are Hildegarde. Patsy Kelly. Jan Murray and Eleanor Teeman.

S 12, 1946

COLT 45: screen play by Thomas Blackburn; directed by Edwin L. Marin; produced by Saul Elkins for Warner Brothers. At the Strand.

Steve Farrell	Randolph Scott
Beth Donovan	Ruth Roman
Jason Brett	Zachary Scott
Paul Donovan	Lloyd Bridges
Miller	Ian MacDonald
Walking Bear	Chief Thundercloud
Judge Tucker	Lute Crockett
Carl	Walter Coy
Redrock Sheriff	Charles Evans

By BOSLEY CROWTHER

One thing is fairly obvious: the Warners weren't in a high-brow mood when they rounded up all the fellows and banged out "Colt .45." This Technicolored Western, which came to the Strand yesterday, is as intellectually simple as one and one are two. And although it is solemnly intended as a tribute to that great six-shooting gun, it is really a monumental sanction of the Western formula.

That is no easy achievement. Plenty of Westerns have been made that were just like plenty of others, yet they haven't occasioned the remark. But here is a whoop-de-do horse opera which is so utterly cut to form, in which the good-man and bad-man encounters occur so patly when you most expect them to, and in which the cowboy acting is so obviously full of clichés that the whole thing shrieks loudly — almost boastfully — of its absolute conformance to rules. In fact, it is such a hackneyed picture that it is actually a lot of fun.

From the moment that Randolph Scott, in innocence, lets a new pair of Colt repeating guns fall into the cowardly and reckless hands of the bandit, Zachary Scott, this latter despicable creature becomes the fearful scourge of the West, racing around the country, robbing stages, killing Indians and all the rest. But, fortunately, Mr. Scott, the former, owns another pair of Colts, so he takes after the latter, with the Indians on his side. In the course of this dauntless pursuance, he gains the support of a girl—a fiery miss, played by Ruth Roman—who doesn't pack guns but, oh boy! And eventually, after the bandit has run through his ammu-

Randolph Scott in "Colt .45"

nition stock—and Thomas Blackburn, the script-writer, has exhausted his supply of clichés—Mr. Scott, the good one, destroys the nemesis, regains the smoking pistols and presumably marries the girl.

That is the elemental story. The acting is in the same groove. You'll never see cornier performing than the people in this picture do. If Eddie Marin, the director, had told them, "Now, listen here, I don't care how much you 'ham' it," they couldn't have done a broader job. Both Mr. Scotts are fantastic. Miss Roman is the noblest dame in pants. And Chief Thundercloud simply slays 'em with his dead pan and his magnetic arrows. As a matter of fact—and incidentally—more damage seems to be done by the swift, silent shafts of the Indians than by the bullets from the celebrated guns. This may be simply inadvertence, or it may be the picture's cryptic point. Anyhow, it is just another humor with which "Colt .45" is charged.

MY, 1950

Six-Shooters Again

FIGHTING MAN OF THE PLAINS, story and screen play by Frank Gruber; directed by Edwin L. Marin; produced by Nat Holt and released by Twentieth Century-Fox. At the Rialto.

Jim Dancer	Randolph Scott
Johnny Tancred	Bill Williams
Dave Oldham	Victory Jory
Florence Peel	Jane Nigh
Ken Vedder	Douglas Kennedy
Evelyn Slocum	Jean Taylor
Cliff Bailey	Berry Kroeger
Chandler Leach	Rhys Williams

Judging by the eager-eyed audience yesterday at the Rialto, where "Fighting Man of the Plains" opened, thundering hooves and barking six-shooters can still fill a theatre when all else fails. No one seems to know this better than Producer Nat Holt, whose formula is to sauce things up in Cinecolor, with vague historical footnotes and several hundred extras milling around.

It's the same old smoked ham, and by now Randolph Scott certainly knows how to slice it for the sagebrush customers. This time he's an ex-bandit who becomes marshal of a post-Civil War town in Kansas and cleans out some white-collar hypocrites, who turn out to be as ruthless as Mr. Scott was—or is. It's hard to tell which side to root for in all the confusion, particularly when the marshal is saved from hanging and sent to his girl's arms by the sudden arrival of his old pal, Jesse James.

The general yell that hit the Rialto ceiling on that one was enough to make the original outlaw sit up in his grave and take a bow.

H. H. T.

N 17, 1949

A Better Western

THE NEVADAN, story and screen play by George W. George and George F. Slavin; directed by Gordon Douglas; produced by Harry Joe Brown for Columbia. At the Palace.

Andrew Barkley	Randolph Scott
Karen Galt	Dorothy Malone
Tom Tanner	Forrest Tucker
Jeff	Frank Faylen
Edward Galt	George Macready
Dyke Merrick	Charles Kemper
Bart	Jeff Corey
Bill Martin	Tom Powers

A better than run-of-mine Western popped up at the Palace yesterday in the shape of a film called "The Nevadan," starring that old cowhand, Randolph Scott. And the margin by which this horse-and-gun show rises above the commonplace is in a couple of minor characters whom Jeff Corey and Frank Faylen play. These fellows are supposed to be brothers and members of the gang of gold-greedy frontier-town villains of whom the good marshal has to dispose. They're just a couple of fellows and could be complete nonentities. But here, at least, someone with humor—the desperate script-writers, perhaps—endowed them with individuality and some very acid lines.

And thus, in the midst of routine slugging and shooting and passing harsh words, all having to do with the endeavors of the marshal to get his men, these two brothers discuss their personal problems and fraternal concerns engagingly. Even in Cinecolor they look good. That's something you can't often say.

B. C.

Ja 13, 1950

ALBUQUERQUE screen play by Gene Lewis and Clarence Upson Young based on a story by Luke Short directed by Ray Enright a Clarion Production produced by William Pine and William Thomas released by Paramount

Cole Armin	Randolph Scott
Letty Tyler	Barbara Britton
Juke	George "Gabby" Hayes
Ted Wallace	Russell Hayden
Celia Wallace	Catherine Craig
Murkil	Lon Chaney
John Armin	George Cleveland
Myrtle Walton	Karolyn Grimes
Huggins	Russell Simpson
Sheriff Linton	Bernard Nedell
Pearl	Jody Gilbert
Jackson	Dan White
Bandit	Saylor Vincent

Old Uncle John Armin who ruled Albuquerque from a wheel chair back in 1878 was the sort of "empire" builder who wouldn't stop at robbery or even murder to wipe out a business competitor. But his nephew Cole, who grew up in Texas and rode for a spell with the Rangers, was a solid six feet of virtuousness, the kind of fellow who believed honesty was more important than blood bonds and that women folk were entitled to a full measure of respect.

Now, you can imagine how Cole reacts when he discovers that Uncle John sent his gun-men to hold up the stage coach and rob Celia Wallace of the $10,000 she was bringing to her brother Ted who was bucking the Armin transportation monopoly. What you can't possibly imagine, however, is the ruthlessness and cunning that Uncle John manifests when he determines to ruin his nephew as well as that Wallace fellow.

For further details, your attention is directed to "Albuquerque," which arrived at the Victoria on Saturday all decked out in Cinecolor photography. It might be remarked in passing that the picture is neither especially good nor bad, as Westerns go; that Randolph Scott as Cole seems well able to take care of himself in the clinches; that Catherine Craig as Celia and Barbara Britton as a femme fatale imported by Uncle John to do some spying on Cole and the Wallaces are equally pretty to look at. And, yes, there is some shooting and a runaway stage to liven up the proceedings. But even this doesn't help very much.　　　　T. M. P.

Mr 1, 1948

RETURN OF THE BADMEN: Screen play by Charles O'Neal, Jack Natteford and Luci Ward: directed by Ray Enright: produced by Nat Holt for RKO Radio Pictures, Inc.

Vance	Randolph Scott
Sundance Kid	Robert Ryan
Cheyenne	Anne Jeffreys
John Pettit	George "Gabby" Hayes
Madge Allen	Jacqueline White
Cole Younger	Steve Brodie
Jim Younger	Richard Powers
John Younger	Robert Bray
Emmett Dalton	Lex Barker
Bob Dalton	Walter Reed
Grat Dalton	Michael Harvey
Billy the Kid	Dean White
Wild Bill Doolin	Robert Armstrong
Wild Bill Yeager	Tom Tyler

Instead of quietly settling for one half of a double bill, RKO yesterday installed what the company terms "the biggest Western epic of 1948" at one of Broadway's larger movie palaces, the Mayfair. But the promoters of "Return of the Badmen" can just lay that trumpet down. This round-up of all the two-legged coyotes on the studio lot, for all its blazing guns and mass villiany, is simply another creaky and endless saga of the tumbleweeds.

The three scenarists deemed necessary for this epic have dusted off that ancient plot, the one about the fearless marshal, Randolph Scott, who single-handedly brings law and order to the new Oklahoma Territory. And Director Ray Enright has seen to it that the outlaws swoop in and out exactly on schedule, prying the sweethearts apart and scaring the daylights out of the quaking settlers. The picture's one bid for spectacle, the Land Rush of 1889, is strangely reminiscent of the studio's bygone "Cimarron," a good Western and a horse opera of another color.

Not content with trying to pass off this antique as a streamlined job, the producers have almost smothered some real talent. Anne Jeffreys, who has been singing lead roles in opera hereabouts, is cast as a pistol-packing mama, spurs and all, and her grappling with the role is both painful and admirable to watch. But Robert Ryan has managed to come through unscathed with a cool, expert performance as a prairie sadist. As for all the others, let us hope they gallop lickety-split back to the RKO stables and stay there.　　　- H.H.T.

Ag 5, 1948

Movie of Railroad

CANADIAN PACIFIC. screen play by Jack DeWitt and Kenneth Gamet, from an original story by Mr DeWitt: directed by Edwin L. Marin: produced by Nat Holt for Twentieth Century-Fox. At the Palace.

Tom Andrews	Randolph Scott
Dr Edith Cabot	Jane Wyatt
Dynamite Dawson	J. Carrol Naish
Dirk Rourke	Victor Jory
Cecille Gautier	Nancy Olson
Cornelius Van Horne	Robert Barratt
Mike Brannigan	Walter Sande
Cagle	Don Haggerty
Dr. Mason	Grandon Rhodes
Mrs. Gautier	Mary Kent
Mr Gautier	John Parrish
Pere Lacombe	John Hamilton

By BOSLEY CROWTHER

Vaudeville wasn't the only thing exhumed at the Palace yesterday. The picture that went along with it brought a whiff of the late departed, too. "Canadian Pacific" is its title, and the best to be said for it is that it rounded out a program of mediocrity.

Pretending to tell the story of how a mighty railroad was built across stretching plains and towering mountains to link two distant coasts, this so-called outdoor action picture very quickly and wearily settles down to trickling along in the old bed of cowboy-and-Indian films. The hero in the proceedings is the railroad's "trouble boss," the fellow who handles all varmints and other rascals who get in the way. And the varmints, of course, are much in evidence, making trouble of a most conventional sort.

Randolph Scott is the hero who speaks the usual hero lines, such as, "Round up all the ammunition! Break out those repeaters! Come with me!" And J. Carrol Naish is his side-kick—the inevitable hairy-faced galoot, to whom he addresses such endearments as "You cock-eyed old terrapin!"

Rivals for Mr. Scott's affections are Nancy Olson, who plays a mountain girl as though she had just come home to Canada from the American School of Dramatic Arts, and Jane Wyatt, cast as a trained nurse, who performs the film's one miracle: she gives a blood transfusion from her own arm to Mr. Scott's in a moving train, with no evident equipment —all this prior to 1885!

The film is in Cinecolor, which imparts to the Canadian Rockies a greenish hue and to the faces of most of the actors an appropriately deathly shade.

My 20, 1949

At the Globe

SUGARFOOT, adapted by Russell Hughes from the novel by Clarence Budington Kelland, directed by Edwin L. Marin, produced by Saul Elkins for Warner Brothers.

Jackson (Sugarfoot) Redan	Randolph Scott
Reva Cairn	Adele Jergens
Jacob Stint	Raymond Massey
Don Miguel	S. Z. Sakall
J. C. Crane	Robert Warwick
Fly-Up-the-Creek Jones	Arthur Hunnicutt
Asa Goodhue	Hugh Sanders
Mary	Hope Landin
Johnny-Behind-the-Stove	Hank Worden
Billings	Gene Evans

In the Globe's week-end arrival, "Sugarfoot," Randolph Scott is driven by "ambition" to the frontier town of Prescott, Ariz., while Raymond Massey is driven by "greed" to the same destination. In fact, these two gents arrive via the same wagon train and in mutual agreement that the town is not big enough to accommodate both of them. Sure as shootin', they will settle their differences down the sights of six-guns, and they do, for "Sugarfoot" is the kind of Western that holds no surprises. In fact, it holds no entertainment, despite the ammunition expended and the exciting complexion of the countryside in Technicolor. T. M. P.

F 12, 1951

Muscular Action

SANTA FE, screen play by Kenneth Gamet, based on a novel by James Marshall and a story by Louis Stevens; directed by Irving Pichel; produced by Harry Joe Brown for Columbia Pictures. At the Palace.

Britt Canfield	Randolph Scott
Judith Chandler	Janis Carter
Terry Canfield	Jerome Courtland
Tom Canfield	Peter Thompson
Clint Canfield	John Archer
Dave Baxter	Warner Anderson
Cole Sanders	Roy Roberts
Luke Plummer	Billy House

By BOSLEY CROWTHER

Randolph Scott builds a railroad in Columbia's "Santa Fe," an iron-horse-and-wooden-men Western that came to the Palace yesterday. At least, he helps build a railroad while attending to such incidental chores as minding three mischievous Southern brethren and sparking a beautiful blonde.

The brethren appear to cause more trouble than does either the railroad or the blonde, since they have a peculiar disposition to hold up banks and do other wayward things. But finally Bat Masterson gets them, with the resigned assistance of Mr. Scott; the Sante Fe railroad gets completed and the blonde presumably gets her just deserts.

As for the audience, all that it gets is a lot of muscular action, Western style, including a fist fight aboard a rolling flat car, and some pretty Technicolored outdoors.

My 4, 1951

Sagebrush Saga

FORT WORTH, screen play by John Twist; directed by Edwin L. Marin and produced by Anthony Veiller for Warner Brothers. At the Palace.

Ned Britt	Randolph Scott
Blair Lunsford	David Brian
Flora Talbot	Phyllis Thaxter
Luther	Dick Jones
Ben Garvin	Emerson Treacy
Amy Brooks	Helena Carter

What's the latest Randolph Scott Western all about? Need anyone ask? Warner Brothers' "Fort Worth," at the Palace, more or less takes up where the gentleman last left off. Just why it does, we can't say. But here it all is again—the same pretty Technicolor and thrifty sets, with an occational splicing in of some spectacular footage from some of the more ambitious Warner sagebrush sagas, another little cast round-up of Western diehards and, more than likely, the same horses. And, of course, the granite-jawed Mr. Scott still hitches up his holsters and purges the premises of any varmint who'd obstruct history in the making.

This time he's a fairly sanctimonious newspaper editor who turns trigger-happy because his old buddy, David Brian, a self-made tycoon, is trying to buy up all the Fort Worth territory and make himself a dictator. Mr. Scott's other near-neurosis is a band of prairie scavengers who are terrorizing the good citizens, and who may or may not be in cahoots with Mr. Brian. It's never made clear. The scenarist named John Twist, instead of coming up with a few, substitutes confusion.

Most of the picture has the two stalwarts snarling at each other one minute and back-slapping the next, while Phyllis Thaxter, Helena Carter and Dick Jones get in a few stock company licks. Mr. Brian, incidentally, has no business in or near a saddle. In fact, he'd better go back to cuffing Joan Crawford around or next time he may see a horse laugh. H.H.T.

Jl 13, 1951

'Starlift' Provides Warners With Opportunity to Parade Its Stable of Stars

STARLIFT, screen play by John Klorer and Karl Kamb, from a story by Mr. Klorer; directed by Roy Del Ruth, produced by Robert Arthur for Warner Brothers. At the Warner.

Nel Wayne	Janice Rule
Sgt. Mike Nolan	Dick Wesson
Cpl. Rick Williams	Ron Hagerthy
Col. Joe Callan	Richard Webb
The Chaplain	Hayden Rorke
Steve Rogers	Howard St. John
Doris Day	
Gordon MacRae	
Virginia Mayo	As themselves
Gene Nelson	
Ruth Roman	

and

James Cagney	Lucille Norman
Gary Cooper	Louella Parsons
Virginia Gibson	Randolph Scott
Phil Harris	Jane Wyman
Frank Lovejoy	Patrice Wymore

By BOSLEY CROWTHER

A slightly embarrassing subject in Hollywood, we are told, is something called Operation Starlift. This was a project designed to shuttle film stars to San Francisco to entertain troops Korea-bound, and, as nearly as we can make out, it sort of died in the planning stage. Same might be said for "Starlift," the film Warner Brothers has made to celebrate this patriotic effort and also to exhibit its stable of stars.

The idea behind this fruitless picture, which came to the Warner yesterday, is the same that inspired any number of grab-bag pictures at the time of World War II. A round-up of Hollywood players is made for a camp or canteen show, thus permitting a little performance or just a nod to the camera from each. And, of course, a romance is included to provide a flimsy story line.

In this case, however, the idea is the only inspiration to be seen. The acts are unspeakably slapdash and the romance is painful beyond words. The latter involves a movie starlet, played by Janice Rule, who meets a flier from Travis Air Base while in San Francisco for a film première and through him dis-

Doris Day in "Starlift."

covers the hunger of the outbound troops to be entertained. Eventually, she also discovers the divine afflatus of love.

Let's be brief about it: the performances given by Miss Rule and Ron Hagerthy as the flier are as sappy as they could possibly be, and Dick Wesson as a pushy pal of the flier is downright insufferable. Among the acts, Doris Day's several warblings of old songs are the easiest to take, while a hula dance by Virginia Mayo reaches the other extreme. In between are such things as James Cagney popping in for a little rough talk and Gary Cooper and Frank Lovejoy doing a burlesque of a barroom shooting, with Phil Harris singing the song.

The washout of Operation Starlift is understandable, if it depended upon such "entertainment" as is exhibited in this film.

D 15, 1951

CARSON CITY: screen play by Sloan Nibley and Winston Miller, from a story by Mr. Nibley; directed by André De Toth, produced by David Weisbart for Warner Brothers.

Jeff .... Randolph Scott
Susan Mitchell .... Lucille Norman
"Big Jack" David .... Raymond Massey
Alan Kincaid .... Richard Webb
Jim Squires .... James Millican
William Sharon .... Larry Keating
Henry Dodson .... George Cleveland

If "Carson City," the Globe's new Randolph Scott Western, sounds like another familiar scramble on the Warner Brothers' cow path, it should. This time Mr. Scott is engineering the construction of the first railroad from Carson City to Virginia City. Raymond Massey, a champagne-swilling bandit, manages to set against the hero the whole town, including Mr. Scott's own brother, Richard Webb, and the local beauty, Lucille Norman, who, of course, sees the light well before the finale. The train goes through, Mr. Massey bites the dust, and the hero and heroine depart on a caboose.

While the film is nothing more than a thoroughly routine little horse opera, "Carson City" nevertheless rates comment on at least two mild counts. The studio's new color process, WarnerColor, tones down the heretofore garish grandeur of the scenery with becoming naturalness. And Sloan Nibley and Winston Miller, the scenarists; André De Toth, who directed, and practically the entire cast have performed their assignments with a competent jauntiness that suggests they weren't out to fool anybody.
H. H. T.

Je 14, 1952

HANGMAN'S KNOT: written and directed by Roy Huggins; produced by Harry Joe Brown; a Randolph Scott-Harry Joe Brown production presented by Columbia.

Matt Stewart .... Randolph Scott
Molly Hull .... Donna Reed
Jamie Groves .... Claude Jarman Jr.
Cass Browne .... Lee Marvin
Rolph Bainter .... Richard Denning
Lee Kemper .... Glenn Langan
Captain Petersen .... Clem Bevans
Plunkett .... Ray Teal
Mrs. Harris .... Jeanette Nolan
Quincey .... Ray Teal
Smitty .... Guinn (Big Boy) Williams
Maxwell .... Monte Blue
Egan Walsh .... John Call
Hank Fletcher .... Reed Howes

The Western, a movie staple often misused and maligned through stereotyped production, is given handsome, credible and edifying treatment in "Hangman's Knot," a taut, action-filled adventure sensibly designed to keep the devotees—especially the older ones—from yawning. For the producers of the newcomer at Loew's State—Harry Joe Brown and Randolph Scott, who also stars—obviously were aware that motion pictures should move, and their robust drama wastes few words and very often digs into the character of its principals to give genuine substance to the brisk action of the story. And, since Technicolor always enhances a rugged Western scene, the producers seem to have guessed right on that score, too.

Credit, of course, must go to Roy Huggins, who not only wrote the yarn but directed it without being patronizing toward it. It is simply a modest tale—which starts with a bang—about a detachment of Confederate volunteers who have been dispatched to the Nevada Territory to ambush a Union wagon load of gold bullion and who find, after this successful but bloody encounter, that the war has been over for a month. Thereafter the harried group, hounded and later trapped in a mountain stage coach station by renegades, greedy for gold but not justice, fight an eventually winning battle against this tough and ruthless opposition.

As a director, Mr. Huggins has centered his cast in plausible situations. The six-shooters and Winchesters are rarely allowed to cool down, the talk is pertinent and there are enough corpses around at the finale to satisfy the most exacting fan. And his principals are human withal. Randolph Scott, as the leader of the embattled Confederates is a troubled but heroic man uncertain as to how to honorably dispose of the loot. Donna Reed, as a Union nurse nabbed as a hostage, is utterly natural as her hate is changed to admiration when she comes to know her captor better. Richard Denning is a weak opportunist as her civilian escort and Claude Jarman Jr., as the callow member of the band; Lee Marvin as the lustful killer and Frank Faylen, as a casually brave "Reb," contribute more meaningful delineation than is usual for this type of muscular play acting.

Although "Hangman's Knot" is only loosely tied to its title, it is a tight little entertainment which does justice to this film form.
A. W.

D 11, 1952

THE STRANGER WORE A GUN: screen play by Kenneth Gamet; based on "Yankee Gold," by John M. Cunningham; directed by André De Toth, produced by Harry Joe Brown; a Scott-Brown Production presented by Columbia.

Jeff Travis .... Randolph Scott
Josie Sullivan .... Claire Trevor
Shelby Conroy .... Joan Weldon
Jules Mourret .... George Macready
Degas .... Alfonso Bedoya
Dan Kurth .... Lee Marvin
Bull Slager .... Ernest Borgnine
Jason Conroy .... Pierre Watkin
Dutch Mueller .... Joseph Vitale
Milt Hooper .... Roscoe Ates
Harve Comis .... Reed Howes
Jim Martin .... Clem Bevans
Poley .... Paul Maxey
Red Glick .... Frank Scannell
Jeb .... Edward Earle
Ike .... Guy Wilkerson

Working with some of the roughest film stereotypes, Randolph Scott, Producer Harry Joe Brown and Columbia Pictures, abetted by Technicolor, three-dimensional photography, stereophonic sound and a wide screen, are proving once again that nothing really new has been added to the Western genre in "The Stranger Wore a Gun."

For this sagebrush saga, which clattered into Loew's State yesterday, is a standard, six-gun adventure, all dressed up but recognizable to any hombre who has been west of the Pecos recently via the movies' magic carpet.

The boys, it should be noted, throw things at the audience with reckless abandon—everything from fists, firebrands, furniture and bullets to a stream of tobacco juice, a gimmick that had been introduced previously. And the view through Polaroid glasses is likely to keep the customers awake, if not continuously startled.

The illusions of roundness and depth so devoutly desired by the producers are apparent, now and again, in the great outdoors, which in this case would be just as spectacular in two dimensions. However, scenes of arid, rock-strewn valleys rimmed by distant, snowy mountain ranges, as well as panoramic vistas from a twisting road, are enhanced by the three-dimensional cameras.

Cliche-Cluttered Tale

The story, on the other hand, gives no illusion of depth. It is as cliché-cluttered as some of the staged bouts and the attempted hold-ups of stagecoaches that abound in this muscular number.

The hero, Mr. Scott, portrays a one-time spy for Quantrell's raiders, who has gotten a bellyful of the outlaw's bloody tactics during the sack of Lawrence, Kan., and becomes involved with some bully boys who are trying to take over post-war Prescott, Ariz.

Although he is a man on the run and is willing to make an unclean dollar, he is basically his usual strong, decent self, a gent who won't see dastardly deeds done, or a town ruined by buccaneers on horseback. Naturally, he sets things straight And, pardner, its hard to tell this Randolph Scott from the scores of heroes he's played before.

The same can be said for Claire Trevor, a gambling lady whose heart belongs to our hero, although she thinks there is competition in the presence of Joan Weldon, pretty daughter of the owner of the stagecoach line. Also, for George Macready, the ringleader and a Southerner but no gentleman, who wants to steal a million dollars out of Prescott, and Alfonso Bedoya, his local opposition for this prospective pot of gold.

Lee Marvin and Ernest Borgnine are villains as familiar as "they went thataway." There's a good chance, come to think of it, that they would hardly be missed if they never came thisaway. A. W.

Jl 30, 1953

THUNDER OVER THE PLAINS, screen play by Russell Hughes; directed by Andre de Toth; produced by David Weisbart for Warner Brothers.
Capt. David Porter..............Randolph Scott
Capt. Bill Hodges..................Lex Barker
Norah..........................Phyllis Kirk
Ben Westman....................Charles McGraw
Lieut. Col. Chandler.............Henry Hull
Standish......................Elisha Cook Jr.
Balfour.........................Hugh Sanders
Faraday.......................Lane Chandler
Conrad..........................James Brown
Kirby...........................Fess Parker
Set. Shaw..................Richard Benjamin
Lieut. Williams...................Mark Dana
Henley..........................Jack Woody
Walter Morgan.................Trevor Bardette
Jurgens.........................Frank Matts
McAvoy.........................Steve Darrell
Auctioneer.....................Earl Hodgins

Square-jawed, indomitable, heroic, incorruptible Randolph Scott, than whom there's no more consistent a pillar of good in Hollywood, is familiarly propping up justice in "Thunder Over the Plains," a routine Warner Brothers western, which came to the Palace yesterday. Fling not a dead cat at the picture nor a missile of scorn at Mr. Scott. It is of such uncomplicated roughage that movie second features are made.

In this particular instance Mr. Scott is in command of a company of cavalrymen in Texas right after the Civil War, valiantly standing in the middle between carpet-baggers and Texas renegades. Battered and badgered on both sides, he gets little comfort or aid from his wife, Phyllis Kirk, a limpid hussy, or his square-headed colonel, Henry Hull. Oppressed, too, by a rival captain (Lex Barker), Mr. Scott perseveres. Being square-jawed, indomitable, heroic and incorruptible, he naturally wins. Texas is admitted to the Union. Mr. Scott is glorified. And the cat-nappers at the Palace are awakened for the eight-act vaudeville bill.   B. C.

D 10, 1953

RIDING SHOTGUN, screen play by Tom Blackburn, from a story by Kenneth Perkins; directed by Andre de Toth; produced by Ted Sherdeman for Warner Brothers. At the Holiday
Larry Delong..................Randolph Scott
Tub Murphy....................Wayne Morris
Orissa Flynn...................Joan Weldon
Tom Biggert......................Joe Sawyer
Dan Marady....................James Millican
Pinto........................Charles Buchinsky
Doc Winkler.....................James Bell

IF Randolph Scott's assignment in "Riding Shotgun," calls for anything he hasn't done before, it's not apparent. In the Warner Brothers Western that opened yesterday at the Holiday the seasoned veteran is in typical, if not top form. Produced by Ted Sherdeman in rather faded-looking WarnerColor, this tired, bony little offering of frontier violence and justice remains about as ordinary as they come.

Once again the lantern-jawed Mr. Scott plays a man among men, a stalwart citizen, mistaken for an outlaw, who has to prove his innocence by wiping out the real varmints single-handed. In case anybody wonders, for Mr. Scott, it's a cinch.

Wayne Morris, Joan Weldon, Joe Sawyer, James Millican, Charles Buchinsky and the others line up on both sides of the hero and the law, waiting for that final, clean sweep. Meanwhile, the gunfire sputters as consistently as the musical background.
                H. H. T.

Ap 2, 1954

RIDE THE HIGH COUNTRY, screen play by N. B. Stone Jr.; directed by Sam Peckinpah; produced by Richard E. Lyons for Metro-Goldwyn-Mayer. At neighborhood theatres. Running time: ninety-four minutes.
Steve Judd.......................Joel McCrea
Gil Westrum...................Randolph Scott
Elsa.........................Mariette Hartley
Heck Longtree...................Ronald Starr
Joshua Knudsen...............R. G. Armstrong
Billy Hammond..................James Drury
Elder Hammond.................John Anderson
Sylvus Hammond................L. Q. Jones
Henry Hammond..................Warren Oates
Judge Tolliver................Edgar Buchanan
and
THE TARTARS, scenario by Sabatino Ciuffini and others; directed by Richard Thorpe; a Lux Film Production, released by Metro-Goldwyn-Mayer. At neighborhood theatres. Running time: eighty-three minutes.
The Tartar Chief................Orson Welles
The Viking Chief...............Victor Mature
The Tartar brother...............Folco Lulli
The Viking wife.................Liana Ortel
The Viking boy...............Luciano Marin
The Viking daughter............Bella Cortez
The Tartar adviser..............Arnaldo Foa

AS for yesterday's new double bill in neighborhood theatres, "The Tartars" (Orson Welles and Victor Mature) is trash and "Ride the High Country" (Joel McCrea and Randolph Scott) is a perfectly dandy little Western.

Let's take care of history first, at least according to Metro-Goldwyn-Mayer, which sponsored the Italian-made color spectacle. Big it is—and loud—and gory, and the biggest thing in sight is Mr. Welles as an evil barbarian chief. At this point in his career he looks like a walking house.

At any rate, Mr. Welles and Mr. Mature, as a noble Viking landlubber, slug it out, as do their yowling armies, trailed by such people as Folco Lulli, Bella Cortez, Luciano Marin and Arnaldo Foa. The last two are quite persuasive. As for the dubbed English, one variation has the "poor Slavs" called "slobs." At least that's what it sounds like in "The Tartars."

In contrast, Metro's uncluttered Western supplement is a downright pleasure to watch. Take two cornbelt veterans like Mr. M
Mr. Scott, give the tangy script (by N. Jr.) a trim supportin. and a good director (Sa. Peckinpah), and you have th. most disarming little horse opera in months."

From the opening scene, when the two stars, as a couple of prairie old-timers, start reminiscing about wilder and woolier days, the picture projects a steady, natural blend of wisdom and humos. Excellently photographed in color against some lovely natural vistas, the picture finds the seasoned derelicts and their young partner, Ronald Starr, protecting a gold shipment (for a change) and salvaging an innocent girl, Mariette Hartley, lusty mining camp.

Symbols of a waning era who eventually clash over right and wrong, Messrs. McCrea and Scott mesh perfectly, with the latter getting the drollest lines — and there are plenty.

In the humor department, the entire film is spur-sharp, though the broad antics of the villains, a cutthroat quartet, could have been toned down somewhat. On the other hand, the salty grotesqueness of a saloon wedding (stunningly tinted) is pure gold. The final line caps the picture like a bottletop.

The two young people are quite good, especially Miss Hartley, a newcomer with real promise. R. M. Armstrong and Edgar Buchanan also contribute telling bits. We know little about the director and scenarist, but Mr. Peckinpah and Mr. Stone certainly have what it takes. And so, if anybody ever doubted it, do a couple of leathery, graying hombres named McCrea and Scott.

Je 21, 1962

THE FILMS

[1] *Sharp Shooters* (Fox) 1928   5,573′ Silent B/W
    Producer: William Fox
    Director: J.G. Blystone
    Scenario: Marion Orth
    Titles: Malcom Stuart Boylan
    From the story "Sharp Shooters" by Randall Faye
    Cast: George O'Brien, Lois Moran, Noah Young, Tom
                        Dugan, William Demarest, Gwen Lee, Josef
                        Swickard, Randolph Scott (unbilled)
    Released: January 15, 1928

[2] *The Far Call* (Fox) 1929   5,313′ Sound B/W   5,282′ Silent B/W
    Producer: William Fox
    Director: Allan Dwan
    Screenplay: Seton I. Miller & H. H. Caldwell
    Cast: Charles Morton, Leila Hyams, Arthur Stone,
                        Warren Hymer, Dan Wolheim, Stanley J.
                        Sandford, Charles Middleton, Charles Gorman,
                        Randolph Scott
    Released: April 28, 1929

[3] *The Black Watch* (Fox) 1929   B/W
    Producer: William Fox
    Director: John Ford
    Screenplay: Talbot Mundy
    Cast: Victor McLaughlin, Myrna Loy, David Rollins,
                        Lumston Hare, Roy D'Orcy, Randolph Scott
                        (unbilled)
    Released: May, 1929

[4] *The Virginian* (Paramount) 1929   90 Mins (8,717′)—Sound B/W
    Producer: Louis D. Lighton
    Director: Victor Fleming
    Screenplay: Howard Estabrook
    From the book "The Virginian" by Owen Wister

Titles:	Joseph L. Mankiewicz
Assistant Director:	Henry Hathaway
Cast:	Gary Cooper, Walter Huston, Richard Arlen, Mary Brian, Chester Conklin, Eugene Pallette, E. H. Calvert, Helen Ware, Vic Potel, Tex Young, Charles Stevens, Jack Pennick, George Chandler, Willie Fung, George Morrell, Ernie Adams, Ethan Laidlaw, Ed Brady, Bob Kortman, James Mason, Fred Burns, Nena Quartero, Randolph Scott (unbilled)
Released:	November 9, 1929

[5] *Dynamite* (Pathe') 1929   11,584' (127 min.) Sound B/W   10,771' Silent B/W

Producer:	Cecil B. DeMille
Director:	Cecil B. DeMille
Screenplay:	Jeanie Macpherson
Cast:	Conrad Nagel, Kay Johnson, Charles Bickford, Julia Faye, Joel McCrea, Muriel McCormac, Robert Edison, William Holden, Randolph Scott
Released:	December 13, 1929

[6] *The Women Men Marry* (Headline) 1931   Sound B/W

Producer:	Charles Hutchison
Director:	Charles Hutchison
Screenplay:	John Francis Natteford
Cast:	Natalie Moorhead, Sally Blaine, Randolph Scott, Kenneth Harlan, Craufurd Kent, James Aubrey
Released:	March 21, 1931

[7] *Sky Bride* (Paramount) 1932   8 reels   Sound B/W

Producer:	Paramount Publix
Director:	Stephen Roberts
Screenplay:	Joseph L. Mankiewicz, Agnes Brad Leahy and Grover Jones

Cast: Warner Baxter, Marian Nixon, Rita Laroy,
Lucille Powers, William Pawley, David Landau,
John Breslau, Randolph Scott

Released: April 28, 1932

[8] *A Successful Calamity* (Warner Bros.) 1932 75 min. B/W

Producer: Paramount Publix
Director: John G. Adolphi
Screenplay: Austin Parker, Maude Howell, Julien Josephson
From the play by Clare Kummer
Cast: Hale Hamilton, Randolph Scott, George Arliss,
Mary Astor, Evelyn Knapp, Grant Mitchell,
David Torrence, William Janney

Released: September 19, 1932

[9] *Heritage Of The Desert* (Paramount) 1932 63 min. B/W

Producer: Paramount Publix
Director: Henry Hathaway
Screenplay: Harold Shumate & Frank Partos
From the book "Heritage of the Desert" by Zane Grey
Cast: Randolph Scott, Sally Blaine, Vince Barnett,
Guinn Williams, J. Farrell MacDonald, David
Landau, Gordon Westcott, Susan Fleming,
Charles Stevens, Fred Burns

Released: September 30, 1932

[10] *Hot Saturday* (Paramount) 1932 73 min. B/W

Producer: Paramount Publix
Director: William A. Seiter
Screenplay: Seton I. Miller
Adapted by: Josephine Lovett & Joseph M. March
From the book "Hot Saturday" by Harvey Ferguson
Cast: Nancy Carroll, Cary Grant, Randolph Scott,
Edward Woods, Lillian Bond, William Collier Sr.,
Jane Darwell, Rita LaRoy, Rose Coughlan, Oscar
Appel, Jessie Arnold, Grady Sutton

[11] *Wild Horse Mesa* (Paramount) 1932   65 min. B/W
  Producer: Paramount Publix
  Director: Henry Hathaway
  Screenplay: Frank Clark & Harold Shumate
  From the book, "Wild Horse Mesa" by Zane Grey
  Cast: Randolph Scott, Sally Blaine, Fred Kohler, James
                     Bush, George Hayes, Charley Grapewin, Buddy
                     Roosevelt, Lucille LaVerne, Jim Thorpe, E. H.
                     Calvert
  Released: November 25, 1932

[12] *Hello Everybody!* (Paramount) 1933   B/W
  Producer: Paramount Publix
  Director: William A. Seiter
  From a story by Fannie Hurst
  Cast: Kate Smith, Randolph Scott, Sally Blaine,
                     Charley Grapewin, George Barbier, Fern
                     Emmett, Frank Darien, Julia Swayne Gordon,
                     Wade Boteler, Jerry Tucker, Marguerite
                     Campbell, Frank McGlynn Sr., Erville Alderson,
                     Jack Pennick, Edward Davis, Ted Collins,
                     Hallene Hill, Paul Kruger, Lon Poff
  Released: January 30, 1933

[13] *The Thundering Herd* (Paramount) 1933   59 min. B/W
  Producer: Paramount Publix
  Director: Henry Hathaway
  Screenplay: Jack Cunningham & Mary Flannery
  From the book "The Thundering Herd" by Zane Grey
  Cast: Randolph Scott, Judith Allen, Barton MacLane,
                     Harry Carey, Larry "Buster" Crabbe, Dick
                     Rush, Frank Rice, Buck Conners, Charles
                     Murphy, Noah Beery Sr., Raymond Hatton,
                     Blanche Frederici, Monte Blue, Al Bridge
  Released: March 1, 1933
  Re-issued as *Buffalo Stampede*

[14] *Murders In The Zoo* (Paramount) 1933   64 min. B/W
    Producer: Paramount Publix
    Director: Edward Sutherland
    Screenplay: Phillip Wylie, Seton I. Miller
    Cast: Charles Ruggles, Lionel Atwill, Gail Patrick, Randolph Scott, John Lodge, Kathleen Burke, Harry Beresford, Edward McWade
    Released: March 30, 1933

[15] *Supernatural* (Paramount) 1933   67 min. B/W
    Producers: Victor & Edward Halperin
    Director: Victor Halperin
    Screenplay: Harvey Thew, Brian Marlowe
    From the story "Supernatural" by Garnett Weston
    Cast: Carole Lombard, Randolph Scott, Vivienne Osborne, Allan Dinehart, H. B. Warner, Beryl Mercer, William Farnum
    Released: May 4, 1933

[16] *Sunset Pass* (Paramount) 1933   61 min. B/W
    Producer: Paramount Publix
    Director: Henry Hathaway
    Screenplay: Jack Cunningham & Gerald Geraghty
    From the book "Sunset Pass" by Zane Grey
    Cast: Randolph Scott, Tom Keene, Kathleen Burke, Harry Carey, Fuzzy Knight, Noah Berry, Vince Barnett, Kent Taylor, Tom London, Pat Farley, Charles Middleton, Bob Kortman, James Mason, Frank Beal, Al Bridge, Leila Bennett, Nelson McDowell, George Barbier, Christian J. Frank
    Released: May 26, 1933

[17] *Cocktail Hour* (Columbia) 1933   8 reels B/W
    Producer: Columbia Pictures Corp.
    Director: Victor Schertzinger

Screenplay: Gertrude Purcell, Richard Sayer
From the book "Pearls & Emeralds" by James K. McGuiness
Cast: Bebe Daniels, Randolph Scott, Muriel Kirkland,
                 Jessie Ralph, Sidney Blackmer, Barry Norton,
                 Phillips Smalley, Marjorie Gateson, Paul McVey
Released: May 29, 1933

[18] *Man Of The Forest* (Paramount) 1933   62 min. B/W
     Producer: Paramount Publix
     Director: Henry Hathaway
     Screenplay: Jack Cunningham & Harold Shumate
     From the book "Man of the Forest" by Zane Grey
     Cast: Randolph Scott, Harry Carey, Verna Hillie, Noah
                      Beery, Larry "Buster" Crabbe, Barton MacLane,
                      Guinn Williams, Vince Barnett, Blanche
                      Frederici, Tempe Piggot, Tom Kennedy, Frank
                      McGlynn Jr., Duke Lee, Lew Kelly, Merrill
                      McCormack
     Released: August 25, 1933

[19] *To The Last Man* (Paramount) 1933   70 min. B/W
     Producer: Paramount Publix
     Director: Henry Hathaway
     Screenplay: Jack Cunningham
     From the book "To The Last Man" by Zane Grey
     Cast: Randolph Scott, Esther Ralsron, Noah Beery,
                      Jack LaRue, Larry "Buster" Crabbe, Fuzzy
                      Knight, Barton MacLane, Gail Patrick, Muriel
                      Kirkland, Egon Brecher, James Eagles, Eugenie
                      Besserer, Harlan Knight, Shirley Temple
     Released: September 15, 1933

[20] *Broken Dreams* (Monogram) 1934   70 min. B/W
     Producer: Ben Verschleiser
     Director: Robert Vignola

Screenplay: Maude Fulton
From the story "Broken Dreams" by Olga Printzlau
Cast: Randolph Scott, Martha Sleeper, Joseph
                  Cawthorne, Beryl Mercer, Buster Phelps,
                  Charlotte Merriam, Sidney Bracy
Released: January 15, 1934

[21] *The Last Roundup* (Paramount) 1934   65 min. B/W
    Producer: Paramount Publix
    Director: Henry Hathaway
    Screenplay: Jack Cunningham
    From the book "The Border Legion" by Zane Grey
    Cast: Randolph Scott, Barbara Fritchie, Barton
                  MacLane, Fuzzy Knight, Monte Blue, Charles
                  Middleton, Richard Carle, Dick Rush, Ben
                  Corbett, Fred Kohler, James Mason, Bud
                  Osborne, Bob Miles, Buck Connors, Frank Rice,
                  Jim Corey, Sam Allen, Jack M. Holmes
    Released: May 1, 1934

[22] *Wagon Wheels* (Paramount) 1934   56 min. B/W
    Producer: Paramount Publix
    Director: Charles Barton
    Screenplay: Jack Cunningham, Charles Logan & Carl A. Buss
    From the book "Fighting Caravans" by Zane Grey
    Cast: Randolph Scott, Gail Patrick, Billie Lee, Leila
                  Bennett, Jan Duggan, Monte Blue, Raymond
                  Hatton, Olin Howland, J. P. McGowan, James
                  Marcus, Helen Hunt, James Kenton, Alfred
                  Delcambre, John Marston, Sam McDaniels,
                  Howard Wilson, Michael Visaroff, Julian
                  Madison, Eldred Tidbury, E. Alyn Warren,
                  Pauline Moore
    Released: September 15, 1934

[23] *Home On The Range* (Paramount) 1935   65 min. B/W
    Producer: Harold Hurley
    Director: Arthur Jacobson
    Screenplay: Harold Shumate
    From the book "Code of the West" by Zane Grey
    Cast: Randolph Scott, Ann Sheridan, Dean Jagger,
                           Jackie Coogan, Fuzzy Knight, Ralph Remley,
                           Philip Morris, Frances Sayles, Addison Richards,
                           Clarence Sherwood, Evelyn Brent, Allen Wood,
                           Howard Wilson, Albert Hart, Richard Carle
    Released: February 1, 1935

[24] *Rocky Mountain Mystery* (Paramount) 1935   63 min. B/W
    Producer: Harold Hurley
    Director: Charles Barton
    Screenplay: Edward E. Patemore Jr. and Ethyl Doherty
    From the book "Golden Dreams" by Zane Grey
    Cast: Randolph Scott, Charles "Chic" Sale, Mrs. Leslie
                           Carter, Kathleen Burke, George Marion Sr., Ann
                           Sheridan, James C. Eagles, Howard Wilson,
                           Willie Fung, Florence Roberts
    Released: March 1, 1935
    Also released as: *The Fighting Westerner*

[25] *Roberta* (RKO) 1935   105 min. B/W
    Producer: Pandro S. Berman
    Director: William A. Seiter
    Screenplay: Jane Murfin, Sam Mintz, Allan Scott and Glenn
                           Tryon
    From the musical play "Roberta" by Jerome Kern, Otto Harbach,
                           Dorothy Fields and Jimmy McHugh
    Cast: Fred Astaire, Ginger Rogers, Irene Dunne,
                           Randolph Scott, Helen Westley, Victor Varconi,
                           Claire Dodd, Louis Alberni, Ferdnand Munier
    Released: March 7, 1935

[26] *Village Tale* (RKO) 1935   9 reels B/W
    Producer: Radio Pictures Inc.
    Director: John Cromwell
    Screenplay: Allan Scott
    From the book "Village Tale" by Phil Strong
    Cast: Randolph Scott
    Released: May 10, 1935

[27] *She* (RKO) 1935   11 reels B/W
    Producer: Merian C. Cooper
    Directors: Irving Pichel, Lansing C. Holden
    Screenplay: Ruth Rose, Dudley Nichols
    From the book "She" by H. Rider Haggard
    Cast: Helen Gahagan, Randolph Scott, Helen Mack,
                        Nigel Bruce, Samuel S. Hinds, Noble Johnson,
                        Lumsden Hare
    Released: July 12, 1935

[28] *So Red The Rose* (Paramount) 1935   83 min. B/W
    Executive Producer: Adolph Zukor
    Producer: Douglas MacLean
    Director: King Vidor
    Screenplay: Laurence Stallings, Maxwell Anderson, Edwin
                        Justus Mayer
    From the book "So Red The Rose" by Stark Young
    Cast: Margaret Sullivan, Walter Connelly, Randolph
                        Scott, Janet Beecher, Elizabeth Patterson, Dickie
                        Moore, Harry Ellerbe, Robert Cummings,
                        Charles Starrett, Johnny Downs, Daniel Haynes,
                        James Burke, Warner Richmond
    Released: November 22, 1935

[29] *Follow The Fleet* (RKO Radio) 1936   110 min. B/W
    Producer: Pandro S. Berman
    Director: Mark Sandrich

Screenplay:	Dwight Taylor and Allan Scott
Music and	
Lyrics by:	Irving Berlin

From the play "Shore Leave" by Hubert Osborne

Cast:	Fred Astaire, Ginger Rogers, Randolph Scott,
	Harriet Hilliard, Astrid Allwyn, Ray Mayer,
	Harry Beresford, Addison Randall, Lucille Ball,
	Betty Grable, Joy Hodges, Jeanne Grey
Released:	February 20, 1936

[30] *And Sudden Death* (Paramount) 1936   70 min. B/W

Producer:	Adolph Zukor
Director:	Charles Barton
Screenplay:	Joseph M. March

From the story by Theodore Reeves

Cast:	Randolph Scott, Frances Drake, Tom Brown,
	Billy Lee, Fuzzy Knight, Terry Walker, Porter
	Hall, Charles Quigley, John Hyams, Joseph
	Sawyer, Oscar Apfel, Don Rowan, Jimmy Conlin,
	Maidel Turner, Charles Arnt
Released:	July 3, 1936

[31] *The Last Of The Mohicans* (United Artists) 1936   91 min. B/W

Producer:	Edward Small
Director:	George B. Seitz
Screenplay:	Philip Dunne

From the book "The Last of the Mohicans" by James Fenimore Cooper

Cast:	Randolph Scott, Binnie Barnes, Henry Wilcoxin,
	Bruce Cabot, Heather Angel, Philip Reed,
	Robert Barrat, Hugh Buckler, Willard
	Robertson, Frank McGlynn Sr., Will Stanton,
	William V. Mong, Reginald Barlow, Olaf H.
	Hare, Lionel Belmore
Released:	September 4, 1936

[32] *Go West Young Man* (Paramount) 1936   80 min. B/W
    Producer: Emanuel Cohen
    Director: Henry Hathaway
    Screenplay: Mae West
    Cast: Mae West, Randolph Scott, Warren Williams,
                              Alice Brady, Elizabeth Patterson, Lyle Talbot,
                              Isabel Jewell, Margaret Perry
    Released: November 19, 1936

[33] *High Wide And Handsome* (Paramount) 1937   104 min. B/W
    Executive Producer: Adolph Zukor
    Producer: Arthur Hornblow
    Director: Rouben Malmoulian
    Screenplay: Oscar Hammerstein II
    Book & Lyrics: Oscar Hammerstein II
    Music: Jerome Kern
    Cast: Irene Dunne, Randolph Scott, Dorothy Lamour,
                              Raymond Walburn, Charles Bickford, Elizabeth
                              Patterson, William Frawley, Akim Tamiroff, Ben
                              Blue, Alan Hale, Irving Pichel, Helen Lowell,
                              Stanley Andrews
    Released: October 1, 1937

[34] *Rebecca Of Sunnybrook Farm* (Fox) 1938   80 min. B/W
    Producer: William Fox
    Director: Allan Dwan
    Screenplay: Karl Tunberg, Don Ettinger
    From the book "Rebecca of Sunnybrook Farm" by Kate Douglas
                    Wiggin
    Cast: Shirley Temple, Randolph Scott, Jack Haley,
                              Gloria Stuart, Phyllis Brooks, Helen Westley,
                              Slim Summerville, Bill Robinson, Allan Dinehart,
                              J. Edward Bromberg, Paul Hurst, William
                              Demarest, Paul Harvey
    Released: March 18, 1938

[35] *The Road To Reno* (Universal) 1938   72 min. B/W
    Producer: Edmund Grainger
    Director: S. Sylvan Simon
    Screenplay: Ray Chanslor and Comandini
    Story: Charles Kenyon and F. Hugh Herbert
    From the book "Puritan At Large" by I.A.R. Wylie
    Cast: Randolph Scott, Hope Hampton, Glenda Farrell,
                        Helen Broderick, Alan Marshall, David Oliver,
                        Ted Osborn, Sam S. Hinds, Charles Murphy,
                        Spencer Charters, Dorothy Farley, Mira
                        McKinney, Renie Riano
    Released: August, 1938.

[36] *The Texans* (Paramount) 1938   92 min. B/W
    Producer: Lucien Hubbard
    Director: James Hogan
    Screenplay: Bertrand Millhauser, Paul Sloane, William Wister
                        Haines
    From the book "North of '36" by Emerson Hough
    Cast: Randolph Scott, Joan Bennett, May Robson,
                        Walter Brennan, Robert Cummings, Robert
                        Barrat, Harvey Stephens, Francis Ford,
                        Raymond Hatton, Clarence Wilson, Jack Moore,
                        Chris-Pin-Martin, Anna Demetrio, Richard
                        Tucker, Ed Gargan, Otis Harlan, Spencer
                        Charters, Archie Twitchell, William Haade,
                        Irving Bacon, Bill Roberts, Francis MacDonald
    Released: August 12, 1938

[37] *Jesse James* (Fox) 1939   105 min. Technicolor
    Producer: Nunnally Johnson
    Director: Henry King
    Screenplay: Nunnally Johnson
    Cast: Tyrone Power, Henry Fonda, Nancy Kelly,
                        Randolph Scott, Henry Hull, Slim Summerville,

J. Edward Bromberg, Brian Donlevy, John
Carradine, Donald Meek, John Russell, Jane
Darwell, George Chandler, Charles Tannen,
Claire Dubrey, Willard Robertson, Harold
Goodwin, Ernest Whitman, Eddy Waller, Paul
Burns, Spencer Charters, Arthur Aylesworth,
Charles Middleton, Charles Halton, Harry Tyler,
Virginia Brissac, Edward J. LeSaint, John
Elliott, Erville Alderson, George Breakston, Lon
Chaney Jr., Ernest Whitman, James Flavin,
Harry Holman, Wylie Grant, Ethan Laidlaw, Don
Douglas, George O'Hara

Released: January 27, 1939

[38] *Susanna Of The Mounties* (Fox) 1939   78 min. Sepiatone

Producer: Keneth MacGowan

Director: William A. Seiter

Screenplay: Fidel La Barba, Walter Ferris, Robert Ellis,
Helen Logan

From the book "Susannah, A Little Girl of the Mounties" by Muriel
Denison

Cast: Shirley Temple, Randolph Scott, Margaret
Lockwood, Martin Good Rider, J. Farrell
MacDonald, Maurice Moscovich, Moroni Olson,
Victor Jory, Lester Matthews, Leyland Hodges,
Herbert Evans, Jack Luden, Charles Irwin, John
Sutton, Chief Big Tree

Released: June 13, 1939

[39] *Frontier Marshal* (Fox) 1939   71 min. B/W

Producer: Sol Wurtzel

Director: Allan Dwan

Screenplay: Sam Hellman

From the book "Wyatt Earp, Frontier Marshal" by Stuart Lake

Cast: Randolph Scott, Nancy Kelly, Cesar Romero,

Binnie Barnes, John Carradine, Edward Norris,
Eddie Foy Jr., Ward Bond, Lon Chaney Jr., Tom
Tyler, Joe Sawyer, Del Henderson, Harry
Hayden
Released: July 28, 1939

[40] *Coast Guard* (Columbia) 1939 70 min. B/W
Producer: Columbia Pictures Corp.
Director: Edward Ludwig
Screenplay: Richard Maibuam, Albert Duffy, Harry Segall
Cast: Randolph Scott, Ralph Bellamy, Frances Dee,
Walter Connolly, Warren Hymer, Robert
Middlemass, Stanley Andrews, Edmund
McDonald
Released: August 4, 1939

[41] *20,000 Men A Year* (Fox) 1939 7,656′ B/W
Producer: Twentieth Century-Fox
Director: Alfred E. Green
Screenplay: Lew Breslow, Owen Francis
From a story by Frank Wead
Cast: Randolph Scott, Robert Preston, Margaret
Lindsay, Mary Healy, Robert Shaw, George
Ernest, Jane Darwell, Kane Richmond, Maxie
Rosenbloom, Douglas Wood, Sen Young, Paul
Stanton
Released: October 27, 1939

[42] *Virginia City* (Warner Bros.) 1940 121 min. B/W
Producer: Robert Fellows
Director: Michael Curtiz
Screenplay: Robert Henry Buckner
Cast: Errol Flynn, Miriam Hopkins, Randolph Scott,
Humphrey Bogart, Frank McHugh, Alan Hale,
Guin (Big Boy) Williams, John Litel, Douglass

Dumbrille, Moroni Olson, Russell Hicks, Dickie
Jones, Frank Wilcox, Russell Simpson, Victor
Kilian, Charles Middleton

Released: March 23, 1940

[43] *My Favorite Wife* (RKO Radio) 1940   88 min. B/W
Producer: Leo McCarey
Director: Garson Kanin
Screenplay: Bella Spewack, Samuel Spewack, Leo McCarey
Cast: Irene Dunne, Cary Grant, Randolph Scott, Gail
                  Patrick, Ann Shoemaker, Scotty Beckett, Mary
                  Lou Harrington, Donald MacBride, Hugh
                  O'Connell, Granville Bates, Pedro De Cordoba
Released: May 17, 1940

[44] *When The Daltons Rode* (Universal) 1940   80 min. B/W
Producer: Universal Pictures
Director: George Marshall
Screenplay: Harold Shumate
From the book "When the Daltons Rode" by Emmett Dalton, Jack
                  Jungmeyer Sr.
Cast: Randolph Scott, Kay Francis, Brian Donlevy,
                  George Bancroft, Broderick Crawford, Andy
                  Devine, Stuart Erwin, Frank Albertson, Mary
                  Gordon, Harvey Stevens, Edgar Dearing, Quen
                  Ramsey, Bob McKenzie, Dorothy Granger, Fay
                  McKenzie, Walter Sodering, Mary Ainslee,
                  Erville Alderson, Sally Payne, June Wilkins
Released: July 26, 1940

[45] *Western Union* (Fox) 1941   94 min. B/W
Producer: Harry Joe Brown
Director: Fritz Lang
Screenplay: Robert Carson
From the book "Western Union" by Zane Grey

Cast:	Robert Young, Randolph Scott, Dean Jagger, Virginia Gilmore, John Carradine, Slim Summerville, Chill Wills, Barton MacLane, Russell Hicks, Victor Kilian, Minor Watson, George Chandler, Chief Big Tree, Chief Thunder Cloud, Dick Rich, Harry Strange, Charles Middleton, Addison Richards, Irving Bacon
Released:	February 21, 1941

[46] *Belle Starr* (Fox) 1941   87 min. B/W

Producer:	Kenneth MacGowan
Director:	Irvin Cummings
Screenplay:	Lamar Trotti

From a story by Niven Busch, Cameron Rogers

Cast:	Randolph Scott, Gene Tierney, Dana Andrews, John Sheppard, Elizabeth Patterson, Chill Wills, Louise Beavers, Olin Howlin, Paul Burns, Joseph Sawyer, Joseph Downing, Howard Hickman, Charles Trowbridge, James Flavin, Charles Middleton, Clarence Muse, George Melford, Mae Marsh, Herbert Ashley, Norman Willis, Billy Wayne, George Reed, Davidson Clark, Hugh Chapman, Clinton Rosemond
Released:	September 12, 1941

[47] *Paris Calling* (Universal) 1941   108 min. B/W

Producer:	Benjamin Glazer
Director:	Edwin L. Marin
Screenplay:	Benjamin Glazer and Charles S. Kaufman
Cast:	Elisabeth Bergner, Randolph Scott, Basil Rathbone, Gale Sondergaard, Lee J. Cobb, Charles Arnt, Eduardo Ciannelli, Elisabeth Risdon, George Renavent, William Edmunds, Gene Garrick, Ian Wolfe, Mary Forbest
Released:	December, 1941

[48] *To The Shores of Tripoli* (Fox) 1942   86 min. Technicolor

Producer:	Twentieth Century-Fox Film Corp.
Associate Producer:	Milton Sperling
Director:	Bruce Humberstone
Screenplay:	Lamar Trotti
Cast:	Randolph Scott, John Payne, Maureen O'Hara, Nancy Kelly, William Tracy, Maxie Rosenbloom, Iris Adrian
Released:	March 26, 1942

[49] *The Spoilers* (Universal) 1942   87 min. B/W

Producer:	Frank Lloyd
Director:	Ray Enright
Screenplay:	Tom Reed

From the book "The Spoilers" by Rex Beach

Cast:	Marlene Dietrich, Randolph Scott, John Wayne, Margaret Lindsay, Harry Carey, Richard Barthelmess, William Farnum, George Cleveland, Samuel S. Hinds, Russell Simpson, Marietta Canty, Jack Norton, Ray Bennett, Forrest Taylor, Art Miles, Charles McMurphy, Charles Halton, Bud Osborne, Robert W. Service
Released:	April 10, 1942

[50] *Pittsburgh* (Universal) 1942   98 min. B/W

Producer:	Charles K. Feldman
Director:	Lewis Seiler
Screenplay:	George Owen and Tom Reed
Cast:	Marlene Dietrich, Randolph Scott, John Wayne, Frank Craven, Louise Allbritton, Shemp Howard, Thomas Gomez, Ludwig Stossell, Samuel S. Hinds, Paul Fix, William Haade, Douglas Fowley, Nestor Paiva, Virginia Sale
Released:	December 1942

[51] *The Desperadoes* (Columbia) 1943 85 min. Technicolor
    Producer: Harry Joe Brown
    Director: Charles Vidor
    Screenplay: Robert Carson
    From the book "The Desperadoes" by Max Brand
    Cast: Randolph Scott, Glenn Ford, Claire Trevor, Edgar Buchanan, Guinn (Big Boy) Williams, Evelyn Keyes, Raymond Walburn, Porter Hall, Joan Woodbury, Bernard Nedell, Irving Beacon, Glenn Strange, Ethan Laidlaw, Slim Whitaker, Edward Pawley, Chester Clute, Bill Wolfe, Francis Ford, Tom Smith, Jack Kinney, Silver Harr
    Released: May 25, 1943

[52] *Bombardier* (RKO) 1943 99 min. B/W
    Producer: Robert Fellows
    Director: Richard Wallace
    Screenplay: John Twist
    From the story by John Twist and Martin Rackin
    Cast: Pat O'Brien, Randolph Scott, Anne Shirley, Eddie Albert, Walter Reed, Robert Ryan, Barton MacLane, Leonard Strong, Richard Martin, Russell Wade, James Newill, Charles Russell
    Released: July 2, 1943

[53] *Corvette K-225* (Universal) 1943 91 min. B/W
    Producer: Howard Hawks
    Director: Richard Rossen
    Screenplay: John Rhodes
    Cast: Randolph Scott, Ella Raines, James Brown, Noah Beery Jr., Barry Fitzgerald, John Frederick, Holmes Herbert, Andy Devine, Fuzzy Knight, David Bruce, Thomas Gomez, Richard Lane, Walter Sande, Peter Lawford, Milburn Stone, Oscar O'Shea, James Flavin

Released: September, 1943

[54] *Gung Ho!* (Universal) 1943   88 min. B/W
    Producer: Walter Wanger
    Director: Ray Enright
    Screenplay: Lucien Hubbard
    From the story "Gung Ho!" by Capt. W. S. LeFrancois, USMC
    Cast: Randolph Scott, Grace McDonald, Alan Curtis,
                  Noah Beery Jr., J. Carrol Naish, David Bruce,
                  Peter Coe, Louis Jean Heydt, Robert Mitchum,
                  Richard Lane, Rod Cameron, Sam Levene,
                  Milburn Stone, Harold Landon, John James
    Released: December, 1943

[55] *Follow The Boys* (Universal) 1944   122 min. B/W
    Producer: Charles K. Feldman
    Director: Edward Sutherland
    Screenplay: Lou Breslow and Gertrude Purcell
    Music: Leigh Harline
    Cast: Large cast of about 150 appeared in speaking
                  parts. In addition, about 50 stars appeared as
                  themselves. Randolph Scott appeared as himself
                  in the "Hollywood Victory Committee" scene.
    Released: March 1944

[56] *Belle Of The Yukon* (RKO) 1944   89 min. B/W
    Producer: William A. Seiter
    Director: William A. Seiter
    Screenplay: James Edward Grant
    From the story by Houston Branch
    Cast: Randolph Scott, Gypsy Rose Lee, Dinah Shore,
                  Bob Burns, Charles Winninger, William Marshall,
                  Guin (Big Boy) Williams, Robert Armstrong,
                  Florence Bates, Edward Fielding, Wanda
                  McKay, Charles Soldani

Released: December 6, 1944

[57] *China Sky* (RKO) 1945   78 min. B/W
    Producer: Maurice Garaghty
    Director: Ray Enright
    Screenplay: Brenda Weisberg, Joseph Hoffman
    From the book "China Sky" by Pearl S. Buck
    Cast: Randolph Scott, Ruth Warrick, Ellen Drew,
                             Anthony Quinn, Carol Thurston, Richard Loo,
                             Ducky Louie, Philip Ahn, Benson Fong
    Released: May 15, 1945

[58] *Captain Kidd* (United Artists) 1945   89 min. B/W
    Producer: Benedict Bogeaus
    Director: Rowland V. Lee
    Screenplay: Norman Reilly Raine
    From the story by Robert N. Lee
    Cast: Charles Laughton, Randolph Scott, Barbara
                             Britton, Reginald Own, John Carradine, Gilbert
                             Roland, Sheldon Leonard, Henry Danielle, John
                             Qualen, William Farnum
    Released: November 23, 1945

[59] *Abilene Town* (United Artists) 1946   89 min. B/W
    Producer: Jules Levey
    Director: Edwin L. Marin
    Screenplay: Harold Shumate
    From the book "Trail Town" by Ernest Haycox
    Cast: Randolph Scott, Ann Dvorak, Edgar Buchanan,
                             Rhonda Fleming, Lloyd Bridges, Helen Boyce,
                             Howard Freeman, Richard Hale, Jack Lambert,
                             Hank Patterson, Dick Curtis, Eddy Waller
    Released: January 11, 1946

[60] *Badman's Territory* (RKO) 1946   98 min. B/W
    Producer: Nat Holt
    Director: Tim Whelan
    Screenplay: Jack Natteford, Luci Ward
    Cast: Randolph Scott, Ann Richards, George Hayes,
                           Lawrence Tierney, Tom Tyler, John Halloran,
                           Phil Warren, Steve Brodie, William Moss, James
                           Warren, Isabel Jewell, Morgan Conway, Nestor
                           Paiva, Chief Thunder Cloud, Ray Collins,
                           Virginia Sale, Andrew Tombes, Harry Holman,
                           Richard Hale, Emory Parnell, Ethan Laidlaw,
                           Kermit Maynard, Bud Osborne, Chuck Hamilton
    Released: April 22, 1946

[61] *Home, Sweet Homicide* (Fox) 1946   90 min. B/W
    Producer: Louis D. Lighton
    Director: Lloyd Bacon
    Screenplay: F. Hugh Herbert
    From the book "Home, Sweet Homicide" by Craig Rice.
    Cast: Peggy Ann Garner, Randolph Scott, Lynn Bari,
                           Dean Stockwell, Connie Marshall, James Gleason,
                           Anabel Shaw, Barbara Whiting, John Sheppard,
                           Stanley Logan, Olin Howlin
    Released: September 12, 1946

[62] *Trail Street* (RKO-Radio) 1947   84 min. B/W
    Producer: Nat Holt
    Director: Ray Enright
    Screenplay: Norman Houston, Gene Lewis
    From the story by William Corcoran
    Cast: Randolph Scott, Robert Ryan, Anne Jeffreys,
                           George Hayes, Madge Meredith, Steve Brodie,
                           Billy House, Virginia Sale, Harry Woods, Phil
                           Warren, Harry Harvey, Jason Robards Sr.,
                           Forrest Taylor, Kit Guard, Stanley Andrews,

Sarah Padden, Frank McGlynn Jr., Ernie Adams,
Roy Butler, Jessie Arnold, Guy Beach, Warren
Jackson, Billy Vincent, Frank Austin, Betty Hill,
Larry McGrath, Chris Willowbird

Released: February 19, 1947

[63] *Gunfighters* (Columbia) 1947   87 min. Cinecolor
Producer: Harry Joe Brown
Director: George Waggner
Screenplay: Alan LeMay
From the book "Twin Sombreros" by Zane Grey
Cast: Randolph Scott, Barbara Britton, Dorothy Hart,
Bruce Cabot, Charley Grapewin, Steven Geray,
Forrest Tucker, Charles Kemper, Grant Withers,
John Miles, Griff Barnett
Released: July 1, 1947

[64] *Christmas Eve* (United Artists) 1947   90 min. B/W
Producer: Benedict Bogeaus
Director: Edwin L. Marin
Screenplay: Laurence Stallings
Cast: Randolph Scott, George Raft, George Brent, Ann
Harding, Joan Blondell, Virginia Field, Reginald
Denny, Dolores Moran, Clarence Kolb, Joe
Sawyer, Walter Sande
Released: November 28, 1947

[65] *Albuquerque* (Paramount) 1948   90 min. Cinecolor
Director: Ray Enright
Screenplay: Gene Lewis, Clarence Upson Young
From the book by Luke Short.
Cast: Randolph Scott, Barbara Britton, George Hayes,
Russell Hayden, Lon Chaney Jr., Catherine
Craig, George Cleveland, Irving Bacon, Bernard

Nedell, Karolyn Grimes, Russell Simpson, Jody
Gilbert, Dan White, Walter Baldwin, John
Halloran

Released: February 20, 1948

[66] *Coroner Creek* (Columbia) 1948   90 min. Cinecolor

Producer: Harry Joe Brown
Director: Ray Enright
Screenplay: Kenneth Gamet
From the book "Coroner Creek" by Luke Short
Cast: Randolph Scott, Marguerite Chapman, George
Macready, Sally Eilers, Edgar Buchanan,
Barbara Reed, Wallace Ford, Forrest Tucker,
William Bishop, Joe Sawyer, Russell Simpson,
Douglas Fowley, Lee Bennett, Forrest Taylor,
Phil Shumaker, Warren Jackson

Released: July 1, 1948

[67] *Return Of The Badmen* (RKO) 1948   96 min. B/W

Producer: Nat Holt
Director: Ray Enright
Screenplay: Charles O'Neal, Jack Natteford, Luci Ward
Cast: Randolph Scott, Robert Ryan, Anne Jeffreys,
George Hayes, Jacqueline White, Richard Powers
(Tom Keene), Tom Tyler, Steve Brodie, Robert
Bray, Lex Barker, Walter Reed, Michael
Harvey, Dan White, Robert Armstrong, Lew
Harvey, Gary Gray, Walter Baldwin, Minna
Gombell, Warren Jackson, Robert Clarke, Jason
Robards Sr., Ernie Adams, Bud Osborne,
Forrest Taylor, Lane Chandler, Charles Stevens,
Kenneth MacDonald, Earle Hodgins, Harry
Shannon, Larry McGrath, Billy Vincent, Brandon
Beach, Ida Moore, John Hamilton, Charles McAvoy

Released: July 17, 1948

[68] *Canadian Pacific* (Fox) 1949   95 min. Color
    Producer: Nat Holt
    Director: Edwin L. Marin
    Screenplay: Jack DeWitt, Kenneth Gamet
    Cast: Randolph Scott, Jane Wyatt, J. Carroll Naish,
        Victor Jory, Nancy Olson, Robert Barratt, Walter
        Sande, Don Haggerty, John Parrish, John
        Hamilton
    Released: May 20, 1949

[69] *The Walking Hills* (Columbia) 1949   78 min. B/W
    A Scott-Brown Production
    Producer: Harry Joe Brown
    Director: John Sturges
    Screenplay: Alan LeMay
    From the story by Alan LeMay
    Cast: Randolph Scott, Ella Raines, William Bishop,
        Edgar Buchanan, Arthur Kennedy, John Ireland,
        Jerome Courtland, Josh White, Russell Collins,
        Charles Stevens, Houseley Stevenson, Reed
        Howes
    Released: March, 1949

[70] *The Doolins Of Oklahoma* (Columbia) 1949   90 min. B/W
    A Scott-Brown Production
    Producer: Harry Joe Brown
    Director: Gordon Douglas
    Screenplay: Kenneth Gamet
    Cast: Randolph Scott, George Macready, Louise
        Allbritton, John Ireland, Virginia Huston,
        Charles Kemper, Noah Beery Jr., Dona Drake,
        Lee Patrick, James Kirkwood, Jock Mahoney
    Released: 1949

[71] *Fighting Man Of The Plains* (Fox) 1949   94 min. Cinecolor
 Producer: Nat Holt
 Director: Edwin L. Marin
 Screenplay: Frank Gruber
 From the book "Fighting Man of the Plains" by Frank Gruber
 Cast: Randolph Scott, Bill Williams, Victor Jory, Jane
       Nigh, Dale Robertson, Douglas Kennedy, Joan
       Taylor, Barry Kroeger, Rhys Williams, Barry
       Kelly, James Todd, James Millican, Burk Symon,
       Herbert Rawlinson, J. Farrell MacDonald, Harry
       Cheshire, James Griffith, Tony Highes
 Released: December, 1949

[72] *The Nevadan* (Columbia) 1950   81 min. Cinecolor
 A Scott-Brown Production
 Producer: Harry Joe Brown
 Director: Gordon Douglas
 Screenplay: George W. George, George F. Slavin, Roland
       Brown
 Cast: Randolph Scott, Dorothy Malone, Forrest
       Tucker, Frank Faylen, George Macready,
       Charles Kemper, Jeff Corey, Tom Powers, Jock
       O'Mahoney, Stanley Andrews, James Kirkwood,
       Kate Drain Lawson, Olin Howlin, Louis Mason
 Released: February, 1950

[73] *Colt .45* (Warner Bros.) 1950   70 min. Technicolor
 Producer: Saul Elkins
 Director: Edward L. Marin
 Screenplay: Thomas Blackburn
 From the story by Thomas Blackburn
 Cast: Randolph Scott, Zachary Scott, Ruth Roman,
       Lloyd Bridges, Alan Hale, Ian MacDonald, Chief
       Thunder Cloud, Walter Coy, Luther Crockett,
       Charles Evans, Buddy Roosevelt, Hal Taliaferro,

Art Miles, Barry Reagan, Howard Negley,
Aurora Navarro, Paul Newland, Franklyn
Farnum, Ed Piel Sr., Jack Watt, Carl Andre,
Royden Clark, Clyde Hudkins Jr., Leroy
Johnson, Ben Corbett, Kansas Moehring, Warren
Fisk, Forrest R. Colee, Artie Ortego, Richard
Brehm, Dick Hudkins, Leo McMahon, Bob
Burrows, William Steele

Released: May 27, 1950

[74] *The Cariboo Trail* (Fox) 1950   81 min. Cinecolor

Producer: Nat Holt
Director: Edwin L. Marin
Screenplay: Frank Gruber
From the story by John Rhodes Sturdy
Cast: Randolph Scott, George Hayes, Bill Williams,
Karin Booth, Victor Jory, Douglas Kennedy, Jim
Davis, Dale Robertson, Mary Stuart, James
Griffith, Lee Tung Foo, Tony Hughes, Mary
Kent, Ray Hyke, Kansas Moehring, Dorothy
Adams, Jerry Root, Cliff Clark, Fred Libby, Tom
Montore, Michael Barrett

Released: August 1, 1950

[75] *Sugarfoot* (Warner Bros.) 1951   80 min. Technicolor

Producer: Saul Elkins
Director: Edwin L. Marin
Screenplay: Russell Hughes
From the story by Clarence Buddington Kelland
Cast: Randolph Scott, Adele Jergens, Raymond
Massey, S. Z. Sakall, Robert Warwick, Hugh
Sanders, Hope Landin, Hand Worden, Gene
Evans, Arthur Hunnicutt, Edward Hearn, John
Hamilton, Cliff Clark, Kenneth MacDonald, Dan
White, Paul Newland, Philo McCullough

Released: March 3, 1951

[76] *Starlift* (Warner Bros.) 1951 Color
Producer: Robert Arthur
Director: Roy Del Ruth
Screenplay: John Klorer and Carl Kamb
Cast: Janis Rule, Dick Wesson, Ron Haggerty, Richard Webb, Hayden Roarke and many Warner Bros. stars who appeared as themselves including Randolph Scott.
Released: 1951

[77] *Santa Fe* (Columbia) 1951 89 min. Technicolor
Producer: Harry Joe Brown
Director: Irving Pichel
Screenplay: Kenneth Hamet
From the story by Louis Stevens from the book by James Marshall
Cast: Randolph Scott, Janis Carter, Jerome Courtland, Peter Thompson, John Archer, Warner Anderson, Roy Roberts, Billy House, Olin Howlin, Alene Roberts, Jock O'Mahoney, Harry Cording, Sven Hugo Borg, Frank Ferguson, Irving Pichel, Harry Tyler, Chief Thunder Cloud, Paul E. Burns, Reed Howes, Charles Meredith, Paul Stanton, Richard Cramer, William Haade, Francis McDonald, Frank O'Connor, Harry Tenbrook, James Mason, Guy Wilkerson, Frank Hagney, William Tannen, James Kirkwood, Stanley Blystone, Edgar Dearing, Al Kunde, Art Loeb, Blackie Whiteford, Bud Fine, Richard Fortune, Lane Chandler, Charles Evans, Chuck Hamilton, George Sherwood, Louis Mason, Lou Butler, Ralph Sanford, William McCormack
Released: April 1, 1951

[78] *Fort Worth* (Warner Bros.) 1951   80 min. Technicolor
Producer: Anthony Veiller
Director: Edwin L. Marin
Screenplay: John Twist
From the story by John Twist
Cast: Randolph Scott, David Brian, Phyllis Thaxter,
                       Helena Carter, Dick Jones, Ray Teal, Lawrence
                       Tolan, Paul Picerni, Emerson Treacy, Bob Steele,
                       Dick Jones, Walter Sande, Chubby Johnson
Released: July 14, 1951

[79] *Man In The Saddle* (Columbia) 1951   87 min. Technicolor
A Scott-Brown Production
Producer: Harry Joe Brown
Director: Andre de Toth
Screenplay: Kenneth Gamet
From the book "Man in the Saddle" by Ernest Haycox
Cast: Randolph Scott, Joan Leslie, Ellen Drew,
                       Alexander Knox, Richard Rober, John Russell,
                       Alfonso Bedoya, Guinn (Big Boy) Williams, Clem
                       Bevins, Cameron Mitchell, Richard Crane, Frank
                       Sully, George Lloyd, James Kirkwood, Frank
                       Hagney, Don Beddoe, Tennessee Ernie Ford
Released: December 2, 1951

[80] *Carson City* (Warner Bros.) 1952   87 min. WarnerColor
Producer: David Weisbart
Director: Andre de Toth
Screenplay: Sloan Nibley, Winston Miller
From the story by Sloan Nibley
Cast: Randolph Scott, Lucille Norman, Raymond
                       Massey, Richard Webb, James Millican, Larry
                       Keating, George Cleveland, William Haade,
                       Thurston Hall, Vince Barnett, Don Beddoe, Jack
                       Woody, James Smith, Guy Tongue, Carle Andre,

Marlin Nelson, Clyde Hudkins, Sarah Edwards,
Iris Adrian, Edmund Cobb, Zon Murray, House
Peters Jr., Pierce Lyden, Kenneth MacDonald
Released: June 14, 1952

[81] *Hangman's Knot* (Columbia) 1952   84 min. Technicolor
A Scott-Brown Production
Producer: Harry Joe Brown
Director: Roy Huggins
Screenplay: Roy Huggins
Cast: Randolph Scott, Donna Reed, Claude Jarman Jr.,
Frank Faylen, Glenn Langan, Richard Denning,
Lee Marvin, Jeanette Nolan, Clem Bevins, Ray
Teal, Guinn (Big Boy) Williams, Monte Blue,
John Call, Reed Howes, Edward Earle, Post
Park, Frank Hagney, Frank Yaconelli
Released: November 15, 1952

[82] *The Man Behind The Gun* (Warner Bros.) 1953   82 min. Technicolor
Producer: Robert Sisk
Director: Felix Feist
Screenplay: John Twist
From the story by Forest Buckner
Cast: Randolph Scott, Patrice Wymore, Dick Wesson,
Philip Carey, Lina Romay, Roy Roberts, Morris
Ankrum, Katherine Warren, Alan Hale, Jr.,
Douglas Fowley, Tony Caruso, Clancy Cooper,
Robert Cabal, James Brown, Reed Howes, Rory
Mallinson, John Logan, Vickie Raaf, Lee Morgan,
Ray Spiker, Edward Hearn, Terry Frost,
Charles Horvath, Art Millian, Rex Lease, Jack
Parker, James Bellah, Billy Vincent, Albert
Morin, Edward Colemans, Herbert Deans
Released: January 31, 1953

[83] *The Stranger Wore A Gun* (Columbia) 1953 83 min. Technicolor 3-D
A Scott-Brown Production
Producer: Harry Joe Brown, Randolph Scott
Director: Andre de Toth
Screenplay: Kenneth Gamet
From the book "Yankee Gold" by John Cunningham
Cast: Randolph Scott, Claire Trevor, Joan Weldon,
George Macready, Alfonso Bedoya, Lee Marvin,
Ernest Borgnine, Pierre Watkin, Joseph Vitale,
Clem Bevins, Roscoe Ates, Paul Maxey, Frank
Scannell, Reed Howes, Edward Earle, Guy
Wilkerson, Mary Newton, Mary Lou Holloway,
Franklyn Farnum, Barry Brooks, Tap Canutt, Al
Haskell, Frank Hagney, Frank Ellis, Francis
McDonald, Phil Tully, Al Hill, Harry Mendoza,
Terry Frost, Diana Dawson, Richard Benjamin,
Herbert Rawlinson, Britt Wood, Harry Seymour,
James Millican, Jack Woody, Rayford Barnes,
Rudy Germaine, Edith Evanson, Guy Teague
Released: August 15, 1953

[84] *Thunder Over the Plains* (Warner Bros.) 1953 82 min. WarnerColor
Producer: David Weisbart
Director: Andre de Toth
Screenplay: Russell Hughes
Cast: Randolph Scott, Lex Barker, Phyllis Kirk,
Charles McGraw, Henry Hull, Elisha Cook Jr.,
Hugh Sanders, Lane Chandler, James Brown,
Fess Parker, Richard Benjamin, Mark Dana,
Jack Woody, Trevor Bardette, Frank Matts,
Steve Darrell, Earle Hodgins, John Carson,
Monte Montague, Carl Andre, Charles Horvath,
John McKee, Gail Robinson, Boyd Morgan, Gayle
Kellogg
Released: December 12, 1953

[85] *Riding Shotgun* (Warner Bros.) 1954   75 min. WarnerColor
    Producer: Ted Sherdeman
    Director: Andre de Toth
    Screenplay: Tom Blackburn
    From the story by Kenneth Perkins
    Cast: Randolph Scott, Wayne Morris, Joan Weldon, Joe
                          Sawyer, James Millican, Charles Buchinsky
                          (Bronson), James Bell, Fritz Feld, Richard
                          Garrick, Victor Perrin, John Baer, William
                          Johnstone, Kem Dibbs, Alvin Freeman, Edward
                          Coch Jr., Eva Lewis, Lonnie Pierce, Mary Lou
                          Holloway, Boyd Morgan, Richard Benjamin, Jay
                          Lawrence, George Ross, Ray Bennett, Jack
                          Kenney, Jack Woody, Allegra Varron, Frosty
                          Royse, Jimmy Mohley, Ruth Whitney, Bud
                          Osborne, Budd Buster, Buddy Roosevelt, Dub
                          Taylor, Joe Brockman, Harry Hines, Clem
                          Fuller, Opan Evard, Morgan Brown, Bob
                          Stephenson
    Released: April 10, 1954

[86] *The Bounty Hunter* (Transconal/Warner Bros.) 1954   79 min.
    WarnerColor
    Producer: Sam Bischoff
    Director: Andre de Toth
    Screenplay: Winston Miller
    Cast: Randolph Scott, Dolores Dorn, Marie Windsor,
                          Howard Petrie, Harry Atrim, Robert Keys,
                          Ernest Borgnine, Dub Taylor, Tyler McDuff,
                          Archie Twitchell, Paul Picerni, Phil Chambers,
                          Mary Lou Holloway, Katherine Marlowe,
                          Dorothy Seese, Hope Miller, Guy Teague,
                          Charles Delaney, Gail Robinson, Vincent Perry,
                          Wanda Barbour, Fess Parker, Shirley Whitney
    Released: September 25, 1954

[87] *Ten Wanted Men* (Columbia) 1955   80 min. Technicolor
A Scott-Brown Production

Producer:	Harry Joe Brown
Director:	Bruce Humberstone
Screenplay:	Kenneth Gamet

From the story by Irving Ravetch, Harriet Frank Jr.

Cast: Randolph Scott, Jocelyn Brando, Richard Boone, Alfonso Bedoya, Donna Martell, Skip Homeier, Clem Bevins, Leo Gordon, Minor Watson, Lester Matthews, Tom Powers, Dennis Weaver, Lee Van Cleef, Louis Jean Heydt, Kathleen Crowley, Boyd "Red" Morgan, Denver Pyle, Francis McDonald, Pat Collins, Paul Maxey, Jack Perrin, Julian Rivero, Carlos Vera, Edna Holland, Reed Howes, Terry Frost, Franklyn Farnum, George Boyce

Released: February 1, 1955

[88] *Rage At Dawn* (RKO) 1955   87 min. Technicolor

Producer:	Nat Holt
Director:	Tim Whelan
Screenplay:	Horace McCoy

From the story by Frank Gruber

Cast: Randolph Scott, Forrest Tucker, Mala Powers, J. Carroll Naish, Edgar Buchanan, Myron Healey, Howard Petrie, Ray Teal, William Forrest, Denver Pyle, Trevor Bardette, Kenneth Tobey, Chubby Johnson, Richard Garland, Ralph Moody, Guy Prescott, Mike Ragan, Phil Chambers

Released: March 26, 1955

(Briefly released under the title *Seven Bad Men*)

[89] *Tall Man Riding* (Warner Bros.) 1955   83 min. WarnerColor

Producer:	David Weisbart
Director:	Lesley Selander

Screenplay: Joseph Hoffman
From the book by Norman A. Fox
Cast: Randolph Scott, Dorothy Malone, Peggie Castle, William Ching, John Baragrey, Robert Barrat, John Dehner, Paul Richards, Lane Chandler, Mickey Simpson, Joe Bassett, Charles Watts, Russ Conway, Mike Ragan, Carl Andre, John Logan, Guy Hearn, Bill Faucett, Nolan Leary, Phil Rich, Eva Novak, Buddy Roosevelt, Jack Henderson, Bob Peoples, William Bailey, Patrick Henry, Joe Brooks, Vernon Rich, Bob Stephenson, Dub Taylor, Roger Creed
Released: June 18, 1955

[90] *A Lawless Street* (Columbia) 1955   78 min. Technicolor
A Scott-Brown Production
Producer: Harry Joe Brown
Director: Joseph H. Lewis
Screenplay: Kenneth Gamet
From the book "Marshal of Medicine Bend" by Brad Ward
Cast: Randolph Scott, Angela Lansbury, Warner Anderson, Jean Parker, Wallace Ford, John Emery, James Bell, Ruth Donnelly, Michael Pate, Don Megowan, Jeanette Nolan, Peter Ortiz, Don Carlos, Frank Hagney, Charles Williams, Frank Ferguson, Harry Tyler, Harry Antrim, Jay Lawrence, Reed Howes, Guy Teague, Hal K. Dawson, Pat Collins, Frank Scannell, Stanley Blystone, Barry Brooks, Edwin Chandler
Released: December 15, 1955

[91] *Seven Men From Now* (Warner Bros.) 1956   78 min. WarnerColor
A Batjac Production
Producer: Andrew V. McLaglen, Robert E. Morrison

Director: Budd Boetticher
Screenplay: Burt Kennedy
From the story by Burt Kennedy
Cast: Randolph Scott, Gail Russell, Lee Marvin, Walter
Reed, John Larch, Donald Barry, Fred Graham,
John Barradino, John Phillips, Chuck Roberson,
Steve Mitchell, Pamela Duncan, Stuart Whitman
Released: August 4, 1956

[92] *7th Cavalry* (Columbia) 1956   75 min. Technicolor
A Scott-Brown Production
Producer: Harry Joe Brown
Director: Joseph H. Lewis
Screenplay: Peter Packer
From the story by Glendon F. Swarthout
Cast: Randolph Scott, Barbara Hale, Jay C. Flippen,
Jeanette Nolan, Frank Faylen, Lee Gordon,
Denver Pyle, Harry Carey Jr., Michael Pate,
Donald Curtis, Frank Wilcox, Pat Hogan, Russell
Hicks, Peter Ortiz, William Leslie, Jack Parker,
Edward F. Stidder, Al Wyatt
Released: December, 1956

[93] *The Tall T* (Columbia) 1957   78 min. Technicolor
A Scott-Brown Production
Producer: Harry Joe Brown, Randolph Scott
Director: Budd Boetticher
Screenplay: Burt Kennedy
From the story by Elmore Leonard
Cast: Randolph Scott, Richard Boone, Maureen
O'Sullivan, Arthur Hunnicutt, Skip Homeier,
Henry Silva, John Hubbard, Robert Burton,
Robert Anderson, Fred E. Sherman, Chris Olsen
Released: April 1, 1957

[94] *Shoot-out At Medicine Bend* (Warner Bros.) 1957   87 min. B/W
    Producer: Richard Whorf
    Director: Richard L. Bare
    Screenplay: John Tucker Battle, D. D. Beauchamp
    Cast: Randolph Scott, James Craig, Angie Dickinson,
                       Dani Crayne, James Garner, Gordon Jones,
                       Trevor Bardette, Don Beddoe, Myron Healey,
                       John Alderson, Harry Harvey Sr., Robert
                       Warwick, Howard Negley, Marshall Bradford,
                       Ann Doran, Daryn Hinton, Dickie Bellis, Edward
                       Hinton, Lane Bradford, Francis Morris, Robert
                       Lynn, Sam Flint, Philip Van Zandt, Guy
                       Wilkerson, Syd Saylor, Harry Rowland, Marjorie
                       Bennett, Jesslyn Fay, Marjorie Stapp, Nancy
                       Kulp, George Meador, Rory Mallinson, Dee
                       Carroll, Gerald Charlebois, Dale Van Sickel, Gil
                       Perkins, Harry Lauter, George Russ, Carol
                       Henry, George Pembroke, Tom Monroe, John
                       Roy, Buddy Roosevelt, George Bell
    Released: May 4, 1957

[95] *Decision At Sundown* (Columbia) 1957   77 min. Technicolor
A Scott-Brown Production
    Producer: Harry Joe Brown, Randolph Scott
    Director: Budd Boetticher
    Screenplay: Charles Lang Jr.
    Cast: Randolph Scott, John Carroll, Karen Steele,
                       Valerie French, Noah Beery Jr., John Archer,
                       Andrew Duggan, James Westerfield, John Litel,
                       Ray Teal, Vaughn Taylor, Richard Deacon, H. M.
                       Wynant, Guy Wilkerson
    Released: November 10, 1957

[96] *Buchanan Rides Alone* (Columbia) 1958   78 min. Technicolor

A Scott-Brown Production

Producer: Harry Joe Brown, Randolph Scott

Director: Budd Boetticher

From the story by Charles Lang Jr., from the book "The Name's Buchanan" by Jonal Wood

Cast: Randolph Scott, Craig Stevens, Barry Kelley, Tol Avery, Peter Whitney, Manual Rojab, William Leslie, Don C. Harvey, L. Q. Jones, Robert Anderson, Joe De Santis, Jennifer Holden, Nacho Galindo, Roy Jenson, Frank Scannell, Barbara James, Al Wyatt, Terry Frost, Riley Hill, Leo Ogletree, Jim B. Leon

Released: August 1, 1958

[97] *Ride Lonesome* (Columbia) 1959   75 min. Eastman Color (CinemaScope)

A Scott-Brown Production

Producer: Harry Joe Brown, Randolph Scott

Director: Budd Boetticher

Screenplay: Burt Kennedy

Cast: Randolph Scott, Karen Steele, Pernell Roberts, James Best, Lee Van Cleef, James Coburn, Duke Johnson, Boyd Stockman, Roy Jenson, Boyd "Red" Morgan, Bennie Dobbins, Lee Marvin

Released: February 15, 1959

[98] *Westbound* (Warner Bros.) 1959   96 min. WarnerColor

Producer: Henry Blanke

Director: Budd Boetticher

Screenplay: Berne Giler

From the story by Berne Giler, Albert Shelby LeVino

Cast: Randolph Scott, Virginia Mayo, Karen Steele, Michael Dante, Andrew Duggan, Michael Pate, Wally Brown, John Day, Walter Barnes, Fred

Sherman, Mack William, Ed Prentiss, Rory
Mallinson, Rudi Dana, Tom Monroe, Jack Perrin,
Buddy Roosevelt, Kermit Maynard, May Boss,
William A. Green, Jack E. Henderson, Felice
Richmond, Creighton Hale, Gertrude Keeler,
Walter Reed, Jack C. Williams, Gerald Roberts,
John Hudkins, Don Happy, Bobby Herron, Fred
Stromscoe

Released: April 25, 1959

[99] *Comanche Station* (Columbia) 1960   74 min. Eastman Color
(CinemaScope)
A Ranown Production

Producer: Harry Joe Brown, Budd Boetticher
Director: Budd Boetticher
Screenplay: Burt Kennedy
Cast: Randolph Scott, Nancy Gates, Claude Akins,
Skip Homeier, Richard Rust, Rand Brooks, Dyke
Johnson, Foster Hood, Joe Molina, Vince St.
Cyr, Paul Holland
Released: March 1960

[100] *Ride The High Country* (MGM) 1962   94 min. Metrocolor
(CinemaScope)

Producer: Richard E. Lyons
Director: Sam Peckinpah
Screenplay: N. B. Stone Jr.
Cast: Randolph Scott, Joel McCrea, Mariette Hartley,
Ronald Starr, Edgar Buchanan, R. G.
Armstrong, John Anderson, L. Q. Jones, Warren
Oates, James Drury, John Davis Chandler, Jenie
Jackson
Released: May, 1962

SELECTED BIBLIOGRAPHY

Adams, Les and Rainey, Buck. *The Shoot-Em-Ups:* Arlington House 1978

American Film Institute Catalog 1921–1930 (2 Vols): R. R. Bowker Co. 1971

Blum, Daniel. *Screen World 1949:* Greenberg-Publisher 1949

Clapham, Walter C. *The Movie Treasury/Western Movies:* Octopus Books 1974

Corneau, Ernest N. *Our Vanished Western Heroes:* Movie Digest, March 1972.

Deschner, Donald. *The Films of Cary Grant:* The Citadel Press 1973

Everson, William K. *A Pictorial History of The Western Film:* The Citadel Press 1969

Eyles, Allen. *The Western/An Illustrated Guide:* A. S. Barnes 1967

Film Superlist-2000 Motion Pictures in the Public Domain: 7 Arts Press 1973

Fitzgerald, Michael G. *Universal Pictures:* Arlington House 1977

Halliwell, Leslie. *The Filmgoer's Companion* (6th Ed.): Hill & Wang 1976

Hintz, H. F. *Horses in the Movies:* A. S. Barnes & Co. 1979

Horwitz, James. *They Went Thataway:* E. P. Dutton 1976

Jeavons, Clyde. *A Pictorial History of War Films:* The Citadel Press 1974

Library of Congress Catalog-The National Union Catalog of Motion Pictures and Filmstrips (1958 Ed.)

Maltin, Leonard. *TV Movies* (several editions): Signet Books (from 1969)

McCarty, Clifford. *Bogey:* The Citadel Press 1965

McClure, Arthur F. and Jones, Ken D. *Heroes, Heavies & Sagebrush:* A. S. Barnes & Company 1972

_____. *Star Quality:* A. S. Barnes & Company 1974

Michael, Paul and Parish, James Robert. *The American Movies:* Prentice-Hall 1969 (re-issue: Garland Books)

_____. *Movie Greats:* Prentice-Hall 1969 (re-issue: Garland Books)

Morella, Joseph, Epstein, Edward Z. and Griggs, John. *The Films of World War II:* The Citadel Press 1973

New York Times, The Film Reviews 1913–1968 (5 Vols/Index): New York Times and Arno Press 1970

Parish, James Robert. *Great Western Stars:* Ace Books 1976

_____and Stanke, Don E. *The All-Americans:* Arlington House 1977

_____. *The Debonairs:* Arlington House 1975.

_____. *The Swashbucklers:* Arlington House 1976.

Ragan, David. *Who's Who in Hollywood 1900–1976.* Arlington House 1976

Ricci, Mark, Zmijewsky, Boris & Zmijewsky, Steve. *The Films of John Wayne:* The Citadel Press 1970

Scheuer, Steven H. *Movies on TV (1978–79):* Bantam Books (Annual Editions)

The Story of the Movies-Volume 2: S. F. Worthington Associates 1974

Thomas, Tony. *The Films of the Forties:* The Citadel Press 1975

Thompson, Fred. *Hollywood's Magic People-Fred Astaire:* Crescent Books 1970

Comanche Station (Columbia-1960) with Nancy Gates, Skip Homeier, Claude Akins, Richard Rust and Rand Brooks (on ground).

Again, Randy proves himself as he outdraws Claude Akins in *Comanche Station* (Columbia-1960).

Comanche Station (Columbia-1960) with Richard Rust and Nancy Gates.

Comanche Station (Columbia-1960) with Nancy Gates.

A serious discussion with Claude Akins in Columbia's *Comanche Station* (1960).

Comanche Station (Columbia-1960) with Skip Homeier, Richard Rust, Nancy Gates, Randolph Scott and Claude Akins (from left).

Comanche Station (Columbia-1960).

Comanche Station (Columbia-1960).

A happy ending as Randy safely delivers Nancy Gates to her family before once again riding into the sunset in *Comanche Station* (Columbia-1960).

INDEX

A.B.C., 161, 165, 169, 173
Abilene Town, 71, 76
Academy Awards, 129, 165
Action in the North Atlantic, 43
Adams, Dorothy, *109*
Adventures of Mark Twain, The, 45
Akins, Claude, *65,* 66, 67, 68, 180, *285, 287*
Albert, Eddie, 49
Albertson, Frank, 36
Albuquerque, 91
Alias Smith and Jones, 61
Allbritton, Louise, 49, 91
Allen, Judith, 9
Allen, Rex, 103, 125
Allied Artists, 103
Allwyn, Astrid, 21
American Cowboy Music Company, 199
Anchors Aweigh, 45
And Sudden Death, 21
Anderson, John, 186
Anderson, Mary, 117
Anderson, Warner, *112,* 144
Andrews, Dana, 39, 45, 49, 61, 71, 118
Angel and the Badman, 149
Angel, Heather, 21
Angeli, Pier, 123
Anna and the King of Siam, 71
Ansco Color (process), 134, 139, 180
Archer, John, 22, 75, *115,* 169
Arliss, George, 7
Armstrong, R. G., 186
Armstrong, Robert, *48, 50,* 93
Arness, James, 173
Asphalt Jungle, The, 101
Astaire, Fred, 19, 21
Atwill, Lionel, 17
Autry, Gene, 87, 101, 118

B

Bacon, Irving, 49, 91
Bacon, Lloyd, 45, 80
Bad Day At Black Rock, 95
Badman's Territory, 76, 81
Baer, Parley, 173
Balenda, Carla, 61
Balsley, Phil, *200*
Bancroft, George, 36
Baragrey, John, 144
Bare, Richard, 169
Bari, Lynn, 76
Barker, Lex, 139, *143,* 145
Barnes, Binnie, 21, 31
Barry, Don 'Red', XIV
Barrymore, Lionel, 43
Barthelmess, Richard, 47
Barton, Charles, 13
Bates, Florence, 51
Batjac Productions, 144
Bausch & Lomb Corporation, 128
Baxter, Anne, 45
Beach, Rex, 47
Bedoya, Alphonso, *121*
Beery, Noah Sr., 9, 11, 47
Beery, Noah Jr., XVI, 51, 60, 75, *94,* 95, 169, *189, 192*
Bel Geddes, Barbara, 118
Bellamy, Ralph, *44*
Belle Starr, 38, 39, 71
Belle of the Yukon, 48, 50, 51, 52
Bellis, Dickie, *41*
Bells of St. Mary's, The, 71
Bend of the River, 123
Bennett, Joan, 25
Beresford, Harry, 21

Bergman, Ingrid, 71
Bergner, Elisabeth, 47
Berlin, Irving, 21
Best, James, 177, *196*
Best Years of Our Lives, The, 71
Bevins, Clem, 129, *136*
Bickford, Charles, 21, 33
Big Sky, The, 125, 165
Bishop, William, 95
B.J. and the Bear, 66
Black Watch, The, 3, 245
Blaine, Sally, 9, 17
Blair, Janet, 61
Blanke, Henry, 177
Blondell, Joan, 80
Blood on the Moon, 118
Blue Gardenia, The, 118
Blue, Monte, 9, 29, *132*
Boettcher, Bud, 149, 165, *170*, 177, 180
Bogart, Humphrey, 33, *34*, 36, 43
Bombardier, 49
Bonanza, 169
Bond, Ward, 31, 45, 169
Boone, Richard, *78*, 139, *154*, 165, *179*
Booth, Karin, *109*, 110
Border Legion, The, 13
Borgnine, Ernest, 134, 139, *142*, *147*
Boyd, William, 47
Bounty Hunter, The, *2*, 139, *146*, *147*, 148
Bowery Boys, 103
Brand, Max, 49
Brando, Jocelyn, 139, *156*
Brando, Marlon, 156
Brennan, Walter, 25
Brian, David, *IX*, 114, *119*
Brian, Mary, 6
Bridge, Al, 9
Bridges, Lloyd, 76, 106
Britton, Barbara, 54, 80, *82*, 91
Broderick, Helen, 25
Brodie, Steve, 76
Broken Wing, The, 3
Bronco, 169
Bronson, Charles, 139, *151*
Brooks, Phyllis, 6
Brown, Harry Joe, 49, 63, 80, 91, 93, 180
Brown, James, 51
Brown, Johnny Mack, XIII, 103
Brown, Peter, 169
Buchannan, Edgar, 49, 76, 91, 95, 139, *160*, 186
Buchannan Rides Alone, XVII, *79*, 173, *193*

Buchinsky, Charles (see Bronson, Charles)
Buck, Pearl S., 54
Buckler, Hugh, 21
Burke, Kathleen, 13
Burns, Bob, *48*
Burton, Robert, *187*
Bush, James, 9
Bwana Devil, 125, 127

C

Cabot, Bruce, 21, 80, *82*, *84*
Cagney, James, 19
Calhoun, Rory, 47
Call, John, *132*
Cameron, Rod, 51, 103
Canadian Pacific, 93, 95
Canyon Passage, 118
Captain Kid, 54, *55*
Captain Midnight, XIII
Carey, Harry, 9, 11, 47
Carey, Macdonald, 49, 93
Carey, Philip, 134
Cariboo Trail, The, 93, *109*, 110
Carlisle, Mary, 6
Carlson, Frank, *99*
Carmichael, Hoagy, 118
Carradine, John, 27, 31, 39, 54
Carrillo, Leo, 3
Carroll, John, 169
Carroll, Nancy, 3
Carson City, *22*, *28*, *58*, *88*, *90*, *127*, 129, *130*
Carson, Sunset, XIV
Carter, Helena, 114, *117*
Carter, Janis, 114, *116*
Carter, Leslie, 13
Cash, Johnny, 144
Castle, Peggy, 144, 161, *162*, *163*
C.B.S., 7, 149, 161, 173
Chandler, Jeff, 47
Chandler, Lane, *X*
Chaney, Lon Jr., 31, 33, 91
Chapman, Marguerite, 91, *92*
Cherrill, Virginia, 3
Chief Thundercloud (film), 110
Chief Thundercloud (actor) (see Thundercloud, Chief)
Cheyenne, 161, 165, 169
China Sky, 51, *52*, *53*, 54
Ching, William, *XVIII*, 144
Christmas Eve, 80, *85*
Ciannelli, Eduardo, 47

Cinecolor (process), 91, 106, 114, 134, 169
CinemaScope (process), 128, 177, 183
Cinerama (process), 125
Cinerama Corporation, 125
Cleveland, George, 47, 91
Coast Guard, *44*, 45
Cobb, Lee J., 47
Code of the West, 13
Colbert, Robert, 169
Cole, Nat King, 118
Coleman, Ronald, 19
Collins, Ted, 17
Colt .45 (film), 106, 110
Colt .45 (tv), 169
Columbia Pictures, IX, XV, XVI, XVII,
        XVIII, XXIII, XXIV, 2, 3, 5, 6 , 8, 10,
        12, 15, 17, 22, 28, 29, 35, 37, 40, 44, 45,
        49, 66, 73, 75 , 77–80, 82–84, 87, 91–96,
        101, 103, 105–107, 112–116, 118, 120, 121,
        123–126, 129, 131–142, 144, 154, 156, 157,
        161, 164–169, 174–181, 187, 189, 191–193,
        196, 197, 285–289
Comanche Station, 66, 67, 68, 180, 183,
        285–289
Conrad, William, 173
Considine, Robert, 43
Conte, Richard, 45
Converse, Frank, 66
Conway, Pat, 169
Coogan, Jackie, 13
Cook, Elisha Jr., 139
Cooper, Gary, 3, 19, 47, 71, 106, 114, 144
Cooper, James Fenimore, 21
Coroner Creek, 91, *92*, 93
Corvette K-225, 51
Cotten, Joseph, 49
Courtland, Jerome, *22*, 95, 114, *115*
Coy, Walter, 106
Crabbe, Larry 'Buster', 9, 11, 15
Craig, James, 169
Crawford, Broderick, 36
Crayne, Dani, *XXII*, *188*
Crosby, Bing, 45, 71
Crowther, Bosley, 31
Cummings, Irving, 39
Cummings, Robert, 21, 25
Cunningham, Jack, 13
Cunningham, John, 134
Curtis, Alan, 51
Curtis, Dick, 76
Curtis, Donald, 59, *175*, *178*

Curtis, Tony, 123
Curtiz, Michael, 33

D

Dallas, 114
Dalton, Emmett, 36
Daniels, Victor (see Thundercloud, Chief)
Dante, Michael, 177, *198*
Darwell, Jane, 27
Death of a Salesman, 123
Decision At Sundown, XVI, *75*, 169, *189*, *191*,
        192
Dehner, John, 144
DeLuxe Color (process), 139, 180
DeMille, Cecil B., 3, 183
Denning, Richard, 129, *135–137*, *140*
Denny, Reginald, 80
Denver & Rio Grande, The, 93
DeSantis, Joe, 193
Desperadoes, The, 49, 91
Destination Tokyo, 43
deToth, Andre, 134, 139
Devil Makes Three, The, 123
Devine, Andy, 36, 51
Dewitt, Lew, *200*
Dial M for Murder, 128
Dickinson, Angie, 169
Dick Powell's Zane Grey Theatre, 7
Dietrich, Marlene, 47
Dinehart, Allan, *19*
Disney, Walt, Productions, 114
Dobbins, Bennie, 177
Donlevy, Brian, 27, 36
Donnelly, Ruth, *8*, *164*
Doolins of Oklahoma, The, *94*, 95, *96*, 106
Doris Day Show, The, 149
Doran, Ann, *41*
Dorn, Delores, 139, *146*
Douglas, Gordon, 95, 106
Douglas, Kirk, 125
Drake, Frances, 21
Drew, Ellen, *28*, *52*, 118, *120*
Driscoll, Bobby, 45
Drury, James, 186
Duel (Deuel), Peter, 61
Duggan, Andrew, 169, 177
Dukes of Hazzard, The, 149, 155
Durango Kid, The (series), 103
Duryea, Dan, 103, 106
Dvorak, Ann, 76
Dynamite, 3, 183

E

Eagles, James, 13
Eastham, Richard, 169
Eastmancolor (process), 139, 180
Eilers, Sally, *92*
Eisenhower, Dwight David, 123, 144
Elliott, William 'Wild Bill', XIII, 103, 110, 125
Ellis, Georgia, 173
Emery, John, *167*
Enright, Ray, 47, 54, 80, 91
Erwin, Stuart, 36
Everson, William K., 190

F

Far Call, The, 3, 31, 245
Farnum, William, 17, 47
Farrell, Glenda, 25
Faylen, Frank, *29, 77*, 129, *132, 137, 140, 141, 176, 178*
Feld, Fritz, *148*
Fellows, Robert, 144
Field, Virginia, 80, *85*
Fighting Caravans, 13
Fighting Man of the Plains, 93, 95, *96–99*
Fitzgerald, Barry, 51
Fix, Paul, 34, 49, *98*
Fleming, Rhonda, 76
Flippen, Jay C., *40, 77*, 149, *176, 178*
Flynn, Errol, 33, 36, 43
Follow the Boys, 51, 110
Follow the Fleet, *21*, 21
Fonda, Henry, 27, 49
For Whom the Bell Tolls, 49
Ford, Glenn, 49
Ford, John, 31, 47, 144, 245
Ford, Tennessee Ernie, 118
Ford, Wallace, *144, 164, 166–168*
Forrest, William, *157*
Fort Worth, IX, 114, *117, 119*
Fortune, Jimmy, *200*
Fox (see 20th Century-Fox)
Foy, Eddie Jr., 31
Francis, Kay, *30*, 36
French, Valerie, 169
Friendly Persuasion, 144
Fritchie, Barbara, 13
From Here to Eternity, 129
Frontier Marshal, *26*, 27, 31
Fugitive, The, 61

G

Gable, Clark, 19, 87
Garfield, John, 43
Garland, Judy, 71
Garner, James, *XXI*, 61, 165, 169, *188*
Garner, Peggy Ann, 76
Gaslight, 45
Gates, Nancy, 180, *285–287, 289*
Gaynor, Mitzi, 103
Gazzara, Ben, 61
Geray, Steven, 80
Giant, 144
Gilmore, Virginia, 39
Girl Crazy, 49
Go West Young Man, 21
Going My Way, 45
Goldwyn, Samuel, 71
Gomez, Thomas, 49, 51
Gone With the Wind, 31, 87
Gordon, Leo, *176*
Grable, Betty, 21
Grainger, Edmund, 25
Grant, Cary, 3, *5*, 6, 7, 33, 43, 71
Grapes of Wrath, The, 33
Grapewin, Charles, 9, 80, *84*
Great Missouri Raid, The, 93
Green Years, The, 71
Grey, Zane, 7, 9, 13, 15, 17, 19, 39, 76, 80
Grizzly Adams, 149
Gruber, Frank, 11, 95, 113
Guadalcanal Diary, 45
Gunfighter, The, 180
Gunfighters, 15, 80, *82–84*
Gung Ho, 51
Gunsmoke, 173
Guthrie, A. B., 123
Guy Named Joe, A, 43

H

Haggard, H. R., 19
Hagney, Frank, *112, 120*
Hale, Alan, 106
Hale, Barbara, 149, *174, 175*
Hamilton, John, *15*
Hammerstein, Oscar, 21, 23
Hampton, Hope, 25
Hangman's Knot, XV, XXIV, *29*, 61, 64, *124, 126*, 129, *131–133, 135–138, 140, 141*, 165
Hardin, Ty, 169

Harding, Ann, 80, *85*
Harrison, Rex, 71
Hart, Dorothy, 80, *82, 84*
Hart, John, 173
Hartley, Mariette, 186
Harvey Girls, The, 71
Hathaway, Henry, 9, 11, 13, 246
Hatton, Raymond, 9
Hawks, Howard, 51, 125
Haycox, Ernest, 76, 118
Hayden, Russell, 91
Hayden, Sterling, 93
Hayes, George 'Gabby', 9, 76, 80, 91, 93, 110, 165
Hayward, Susan, 118, 123
Hayworth, Rita, 80
Headline Pictures, 3
Heaven Can Wait, 49
Hello Everybody, 17, *18*
Herbert, F. Hugh, 25
Heritage of the Desert, 9
Heydt, Louis Jean, 51, *154, 156*, 165
Hicks, Russell, 34, *77, 175*
High Noon, 106, 114
High, Wide and Handsome, 21
Hilliard, Harriet, 21
Hitchcock, Alfred, 33, 49, 71, 128
Hodiak, John, 71
Hoey, Dennis, *85*
Hogan, James, 25
Holden, William, 80
Holt, Jack, 9
Holt, Nat, 76, 80, 93, 95, 110, 139
Holt, Tim, 101, 125
Home On the Range, 13
Home, Sweet Homicide, 76
Homeier, Skip, *157*, 180, *285, 287*
Hop Harrigan, XIII
Hope, Bob, 45
Horton, Robert, 169
Hot Saturday, 3
Howard, Shemp, 49
Howlin, Olin, *38*
Hough, Emerson, 25
Hudson, Rock, 123
Huggins, Roy, 61–64, 129, 132
Hughes, Howard, 1
Hull, Henry, 27, 139, *143*
Human Comedy, The, 49
Hunnicutt, Arthur, 125, 165, *187*
Hunter, Jeffrey, 144
Hutchins, Will, 169

I

I Love Trouble, 61
Ireland, John, 95, *96*

J

Jacobson, Arthur, 13
Jagger, Dean, 13, 39, 93
Jarman, Claude Jr., *29*, 71, 129, *132, 135–137, 140*
Janssen, David, 61
Jeffreys, Anne, 80, 93
Jenks, Frank, *20*
Jenson, Roy, 177, *193*
Jergens, Adele, 110, *111*
Jesse James, 25, 27
Johnson, Duke, 177
Johnson, Kay, 246
Johnson, Nunnally, 27
Johnson, Van, 43
Jones, Gordon, *XXI*, 169
Jones, L. Q., 173, 186
Jory, Victor, 93, 95, *98*, 110
Jungmeyer, Jack Sr., 36

K

Kanin, Garson, 33
Keene, Tom, 9, 15
Kelly, Barry, *98*, 173
Kelly, Gene, 123
Kelly, Jack, 61, 169
Kelly, Nancy, 27, 31, 47
Kemper, Charles, *94*
Kennedy, Arthur, 95, 123
Kennedy, Burt, 149, 165, 177
Kennedy, Douglas, 95, *97*, 110
Kennedy, Tom, 11
Kentucky, 25
Kenyon, Charles, 25
Kern, Jerome, 21, 23
Keyes, Evelyn, 49
King, Henry, 27
King of the Mounties, 7
King of the Royal Mounted, 7
Kings Row, 45
Kirk, Phyllis, *14, 102*, 139, *145*
Kitty Foyle, 33
Knight, Fuzzy, 9, 11, 51
Knox, Alexander, *120*
Kohler, Fred, 9

Kraft Television Theatre, 161
Kramer, Stanley, 114, 118

L

Ladd, Alan, 106
Lady Gambles, The, 61
Lake, Stuart N., 31
Lamour, Dorothy, 21, 45
Lang, Fritz, 39
Langan, Glenn, 129, *132*
Lansbury, Angela, *XVIII, 78,* 144, *168*
LaRue, Jack, 11
LaRue, Lash, XIV
Lassie Come Home, 45
Last of the Mohicans, 21
Last Roundup, The, 13
Laurie, Piper, 123
Lawless Street, A, XVIII,XXIII, 7, 12, 35, 78,
     144, *164, 166, 167, 168*
Lawman, 169
Lawson, Ted, 43
Laughton, Charles, 54, *55*
Laura, 45
Lease, Rex, 134
Lee, Gypsy Rose, *50,* 51, *52*
LeMay, Alan, 80
Leslie, Joan, 118, *120*
Levy, Jules, 76
Lewis, Joseph, 144, 149
Life & Legend of Wyatt Earp, The, 169
Lindsay, Margaret, 47
Lippert, Robert L., 106, 118
Litel, John, 189
Lombard, Carole, 17, *19*
Lona Hanson, 80
London, Tom, 9
Lone Cowboy, 7
Lone Ranger, The, XIII, 144, 173
Long, Richard, 123
Long Voyage Home, The, 33
Loo, Richard, 54
Lost Weekend, The, 45, 71
Loy, Myrna, 71, 245
Lusitania Secret, 7
Lusty Men, The, 123
Lyons, Richard, 183

M

Ma & Pa Kettle (series), 123
Macao, 123

MacLane, Barton, 9, 39, 49
Macready, George, 91, 95, 106, *108,* 134, *142*
Mahoney, Jock, 73, 95, *96*
Magnificent Seven,The, 95
Malone, Dorothy, *6, 106,* 106, 144, *163*
Man Behind the Gun, The, 134
Man in the Saddle, 28, 118, *120, 121*
Man of the Forest, 9, 11
March, Fredric, 71
Marin, Edwin L., 76, 93, 110, 114
Marion, George, 13
Mark of Zorro, The, 33
Marshal of Medicine Bend, The, 144
Marshall, Alan, 25
Marshall, James, 114
Marshall, Trudy, 45
Marshall, William, 51
Martell, Donna, *157*
Martin, Chico, 125
Martin, Dewey, 125
Marvin, Lee, *29, 40, 70,* 129, *132, 134–138, 140,*
     142
Massey, Raymond, 43, 110, 129
Maverick, 61, 165
Maverick Queen, The, 7
Maxey, Paul, *142*
May, Donald, 169
Maynard, Kermit, 76, *167,* 177
Mayo, Virginia, 177, *197, 198*
McCoy, Tim, 27
McCrea, Joel, 3, 19, 103, 114, 183, *184,* 186, 190
McDonald, Francis, *142*
McDonald, Grace, 31
McDonald, Ian, 106
McDonald, J. Ferrell, 9
McGraw, Charles, 139
McLaglen, Andrew V., 149
McNamara, Alexander, 47
McNear, Howard, 173
Meet John Doe, 33
Meet Me In St. Louis, 45
Megowan, Don, *12, 166*
Metro-Goldwyn-Mayer (MGM), 1, 21, 27, 31, 33,
     43, 45, 49, 71, 87, 89, 95, 101, 123 , 134,
     161, 180, 183, 184, 185, 186
MetroColor (process), 139, 180, 183
Mercer, Beryl, 17
Mercury Records, 199
Meredith, Burgess, 33
Miles, John, *84*
Miles, Vera, 144
Milland, Ray, 71

Millican, James, 139
Mirisch Brothers (producers), 95
Misadventures of Sheriff Lobo, The, 66
Mitchell, Margaret, 31
Mitchell, Thomas, 45
Mitchum, Robert, 43, 51, 101, 118, 123
Moehring, Kansas, *109*
Monogram Pictures, 3, 17, 103, 125
Monroe, Marilyn, 118
Moore, Clayton, 144, 173
Moore, Roger, 169
Morgan, Boyd, 177
Morris, Wayne, 103, 125, 139
Morrison, Robert, 149
Motion Picture Herald Poll, The, 101, 118
Movin' On, 66
Murders in the Zoo, 17
Murphy, Ben, 61
Murphy, Audie, 103, 123
My Favorite Wife, 33
My Six Convicts, 123

N

N.B.C., 149, 161, 169
Naish, J. Carrol, 51, 93, 139
Naked Spur, The, 123
Name's Buchannan, The, 173
Nashville 99, 66
National Broadcasting Co. (see N.B.C.)
National Velvet, 45
Natural-Vision (process), 125, 127, 128, 134
Nevadan, The, IX, *5, 6, 105*, 106, *107, 108*
New York Times, The, 3, 203
New York Times News Service, The, 207
Nigh, Jane, 95, *97, 98*
Nolan, Jeanette, *136, 137*, 144, 149
Norman, Lucille, *28, 58, 127*, 129
Norris, Edward, 31
North of '36', 25
North Star, The, 45
Northwest Passage, 21
Notorious, 71

O

O'Brian, Hugh, 169
O'Brien, Edmond, 93
O'Brien, George, 1, 31
O'Brien, Pat, 49
Objective Burma, 43
Of Mice and Men, 33
Oh Judge, 3
O'Hara, Maureen, 47

Olsen, Moroni, 34
Olson, Nancy, 93
Ormond, Ron, 106
Osborne, Vivienne, 17
O'Sullivan, Maureen, 165
Owen, Reginald, 54
Ox-Bow Incident, The, 45, 49

P

Palladin, 165
Pan-American Road Race, 123
Panavision (process), 128
Paramount Pictures, 3, 6–9, 11, 13, 17–19, 21, 25, 39, 45, 47, 49 , 71, 76, 80, 91, 93, 101, 106
Paris Calling, 45, 76
Parker, Jean, 144
Pasadena Playhouse, 3
Pate, Michael, 144, *167*
Patrick, Gail, 11, 13
Patrick, Lee, *94*
Patterson, Elisabeth, *38*, 39
Patterson, Hank, 76
Payne, John, *44, 46, 47, 48*
Peck, Gregory, 71, 180
Peckinpah, Sam, 183, 186
Perrin, Jack, 177
Perry Mason, 11
Peter Gunn, 173
Petrie, Howard, 139, *160*
Philadelphia Story, The, 33
Picerni, Paul, *29*
Pittsburgh, 47, 49, 149
Polaroid Corporation, 125
Power, Tyrone, 27
Powers, Mala, 139, *160*
Powers, Tom, *154*
Presley, Elvis, 144
Preston, Robert, 61
Preston, Wade, 169
Prince, William, 43
Purple Heart, The, 45
Pyle, Denver, 139, 149, *160*

Q

Quiet Man, The, 125
Quinn, Anthony, 54

R

Raft, George, 80
Ragan, Mike, *157*

Rage At Dawn, *4*, 93, 139, *157*, *159*, *160*
Raines, Ella, 51, 95
Ranown Productions (see Scott-Brown)
Rathbone, Basil, 45
Rebecca of Sunnybrook Farm, 25
Reed, Donna, *124*, *126*, 129, *132*, *135–137*
Reed, Jerry, 66
Reed, Walter, *12*, 149, *172*
Regas, George, 34
Reid, Don, 199, *200*, 201
Reid, Harold, 199, *200*, 201
Republic Pictures, 7, 87, 103, 125, 139, 144,
    149
Return of the Bad Men, 93
Richards, Ann, 76
Ride Lonesome, 177, *196*, *197*
Ride the High Country, 1, 67, 183, *184*, *185*,
    186, 190, 195
Riders of the Purple Sage, 7
Riding Shotgun, X, *14*, *29*, *37*, *88*, 139, *150*,
    151–153
Ritter, Tex, 114, 118
River of No Return, 118
RKO Radio Pictures, 3, 4, 9, 19, 20, 21, 33, 45,
    48, 49, 50–54, 71, 76, 80, 81, 93, 101, 114,
    118, 123, 125, 139, 157, 159, 160, 165
Road to Morocco, The, 45
Road to Reno, 25
Roberta, 19, 21
Roberts, Allene, *22*
Roberts, Florence, 13
Roberts, Pernell, 177, *196*
Roberts, Roy, 45
Robertson, Dale, 95, 103, 110
Robson, May, 25
Rockford Files, The, 61
Rocky Mountain Mystery, 13
Rogers, Ginger, 6, 19, 21
Rogers, Roy, 87, 103, 110, 118
Roland, Gilbert, 54
Roman, Ruth, 106
Romero, Cesar, 31
Roosevelt, Buddy, 9, 177
Rosen, Richard, 51
Royale, Selena, 45
Rule, Janice, 110
Run For Your Life, 61
Russell, Gail, *XIX*, *12*, 149, *171–172*
Russell, Jane, 101, 123
Russell, John, 169
Rust, Richard, *285–287*
Ryan, Robert, 49, 80, 93, 123

S

Sale, Charles 'Chic', 13
Sakall, S. Z., *15*, 110
Sande, Walter, 51
Sandrich, Mark, 21
Santa Fe, *73*, *112*, *113*, 114, *115*, *116*, *222*
Santschi, Tom, 47
Saratoga Trunk, 71
Sawyer, Joe, 31, *38*, 139
Schwartz, Bernard (see Curtis, Tony)
Scott-Brown Productions, 49, 64, 93, 95, 106,
    114, 129, 134, 139, 144, 149, 169, 177, 180
Scott, Christopher, 6
Scott, Sandra, 6
Scott, Zachary, 106
Screen Gems (Columbia), 161
Sea Wolf, The, 33
Sealed Cargo, 61
Searchers, The, 144
See Here, Private Hargrove, 49
Seitz, George B., 21
Selander, Leslie, 144
Selig Company, The, 47
Selznick International Pictures, 31, 87
Seven Men from Now, *XIX*, *12*, *40*, *70*, 149,
    165, *170–172*
7th Cavalry, *40*, *77*, 149, 155, *174–178*
Shadow of a Doubt, 49
Shane, 106
Sharp Shooters, 1, 3, 31
She, 19
Sheridan, Ann, 13
Shirley, Anne, 49
Shoot-Out at Medicine Bend, *XXI*, *XXII*, *41*,
    106, 165, *188*, *189*
Shore, Dinah, 51
Short, Luke, 91
Shumate, Harold, 76
Sills, Milton, 47
Silver Star, The, 118
Silverheels, Jay, 144
Simon, Sylvan, 25
Simpson, Russell, 47, 91
Singing in the Rain, 123
Sinner's Holiday (see *Christmas Eve*), 80
Smith, Kate, 17
So Red the Rose, 19, 21
Somerville, Marianna duPont, 6
Sondergaard, Gale, 46, 47
Spoilers, The, 36, 47, 49, 149
Stack, Robert, 125

Stagecoach, 47, 134
Stanwyck, Barbara, 61
Starlift, 80, 110, 177
Starr, Ronald, 186
Starrett, Charles, 101, 103, 125
State Fair, 45
State Fair of Texas, The, 165
Statler Brothers, The, 199, *200*
Steel (horse), *82*
Steele, Bob, XIII, 33
Steele, Karen, 169, 177, *196–198*
Steve Allen Show, The, 165
Stevens, Craig, 173, *193*
Stevens, George, 144
Stevens, Louis, 114
Stewart, James, 103, 106, 123
Stillman, Marie Patricia, 6, 195
Stockwell, Dean, 76
Stone, N. B. Jr., 183
Strange, Glenn, 49
Stranger Wore a Gun, The, 10, *37*, 128, 134, *142*
Stuart, Gloria, 25
Studio One (see *Westinghouse Studio One*)
Sturges, John, 95
Successful Calamity, A, 7, 177
Sugarfoot, *15*, 110, *111*, 169
Sullivan, Margaret, 21
Sullivans, The, 45
Sully, Frank, *120*
Summerville, Slim, 39
Sunset Pass, 9
Superman, XIII
Supernatural, 17, *19*
Susannah of the Mounties, 25, *27*
Swirl of Glory, 110

T

Tall Man Riding, XVIII, *73*, *144*, *162*, *163*
Tall T, The, *78*, 165, *179*, *181*, *187*
Taylor, Dub, 144
Taylor, Joan, *97*
Taylor, Kent, 9
Taylor, Robert, 89, 123
Taylor, Vaughn, *189*
Teal, Ray, 169
Technicolor (process), 27, 39, 49, 93, 106, 114, 123, 134, 139, 169, 177, 180
Temple, Shirley, 11, 25
Ten Wanted Men, *2*, *139*, *154*, *156*, *157*
Terry & the Pirates, XIII
Texans, The, 25

Thaxter Phyllis, 114
Thirty-Seconds Over Tokyo, 43
This Is Cinerama, 125
This Week Magazine, 205
Thomas, J. P., 87
Thompson, Peter, *115*
Thorpe, Jim, 9
Three-Dimension (see Natural-Vision)
Thunder Over the Plains, X, XX, *10*, *14*, *102*, 134, 139, *143*, *145*
Thundercloud, Chief, 106
Thundering Herd, The, 9
Tierney, Gene, *38*, 39
Tierney, Lawrence, 76
To the Last Man, 9, 11
To the Shores of Tripoli, *44*, *46*, 47, *48*
Tombstone Territory, 169
Tone, Franchot, 43, 61
Tracy, Spencer, 43
Trail Street, 80
Trevor, Claire, *10*, *37*, 49, 134, *142*
Trucolor (process), 180
Tucker, Forrest, *4*, *5*, 80, 91, *92*, *105*, 106, *107*, *108*, 139
20th Century-Fox, 3, 11, 15, 25–27, 31, 33, 38, 39, 43–49, 71, 76, 93 , 95–98, 103, 109, 110, 118, 128, 134, 139, 161, 180
20, 000 Men a Year, 31, 45
Tyler, Tom, 31, 76

U

Under a Virginia Moon, 3
United Artists, 3, 21, 33, 54, 55, 71, 80, 85, 106, 114, 125, 144, 180
Universal Pictures, 3, 25, 30, 36, 45, 47, 49, 51, 103, 110, 118, 123, 180

V

Valez, Lupe, 7
VanCleef, Lee, 177
Varsity Theatre, XIII
Vidor, Charles, 49
Village Tale, A, 19
Virginia City, 33, *34*, 36, 106
Virginian, The, 3

W

Waggner, George, 80
Wagner, Robert, 103

Wagon Train, 169
Wagon Wheels, 13
Wake of the Red Witch, 144, 149
Wakely, Jimmy, 118
Walk in the Sun, A, 45
Walker, Clint, 161, 169
Walker, Robert, 43
Walking Hills, The, 95
Waller, Eddie, 76
Wanger, Walter, 37
Ware, Helen, 246
Warner Bros., IX, X, XVIII, XIX, XX, XXI,
    XXII, 2, 7, 10, 12, 14, 15, 22, 28, 29, 33,
    34, 37, 40, 41, 43, 45, 58, 70, 71, 80, 88,
    89, 101, 102, 103, 106, 110, 111, 114, 117,
    118, 119, 127–130, 134, 139, 143–153,
    161–163, 165, 169–172, 177, 187, 189
Warner, H. B., 17, *19*
Warner, Jack, 180
WarnerColor (process), 134, 139, 177, 180
Warren, James, 76
Warrick, Ruth, 54
Warwick, Robert, *15*
Watson, Minor, 139, *154, 156*
Wayne, John, XIII, 33, 36, 47, 49, 103, 106,
    125, 134, 144, 149, *170*, 173, 183
Webb, Richard, *28, 130*
Weldon, Joan, *14, 88*, 134, 139, *151–153*
Wesson, Dick, 114, 134
West, Mae, 21
Westbound, 177, *197, 198*
Westcott, Gordon, 8
Westerfield, James, *XVI*, 169
Western Union, 15, 39, 49, 71, 91, 180
Westinghouse Studio One, 161
Westward the Women, 123
Whatever Happened to Randolph Scott?, 199,
    200, 201
Whelan, Tim, 76, 139
When the Daltons Rode, *36*, 39

White, Josh, 95
Whitney, J. V., 144
Whitney, Peter, 173, *193*
Wilcoxon, Henry, 21
Wild Bunch, The, 186
Wild Horse Mesa, 9
Wilkerson, Guy, *112*
Williams, Bill, 95, *98, 109*, 110
Williams, Guinn 'Big Boy', 9, 11, *48*, 49, *120*
Williams, Rhys, *97, 98*
Wills, Chill, *38*, 39
Windsor, Marie, 139, *148*
Winninger, Charles, *48*, 51
Wister, Owen, 3, 245
Withers, Grant, *82*
Woman in the Window, The, 45
Women Men Marry, The, 3, 246
Wood, Britt, *142*
Wood, Jonal, 173
Wright, Teresa, 49
Wyatt, Jane, 93
Wyatt Earp—Frontier Marshal, 27, 31
Wyler, William, 71, 144
Wyman, Jane, 71
Wymore, Patrice, 134

Y

Yankee Gold, 134
Yates, Herbert J., 103
Yearling, The, 71
Young, Robert, 15, 39

Z

Zane Grey (book), 11
Zane Grey Theatre (see *Dick Powell's Zane
    Grey Theatre*)
Zanuck, Daryl F., 27

J. Brim Crow III

ABOUT THE AUTHOR

Jefferson Brim Crow III has been a writer, publisher, and film historian, for more than 40 years. Like many seven-year-olds during the early forties, he saw his first Randolph Scott movie at a small neighborhood theatre during a special Saturday morning event called a "Kid Show". Since his youth, he has seen 95 of Scott's 100 films, missing only the pre-1935 bit part films during Scott's early career.

Brim Crow is an unashamed film buff, and an authority on the films of Randolph Scott. He maintains a library of over 1,000 books on the movie industry and is a voting member of the American Film Institute. Two of his books, *Randolph Scott / The Gentleman from Virginia*, and *The Cowboy and the Kid*, received glowing reviews and were chosen by two major book clubs. He founded WindRiver Publishing Company in 1986. He has since retired from the day-to-day activities of publishing, but continues to write. Brim and his wife Pattie live in Carrollton, Texas, and have two grown daughters.

Other Western books available from Empire Publishing, Inc.:

The Roy Rogers Reference-Trivia-Scrapbook Book by David Rothel
The Gene Autry Reference-Trivia-Scrapbook Book by David Rothel
More Cowboy Shooting Stars by John A. Rutherford and Richard B. Smith, III
Allan "Rocky" Lane, Republic's Action Ace by Chuck Thornton and David Rothel
Tom Mix Highlights by Andy Woytowich
An Ambush of Ghosts by David Rothel
Tim Holt by David Rothel
Saddle Pals by Garv Towell and Wayne E. Keates
Whatever Happened to Randolph Scott? by C. H. Scott
Candid Cowboys, Volumes 1 & 2 by Neil Summers
The Official TV Western Books, Volumes 1, 2, 3, & 4 by Neil Summers
The Dick Powell Story by Tony Thomas
Don Miller's Hollywood Corral by M. P. Smith and Ed Hulse
Joel McCrea, Riding the High Country by Tony Thomas
King Cowboy: Tom Mix and the Movies by Robert S. Birchard
Films of Hopalong Cassidy by Francis M. Nevins, Jr.
The Life and Films of Buck Jones: The Silent Era by Buck Rainey
The Life and Films of Buck Jones: The Sound Era by Buck Rainey
Those Fabulous Serial Heroines by Buck Rainey
Those Great Cowboy Sidekicks by David Rothel
The Tom Mix Book by M. G. "Bud" Norris
The Cowboy and the Kid by J. Brim Crow III and Jack H. Smith
The Jimmy Wakely Story by Linda Lee Wakely
The Real Bob Steele and a Man Called Brad by Bob Nareau
Republic Confidential: Volume 2 - The Players by Jack Mathis
Classic TV Westerns by Ronald Jackson
Complete Films of John Wayne by Mark Ricci, Boris and Steve Zmijewsky
Films of Clint Eastwood by Boris Zmijewsky and Lee Pfeiffer
Hollywood Western by William K. Everson
John Wayne Scrapbook by Lee Pfeiffer
The Official John Wayne Reference Book by Charles John Kieskalt
The Western Films of John Ford by J. A. Place
The West that Never Was by Tony Tomas

Future books to be published by Empire Publishing, Inc.:

Lash LaRue, The King of the Bullwhip by Chuck Thornton and David Rothel
Saddle Gals by Steve Turner and Edgar M. Wyatt

Write for complete catalog of Empire Books:

Empire Publishing, Inc.
Box 717
Madison, NC 27025-0717